A Commentary on Acts

SPCK International Study Guide 48

A Commentary on Acts

Yon Gyong Kwon

First published in Great Britain in 2012

Society for Promoting Christian Knowledge
36 Causton Street
London SW1P 4ST
www.spckpublishing.co.uk

British Library Cataloguing-in-Publication Data
A catalogue record for this book is available from the British Library

ISBN 978–0–281–06409–0
eBook ISBN 978–0–281–06686–5

Maps by Pantek Arts Ltd, Maidstone, Kent, UK

Typeset by The Manila Typesetting Company
First printed in Great Britain by Ashford Colour Press
Subsequently digitally printed in Great Britain

Produced on paper from sustainable forests

To the memory of Professor Graham Stanton

Contents

Contents

Contributors

Yon Gyong Kwon is a Professor of New Testament at Soongsil University, Korea. His scholarly interest is the ethical and futuristic dimension of Paul's gospel. He has published *Eschatology in Galatians: Rethinking Paul's Response to the Crisis in Galatia* with Mohr Siebeck, Germany, as well as several other books in Korean. He is also very active in preaching and teaching in local churches, especially in the area of biblical interpretation. He is married to Inhwa and they have a daughter, Sarah.

Emmanuel Anim is Dean of the Faculty of Theology and Mission, Pentecost University College, Accra, and Associate Pastor, Pentecost International Worship Centre, Accra, Ghana. Dr Anim is also Visiting Lecturer at All Nations Christian College, UK, and a member of the Translations Committee of the Bible Society of Ghana. He is married to Emily Ama Ofeibea and they have two children, Edna and Kweku.

Mercy Ah Siu-Maliko studied in Auckland, New Zealand, and Fiji. For a number of years, she lectured at the National University of Samoa, and from Fiji coordinated the Weavers (women in theological education) Program of the South Pacific Association of Theological Schools. She is currently the Country Coordinator for Manahine Pasefika (Association of Oceanian Women Theologians) and a freelance consultant on women and gender issues.

Víctor Hernández-Ramírez is a pastor of the Evangelical Church Betlem (Spanish Evangelical Church) in Barcelona and also works as a psychologist. He studied theology at the Presbyterian Theological Seminary of Mexico and studied psychology at the National Autonomous University of Mexico. He is a doctoral candidate in social psychology at the Autonomous University of Barcelona and a member of the Latin American Theological Fraternity. Víctor is married to Gabriela Leal and they have two children, Laura and Emilio.

Andrea Zaki Stephanous gained a PhD from the University of Manchester in 2003. He is Vice-President of the Protestant Churches of Egypt, Director General of the Coptic Evangelical Organization for Social Services, Adjacent Professor of Cairo Evangelical Theological Seminary, and President of the Fellowship of Middle East Evangelical Churches.

The SPCK International Study Guides

For over forty years, SPCK Worldwide's International Study Guides have provided resources for students training for service across a wide range of church traditions. The series contains biblical commentaries, books on pastoral care, church history and theology, as well as those on contemporary issues such as HIV & AIDS, and each title includes resources for discussion and further reading. Primarily aimed at those for whom English is an alternative language, the Study Guides are clear and accessible resources designed to enable students to explore their own theologies and discern God's mission in their own context. Many other Christians will also find the ISGs useful.

Today, with such plurality within the Church of God, the Study Guides draw upon the breadth of Christian experience across the globe. The contributors come from different countries and from a variety of church backgrounds. Most of them are theological educators. They bring their particular perspectives to bear as they demonstrate the influence of their contexts on the subjects they address. They provide a practical emphasis alongside contemporary scholarly reflection.

David Craig
Editor, International Study Guides

Acknowledgements

I first of all wish to thank the editors of the series, first Emma Wild-Wood, and then David Craig and Lauren Zimmerman. With confidence and unending patience, Emma guided virtually the whole process of preparing the manuscript, offering many perceptive suggestions as I went along. Both David and Lauren, who took over the project toward the end of the process, made sure that the book was brought to its expected destination. I thank all three for their expertise and hard work.

Writing a book is one of the surest ways of learning how much we are dependent upon others, their hard work, good will and willingness to sacrifice themselves. The writing of this Study Guide was no exception. This is especially true because this book does not purport to be an original contribution to Acts scholarship but is a basic guide for those who embark on a serious study of Acts, providing necessary information about the text and helpful reflections on various themes found within it. So I took the liberty of borrowing whatever I deemed helpful to readers from the works of others, including the earlier version of the Study Guide by John Hargreaves. It would be impossible to acknowledge all the debts that I have incurred to other scholars in the course of writing the book, but any expert on Acts who reads this Guide will immediately see what I mean. I also extend my gratitude to Emmanuel Anim, Mercy Ah Siu-Maliko, Víctor Hernández-Ramírez and Andrea Zaki Stephanous for adding variety and depth to the book by contributing the stimulating essays on some important topics.

As always, I am indebted to my dear wife, Inhwa, and our daughter, Sarah, for the love and support they have given me for all these years of our life together.

As I bring the work to completion, I cannot help remembering my teacher, the late Professor Graham Stanton, since it was he who first suggested my name to Emma. He was such a wonderful person and a wonderful teacher to me in many different ways. I only hope that I am not staining his worthy name by dedicating this work to his memory.

Using this Commentary

The plan of this Commentary follows much the same pattern as that of other biblical Guides in the series.

In the **Introduction** the authors set the scene for our study of the biblical book that is selected by providing a brief note on its background. Its relationship with other biblical books may also be explored.

The study of the biblical book itself has been divided into short sections according to natural breaks in the text. But before beginning their work readers may find it helpful to consider how they can make the best use of this Commentary.

Each section consists of:

 1   A **summary** of the passage, briefly indicating the subject-matter it contains. Of course the summary is not intended as a substitute for the words of the Bible itself, which need to be read very carefully at each stage of our study.

 2   **Notes** on particular words and points of possible difficulty, especially as relating to the purpose of the writing, and to the situation which gave rise to the writing.

 3   An **interpretation** of the passage and the teaching it contains, both as it applied to those to whom it was addressed, and as we should understand and apply it to our own situation today.

Theological essays

Topics that warrant extended attention because of their implications for theology and the current situation of many churches today are covered in 'Theological essays'. The authors of these essays show one way in which a theme, a biblical text and a particular context can be read together to discern God's will in our world today.

Study suggestions

Suggestions for further study and review are included at the end of each section. Besides enabling students working alone to check their own progress, they provide subjects for individual and group research, and topics for discussion. They are of four main sorts:

1   **Word study**, to help readers check and deepen their understanding of important words and phrases.

2   **Review of content**, to help readers check the work they have done, and make sure they have fully grasped the ideas and points of teaching given.

3   **Bible study**, to link the ideas and teaching of the biblical passage with related ideas and teaching in other parts of the Bible.

4   **Discussion and application**, to help readers think out the practical significance of the passage being studied, both to those to whom the biblical author was writing, and for the life and work of the churches and of individual Christians in the modern situation. Many of these are suitable for use in a group as well as for students working alone.

The best way to use these study suggestions is:

*   to reread the Bible passage;

*   to read the appropriate section of the Commentary once or twice;

*   to do the work suggested, either in writing or in group discussion, without looking at the Commentary again unless instructed to do so.

Please note that all these are only **suggestions**. Some readers may not wish to use them. Some teachers may wish to select only those most relevant to the needs of their particular students, or may wish to substitute questions of their own.

A list of books suggested for **further reading** is provided on p. xiv, and **maps** of the countries around the Eastern Mediterranean at the time when Paul was writing may be found on pp. xv–xvi.

Index

The Index includes only the more important names of people and places and the main subjects treated in Acts or discussed in the Commentary. Bold-print page references are provided to show where particular subjects are treated in detail.

Bible versions

The English translation of the Bible used in the Commentary is the New Revised Standard Version (NRSV). Reference is also made to the following versions, where these help to show the meaning more clearly:

*   the Jerusalem Bible

*   the Authorized (King James) Version (KJV)

*   the New American Standard Version (NASB)

*   the New International Version (NIV)

*   the New King James Version (NKJV)

*   the Revised New Korean Standard Version.

Further reading

Commentaries for exegesis

Bruce, F. F. *The Acts of the Apostles*. 3rd edition. Grand Rapids, Mich.: Eerdmans, 1990.

Marshall, I. H. *The Acts of the Apostles*. Leicester: IVP, 1980.

Talbert, C. H. *Reading Acts: A Literary and Theological Commentary on the Acts of the Apostles*. Macon, Ga.: Smyth & Helwys, 2005.

Williams, D. J. *Acts*. New International Biblical Commentary. Peabody, Mass.: Hendrickson, 1985.

Witherington III, B. *The Acts of the Apostles: A Socio-Rhetorical Commentary*. Grand Rapids, Mich.: Eerdmans, 1998.

More practical commentaries

Comfort, P. W. (ed.) *Acts*. Life Application Bible Commentary. Carol Stream, Ill.: Tyndale House, 1999.

Fernando, A. *Acts*. NIV Application Commentary. Grand Rapids, Mich.: Zondervan, 1998.

Willimon, W. H. *Acts*. Interpretation (A Bible Commentary for Teaching and Preaching). Minneapolis, Minn.: John Knox, 1988.

Other studies of Acts

Bruce, F. F. *New Testament History*. New York: Doubleday, 1971.

Jervell, J. *The Theology of the Acts of the Apostles*. Cambridge: Cambridge University Press, 1996.

Liefeld, W. L. *Interpreting the Book of Acts*. Guide to New Testament Exegesis. Grand Rapids, Mich.: Eerdmans, 1995.

Marshall, I. H. *Luke: Historian and Theologian*. Exeter: Paternoster, 1988.

Marshall, I. H. (ed.) *Witness to the Gospel: The Theology of Acts*. Grand Rapids, Mich.: Eerdmans, 1998. (A collection of important essays on various topics of Acts.)

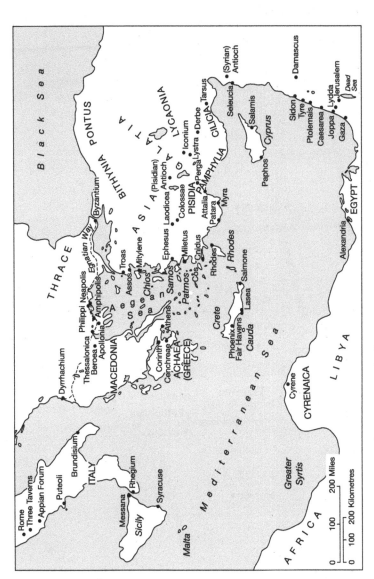

Map 1 The Eastern Mediterranean in the first century AD
Source: Tom Wright, *The New Testament for Everyone* (SPCK, 2011), p. 244.

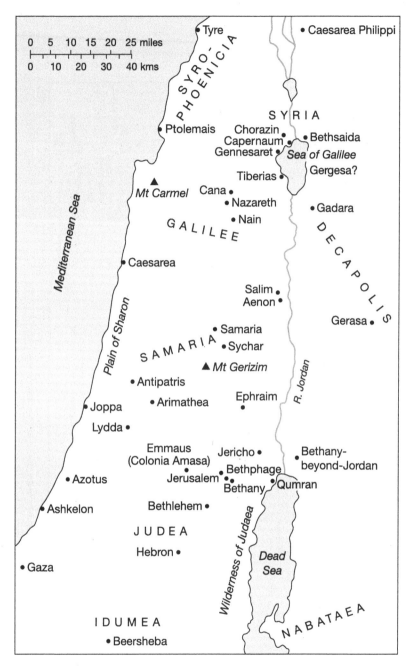

Map 2 Galilee, Samaria and Judea in the first century AD
Source: Tom Wright, *The New Testament for Everyone* (SPCK, 2011), p. xx.

Introduction

How do we know that Christianity is true? This has been a key question people have been asking ever since the birth of the Christian Church. Naturally, an important part of Christian evangelism has always been convincing people of the truth of the Christian gospel. What we have in the Gospel of Luke and the Acts of the Apostles is one of the earliest answers to this ongoing question: is Christianity true? So Luke tells stories about Jesus and his followers, and he does so with a view to helping us see why Christianity has to be true and thus worthy of our devotion.

The book of Acts within the New Testament

The Acts of the Apostles occupies a unique place in the New Testament (NT). As is indicated by its location within the NT, Acts serves as an indispensable bridge between the Gospels and the Letters of the NT. It shares the same narrative form with the four Gospels; the four Gospels tell us about the earthly ministry of Jesus of Nazareth, while Acts deals with the expansion of the movement after his Ascension into heaven. Thus Acts can be read as the second half of a single story. This can be seen from the fact that Luke has planned both the Gospel of Luke and the Acts of the Apostles as two volumes of a single work about 'the events that have been fulfilled among us' (Luke 1.1).

Acts is also closely related to the apostolic Letters (Epistles) in the NT, since both deal with the life of the Church in her earliest stage. Acts tells us the activities of many of Jesus' apostles such as Peter, John, and James the brother of Jesus. And in the NT we have those Letters under their names, which we usually call 'general Letters' or 'catholic (i.e. common) Epistles'. Acts also devotes a large amount of space to Paul's ministry from his conversion until his arrival at Rome, and it was during this period that he wrote most of his major Letters now collected in the NT. Connecting Acts with these various Letters is not always easy, but ignoring Acts will surely make our understanding of these Letters much more difficult, if not impossible (for instance, we learn that Paul was born in Tarsus of Cilicia from Acts, not from his own Letters).

Who wrote Luke–Acts?

We know that both the Gospel of Luke and Acts are written by the same author and dedicated to the same Theophilus (Luke 1.3; Acts 1.1). The works themselves are anonymous (the author is not named anywhere in the text), but ancient tradition is virtually unanimous in attributing them to Luke, a physician and companion of Paul (Philemon 23–24;

Colossians 4.10–17). Scholars disagree on the reliability of this tradition. Some think that there is no reason to disbelieve such an early tradition, but others raise questions about its reliability. But even those who dispute the authorship of Luke continue to use the name 'Luke' to refer to the supposedly anonymous author, simply for convenience's sake.

Whether it is Luke or not, it is clear that both Luke and Acts were written by the same author. Does this mean that we should read both books together as a single work? Many people think that the two works reveal basically the same literary style and theological outlook, and thus should be studied together. They say that we will miss Luke's theological richness if we read one and ignore the other. But there are also others who treat them as two different works which happen to have been written by the same author, like the different plays of the same Shakespeare. They are separated from each other in the NT, and we do not have any evidence that they were read together in ancient days. Perhaps this is not a problem of an either/or choice. We can read both the Gospel and Acts in their own right, but our interpretation of one will be greatly enhanced by serious consideration of the other. The present volume is on Acts but we will frequently bring the Gospel of Luke to bear on our reading of Acts.

Acts as history

What kind of book is Acts, then? Is it a work of history or should we rather call it a piece of theology? There is no denying that Acts should be read as a historical account of the Earliest Church. Luke's intention was to write 'an orderly account' of the ministry of Jesus and of the Early Church (Luke 1.3). So we read Acts in order to find out what happened at the beginning of the Christian movement. Indeed, we can hardly overestimate the historical value of Acts, since it is often the only source of information about the formative period of the Church, i.e. from her birth in Jerusalem in the 30s to Paul's arrival at Rome in the 60s of the first century. Without Acts we are left in the dark about so much of what happened during this critical period.

But there is a constant debate about the historical reliability of Acts. Many believe that Acts presents us with a fairly reliable account of what actually happened. But there are those who think that Acts is inadequate as a historical source since the account is heavily influenced by the author's theological intention. They claim that Luke minimized the extent of the conflict between the Jewish and the Gentile communities out of his desire to create a picture of the Church as a unified and harmonious community of faith.

An important case in point here is the so-called 'we' passages (16.10–17; 20.5–15; 21.1–18; 27.1—28.16). Those who value the historical trustworthiness of Acts, including the present author, naturally find in them a strong piece of evidence for the eyewitness character of Acts, but those who consider Acts historically unreliable tend to brush them aside as nothing more than a literary device. Another point in dispute is the alleged discrepancy between Luke's portrait of Paul and the Paul of his own Letters. We know that Paul was an avid letter-writer but Luke says nothing about it. Luke's knowledge of Paul's doctrine of justification seems singularly inadequate. The Paul as a traditional Jew in the latter part of Acts does not fit comfortably with the Paul of the law-free gospel.

The present Guide assumes the general trustworthiness of Acts as a work of history. The hypothesis that the 'we' passages are merely a literary device is not easy to establish historically. And the alleged discrepancy between Acts and Paul's Letters is not as great as some scholars would make it out to be. We can satisfactorily explain most of the gaps between the two if we pay sufficient attention to their differences in genre and historical circumstances.

Acts as theology

Nevertheless, it is also clear that we cannot read Acts as a history in the modern sense of the word. We can trust that Luke draws for us a fairly accurate picture of the Early Church, but it is also clear that Luke uses much freedom in describing the scenes and recording the words of his characters. For example, in Acts we have many sermons preached by such people as Peter, Stephen and Paul. We can suppose that Luke could learn the general thrust of such sermons from various sources but it is unreasonable to expect him to reproduce minute details of these speeches. So what we have in Acts is Luke's own summary of the sermons preached by these people, not exact reproductions of them.

More importantly, we also remember that Luke has his own points to make and he tells his stories accordingly. Luke is a historian, not a mere chronicler. His report of the lives of the Early Church is at the same time an interpretation of it. That is, Luke is as much a theologian as he is a historian. Luke tells us a lot about the Early Church but he has no intention of being either comprehensive or 'objective' in the modern sense of the word. Luke is clearly selective in telling his stories, focusing his attention only on those stories which are relevant to his purpose. For example, he devotes much space to Peter but is virtually silent about the other apostles. He is also more focused on Paul than on Barnabas. We do not hear anything about the evangelization of Galilee. We do not know how the church was established in Rome either. It is also clear that Luke employs many literary devices in Acts, such as numerous parallels between different characters in both Luke and Acts, literary repetition and litotes (understatement). This does not mean that Luke is making up fictitious stories but rather that he is making a conscious effort to help us see the theological significance behind the stories.

So as we go along, we will often stop to reflect upon the theological and spiritual significance of the stories that we are reading. For example, throughout his narrative Luke puts a strong emphasis on the role of the Holy Spirit in the ministries of both Jesus (the Gospel of Luke) and his disciples (Acts). In this respect, it is noteworthy that Luke portrays the major players in Acts, such as Peter, Stephen and Paul, as recapitulating the pattern set by Jesus in the Gospel. We can also see that resurrection takes a central place in the proclamation of the Early Church. Another prominent theme in Luke–Acts is prayer: Jesus in Luke is a man of prayer, and the same goes for his followers in Acts. Acts also follows the Gospel in its emphasis on the role of women for the ministry of the Church, as is illustrated by such names as Priscilla or Lydia. The interest in economic sharing continues in Acts, as is clearly seen in the ideal portrait of the earliest Jerusalem church where believers shared all things in common and there was no needy person in the Spirit-empowered community. The relationship between Jews and Gentiles also receives special treatment, and Luke is at pains to show that the Church is not a new religion but the long-awaited fulfilment of God's promise to the people of Israel. It is also noteworthy that Luke depicts many of the pagan leaders as favourable to Christianity, often in contrast to the hostile attitude of the Jews. To be sure, there are numerous other themes to be explored in Acts but we list a few of them in advance simply to help readers to have some ideas about what we are going to read.

The source of Acts

In Acts, Luke tells us many interesting stories about the earliest phase of the Church. It starts from Jerusalem and ends in Rome. During the course of the story we come across a wide variety of people in remarkably diverse settings: a mountain, an upper room, the temple precinct, the Sanhedrin, prisons, the law courts, the Jewish synagogues, the public theatre, a market-place, a sea voyage, etc. A natural question to ask is: where did Luke learn all about these? Luke also records a number of sermons by different people such as Peter, Stephen and Paul. How was he able to record all those sermons in such detail? Did he have certain written sources before him? Did he reproduce them out of his memory? Or, as some critics claim, did he just make them all up?

No definite answer is possible, but we can make some probable specu-lations. In the preface to the Gospel, Luke explicitly says that he had stud-ied the available sources to the best of his knowledge (Luke 1.3). We can assume that the same applies to the writing of Acts. For the earlier chap-ters, which largely deal with the Jerusalem community, many scholars sug-gest that Luke probably had certain Aramaic sources already translated into Greek. The frequency of Semitic expressions is in support of such a supposition. We can also think of numerous figures Luke could have con-sulted for his information. He must have obtained much of his knowledge of Paul from Paul himself as well as from his own experience in Paul's mission. There are also others who could help him in this regard, such as Timothy, Priscilla and Aquila and many others. According to the 'we' passages, Luke also stayed with Philip in Caesarea. That may explain his knowledge of the activities of the Hellenists, such as Stephen, and Philip himself. Luke's references to the family of Herod are also noteworthy (Acts

13.1; Luke 8.3); we may suppose that Luke obtained the 'inside information' about the Herod family from people like 'Manaen (who had been brought up with Herod)' (Acts 13.1, NIV). Ancient tradition says that Luke was an Antiochene. If so, he could probably learn a lot from Barnabas, the first leader of the church in Antioch. There are many others whom we can think of as the possible sources of Luke's knowledge.

The manuscripts of Acts

Like all the other NT books, we do not have the original text (autograph) of Acts. What we now have are a large number of copied manuscripts whose relationship with the original is not immediately clear. These manuscripts are all different from one another to various degrees, and scholars have to study each of these manuscripts closely and compare them with one another with a view to recovering the original text of the book. This area of study is called textual criticism. Having compared all these manuscripts, scholars have come to the conclusion that they can be divided into a few large categories or 'textual traditions'. One of them is called the 'Western text' or the 'Western textual tradition', of which the best example is the manuscript named Codex Bezae. (Codex means a manuscript bound in book form. Codex Bezae is called so, since Theodore Beza found it and donated it to Cambridge University. In textual criticism it is represented by the capital letter 'D'.) Interestingly, the Western text of Acts is almost a third longer than other textual traditions with many interesting additions of its own. Most of such additions seem secondary (i.e. not written by Luke himself), but nevertheless they often provide important helps in understanding the meaning of the text. (See the notes on 19.9–10, for example.)

Reading Acts today

As we said earlier, the whole of Luke–Acts is Luke's attempt to show the truth or relevance of the Christian gospel for his own generation. We live in a world which is very different from the world of Acts, and much of what we find in it may not apply to us on a literal level. But the basic need Luke tried to meet is as much ours as theirs: the need to ascertain the truth of the gospel and affirm its relevance for us today. So we read what the first disciples of Jesus did to be faithful to the gospel with a view to discovering what we are to do in order to be faithful witnesses of Jesus in a world like ours. And we may ask the guidance of the same Spirit of God as we journey through the exciting world of the Acts of the Apostles.

Acts 1.1–11

Forty days with the risen Jesus

 Summary

Luke begins the second part of his story by summarizing the first (the Gospel of Luke) and expanding the last phase of Jesus' earthly ministry, with the promise of the Holy Spirit.

 Notes

1.1a. In the first book: The 'first book' refers to the Gospel of Luke, which is about 'all that Jesus did and taught from the beginning' until the day of his Ascension. Luke now begins the second half of his 'orderly account' about what Jesus did through his followers. Luke's Gospel describes his subject: 'the events that have been fulfilled among us', suggesting the continuing relevance of the story (Luke 1.1).

1.1b. Theophilus: Luke follows the literary convention of the day by dedicating Luke–Acts to Theophilus, possibly a Roman official ('most excellent', Luke 1.3). The name means 'lover of God' (*theo-philos*) and some think that the name is a fictitious literary convention.

1.2a. Until the day when he was taken up: Verses 2–11 repeat, and partly add to, the conclusion of the first book (Luke 24.36–53).

1.2b. Through the Holy Spirit: Luke depicts the whole of Jesus' earthly ministry as one empowered by the Holy Spirit (Luke 4.18; Acts 10.38).

1.2c. The apostles whom he had chosen: By 'apostles' Luke usually means 'the Twelve' (Luke 6.13–16). One glaring exception is Acts 14.4 and 14.14 where it refers to Paul and Barnabas (cf. Acts 1.21–22). The word, literally meaning 'someone who has been sent', can sometimes be used more broadly (Luke 11.49; John 13.16; 2 Corinthians 8.23; Philippians 2.25). In Hebrews it is used of Jesus (3.1).

1.3a. He presented himself alive to them by many convincing proofs: So these disciples are 'eyewitnesses' (Luke 1.2) of Jesus' resurrection. Empowered by the Holy Spirit, they will soon act as its witnesses (Acts 1.8, 22; 3.15; 4.2; 5.30–32; 10.39–41; 13.31).

1.3b. Over the course of forty days: Only here do we learn that the risen Jesus spent 40 days with his disciples before his Ascension. In Luke 24 one gets the impression that the period was only one day. It does not mean that Jesus stayed with them throughout these 40 days but that he made frequent visitations during this period. The number 40 may be symbolic; just as Jesus prepared for his ministry for 40 days (Luke 4.1–2), now his disciples prepare for theirs by being instructed by the risen Jesus for 40 days.

1.3c. Speaking about the kingdom of God: In the Synoptic Gospels Jesus' preaching focuses on the kingdom (or reign) of God. In Acts it summarizes the content of the gospel (8.12; 19.8; 20.25; 28.23, 31). Although there are some indications of its presence (Luke 17.21), it predominantly refers to the future kingdom that believers are to enter or inherit (Acts 14.22).

1.4a. While staying with them: The word 'staying' literally means 'eating (salt) with'. Meals provide important contexts for the ministry of Jesus (Luke 5.29; 7.36; 11.37) as well as for the resurrection appearances, especially for proving the bodily resurrection of Jesus (Luke 24.30–31, 36–43). See what Peter says in Acts 10.41.

1.4b. He ordered them not to leave Jerusalem: Luke accords Jerusalem special importance as the salvation-historical centre: the final destination of the way of Jesus, the place of receiving the eschatological Spirit, and the birthplace of first community and its mission. The disciples naturally followed this order (1.12–14; Luke 24.52).

1.4c. Wait there for the promise of the Father: The promise of the Father means what the Father promised, i.e. the Spirit (2.33; Luke 24.49; John 14.16). Jesus repeats the promise in 1.8.

1.5a. John baptized with water: John's baptizing ministry appears in Luke 3.1–20. There John contrasts his water baptism with that of the Holy Spirit by Jesus (cf. Acts 11.16).

1.5b. Baptized with the Holy Spirit: This promise continues in 1.8 with more detailed information. It finds its initial fulfilment in Acts 2 ('not many days from now'), but its validity extends to subsequent comings of the Spirit (8.14–17; 9.17; 11.16; 19.1–7).

There are considerable debates over the precise nature of the 'baptism of the Holy Spirit', but the diverse modes of the Spirit's coming in Luke–Acts makes a systematic description impossible. In Acts 10.44–48 the outpouring of the Spirit even precedes the confession of sin, let alone water baptism.

1.6. Is this the time when you will restore the kingdom to Israel?: The disciples mean restoring Israel's political independence. Interestingly enough, however, Jesus does not rebuke them for such a misunderstanding; he simply warns them not to concern themselves with 'the times and periods that the Father has set by his own authority'. Instead ('not . . . but'), they have to 'mind their own business'; the task set before them by the risen

Jesus in 1.8. One should not press the distinction between 'the spiritual' and 'the political' too far here, since God's sovereignty covers both.

1.8a. But you will receive power when the Holy Spirit has come upon you; and you will be my witnesses . . . to the ends of the earth: This verse is a succinct summary of the whole book. The promise, setting the outpouring of the Spirit as the prerequisite of effective witness, recalls the preaching of Jesus at the synagogue of Nazareth (Luke 4.18–19). The Holy Spirit gives the disciples the power necessary for effective witnessing. Not surprisingly, therefore, it is the Spirit that takes the initiative in the Church's witness to Jesus (e.g. Acts 8.26, 39; 10.19–20; 16.6–7). Hence the popular epithet: 'Acts of the Holy Spirit'.

1.8b. In Jerusalem: See 2.14–36; 3.12–26; 4.1–5; 5.27–32; 7.1–56.

1.8c. In all Judea and Samaria: See 8.1, 4–40; 9.31—11.18.

1.8d. To the ends of the earth: The reference is somewhat ambiguous. It may refer to:

1 the end of the inhabited world (geographically);

2 Paul's arrival in Rome (politically, 28.16); or

3 the conversion of the Gentiles (racially, 10.1—11.18).

Luke 24.47 renders (2) most likely. In this sense it provides a corrective to the disciples' nationalistic attitude.

1.9a. As they were watching: In vv. 9–11 Luke emphasizes that the disciples saw the Ascension of Jesus no less than five times, also stating: 'out of their sight'; 'they were gazing up towards heaven'; 'stand looking up towards heaven'; 'as you saw him go into heaven'.

1.9b. He was lifted up, and a cloud took him out of their sight: Both are related to each other. In the Bible the 'cloud' often signifies divine presence (Exodus 19.9, 16; 24.15–16; 34.5; Daniel 7.13; Revelation 1.7). So what Luke means is that Jesus has now 'entered into his glory' (Luke 24.26) and is 'exalted at the right hand of God' (Acts 2.33). Jesus' Ascension marks the end of his resurrection visitations (appearing and disappearing).

1.10. Two men in white robes: They are probably angels. They remind us of the 'two men in dazzling clothes' in Luke 24.4, as well as Moses and Elijah conversing with Jesus on a mountain (Luke 9.30–31). Luke views them as witnesses (Deuteronomy 19.15) to Jesus' resurrection and his future *parousia*, i.e. the second coming.

1.11a. Men of Galilee: This reference seems to be related to one of the apostolic qualifications set down in 1.21–22. Mere 'standing' and 'looking up towards heaven' is not a proper thing to do at this point of time; they should set to the task entrusted to them by Jesus. Just as the two women returned 'from the tomb' and reported what they saw to the disciples (Luke 24.9), so now these Galileans should return 'to Jerusalem' (v. 12) and begin to obey the orders given by Jesus.

1.11b. This Jesus . . . will come in the same way as you saw him go into heaven: Jesus will come as the Son of Man on the clouds of heaven (Daniel 7.13), bringing the whole of history to its proper end (Mark 13.26; 14.62). Yet Jesus continues to work with his disciples through his Spirit, as the whole of Acts makes clear. In that sense, the Ascension signifies the beginning of the reign of Christ which will last until the time of final consummation.

 Interpretation

Bridging the Gospel and Acts

Luke sets out to write an 'orderly account' of the 'events that have been fulfilled among us' to convince Theophilus of the truth of the Christian gospel he has learned (Luke 1.1–4). In the Gospel of Luke, the first of his two-volume project, Luke wrote 'all that Jesus began to do and to teach until the day he was taken up to heaven' (Acts 1.1–2, NIV). Now in the second part of this account, he describes how the apostles, commissioned by Jesus and empowered by the Holy Spirit, continued what Jesus himself began.

Acts of the Apostles, dedicated to the same Theophilus, begins with a brief résumé of the first volume (1.1–2). Luke then proceeds to recount those stories originally told at the conclusion of the Gospel (Luke 24). But as he does so, he also adds some new facts and explanations necessary for the unfolding of the new story. In this way the last phase of the Gospel grows smoothly into the beginning of Acts. The point is: we are reading the latter part of one and the same story.

Certainty of the resurrection

This bridging section highlights a few themes which will dominate the book. First, the risen Jesus has left the apostles with no shred of doubt about the reality of his resurrection. It is already clear in Luke 24, but Luke further adds that Jesus convinced them 'by many convincing proofs' over the long period of 40 days. He spoke to them about the kingdom of God, just as he had done in his earthly ministry, before his suffering. At the Ascension too, Luke repeatedly emphasizes that the disciples saw Jesus leave with their own eyes. In the following stories, the apostles will be testifying to the resurrection of Jesus (1.22), even at the cost of their lives. So they need such assurance, for otherwise they will not be able to proclaim its truth so boldly (cf. 1 John 1.1–4).

Acts of the Holy Spirit

The importance of the Holy Spirit also stands out quite clearly. The risen Jesus tells his disciples to wait for the empowerment of the Holy Spirit before they set to work as his witnesses. Even such extensive and intensive instruction by the risen Jesus is not enough; they have to be 'clothed with power from on high' through the Holy Spirit (Luke 24.49). Thus what we hear in Acts is the story of how the Holy Spirit empowers and guides the disciples in their work of witnessing to the risen Jesus. Jesus began his ministry with the anointing of the Holy Spirit (Luke 4.18); so will his disciples. In this sense we can say that the story of Acts still continues in the lives of faithful Christians, including ourselves.

The spread of the gospel

The empowered disciples were to proclaim the gospel 'in Jerusalem, in all Judea and Samaria, and to the ends of the earth' (1.8). This did not mean just crossing rivers and climbing mountains but also taking down the barrier of racial prejudice, especially on the part of the Jews. Yet, this was not an easy thing to do, as we will see over and over again in the following chapters of the book.

Witnesses need power

We should also note Luke's interest in power. His purpose for writing is to show the 'truth' or 'certainty' (NIV) of the Christian gospel (Luke 1.4). But this truth cannot be proven by mere words; it also takes power. Luke repeatedly stresses that the apostles' confident testimony to Jesus was accompanied by 'many wonders and signs' (Acts 2.43; 3.1–10; 4.13–14, 29–30; 5.12; 6.8). This recapitulates the pattern found in Jesus himself (10.38). We also remember that Paul defines the gospel in terms of the 'power of God' and tells us how Christ works through him 'with words and deeds' (Romans 1.16; 15.18). In a way, this is the biggest question 'Acts of the Holy Spirit' poses before us modern Christians: how effective are we in demonstrating the power of the name of Jesus?

 STUDY SUGGESTIONS

Word study

1 What is the meaning of 'power' in the New Testament?

2 What did Jesus say about the 'kingdom of God' in the Gospel of Luke?

Review of content

3 How does Luke summarize the content of 'the first book'?

4 What promises did Jesus make to his disciples?

5 Why do the disciples need the gift of the Holy Spirit?

6 What is the intent of the two men's question?

Bible study

7 Read Matthew 3.11–12; Mark 1.7–8; Luke 3.15–17; Acts 2.33. What does it mean that Jesus will baptize people with the Holy Spirit?

8 In both Luke 17.21–22 and Acts 1.6–8, Jesus receives questions about the 'time' of the kingdom. Compare the answers Jesus gives. How are they similar to or different from each other?

Discussion and application

9 The disciples asked Jesus about the 'time' but he said, 'It is not for you to know the times or periods' (1.7). Instead he drew their attention to what they would have to do. Can you think of any situations or incidents around you where this phrase might apply?

10 Luke says that Jesus 'was lifted up and a cloud took him out of their sight' (1.9). How are we to understand this depiction of Jesus' Ascension?

11 What are the ways in which the power of the gospel becomes manifest in our lives? And what are the barriers to effective witness?

Acts 1.12–26

Waiting and preparation

 Summary

The Church waits for the gift of the Holy Spirit in earnest prayer and prepares itself for the ministry of witnessing to the risen Jesus.

 Notes

1.12a. Then they returned to Jerusalem: The disciples had returned to Jerusalem on first encountering the risen Jesus (Luke 24.33). Interestingly, Luke says nothing about their going to Galilee (Matthew 28.7, 10; Mark 16.7; John 21).

1.12b. The mount called Olivet: It is located east of Jerusalem across the Kidron valley. In Zechariah, this is the place where Yahweh will visit his people on the Day of the Lord (14.4).

1.12c. A sabbath day's journey away: Taking Exodus 16.29 and Numbers 35.5 together, this is a distance of 2,000 cubits, which is about one kilometre. The point is: the distance was short, and everything happened within the vicinity of Jerusalem (Acts 1.4; Luke 24.49).

1.13a. The room upstairs where they were staying: This could either have been an upper storey of a large house or a room on the flat roof of a house (9.37, 39; 20.8). Some identify it with the room of the Last Supper (Luke 22.12) and/or the house of John Mark (Acts 12.12), but it could have been any upper room in Jerusalem. The word is used only in Acts (9.37, 39; 20.8); in the Gospel of Luke a different word is used.

1.13b. Peter, and John, and James . . . : The list essentially agrees with the one found in Luke 6.14–16, with Judas Iscariot naturally deleted. Only the first three in the list appear again in the rest of Acts. The order reflects the importance of their roles in Acts.

1.14a. Constantly devoting themselves to prayer: Luke emphasizes the persistence of the Church in prayer: it was both continuous and resolute (2.42, 46; 12.12; Colossians 4.2). Luke regularly portrays the

Early Church at prayer (Acts 2.42; 6.4, 6; 10.9; 13.3; 28.8). In the Gospel Luke also describes Jesus as a man of prayer (Luke 3.21; 5.16; 6.12). The Church waiting for the Spirit in ardent prayer echoes what Jesus had taught about prayer (Luke 11.9–13; 18.1). The Greek text contains a word (*homothymadon*) which means 'with one accord' (KJV) or 'with one mind' (NASB). It stresses the harmonious and prayerful nature of the Church (2.46; 4.24; 5.12).

1.14b. With certain women: They could be wives of the apostles (cf. 1 Corinthians 9.5) or those ministering to Jesus (Matthew 27.55; Luke 8.2–3; 24.22). Among the Gospel writers, Luke pays special attention to women (Luke 8.1–3; 23.49).

1.14c. Mary the mother of Jesus, as well as his brothers: They receive a special mention due to her relationship with Jesus. This is the last reference to Mary in the NT. The Gospels mention four as Jesus' brothers: James, Joseph, Simon and Judas (Matthew 13.55; Mark 6.3). Earlier Jesus' family had been opposed to him; now they were among the disciples (Luke 8.21). Very probably, the appearance of the risen Jesus to James brought about such a drastic change (1 Corinthians 15.7). This James plays an important role later in Acts (12.17; 15.13; 21.18; cf. Galatians). Luke, however, never identifies him as a brother of Jesus; Paul does (Galatians 1.19).

1.15a. In those days: Interestingly, the same 'time notice' is used in the other election stories: of the apostles (Luke 6.12) and of the seven leaders (Acts 6.1). The replacement of Judas is located between the Ascension and Pentecost as a preparatory step for receiving the gift of the Spirit.

1.15b. Peter stood up . . . and said: This is the first speech in Acts. The Greek participle here ('standing up') often signals the beginning of a speech (13.16; 15.7). Peter was the spokesperson for the disciples in the Gospel (Luke 5.1–11; 8.45; 9.32–33, etc.). He also plays a leading role in the first half of Acts (cf. Luke 22.32), but disappears completely after chapter 15. John 21 tells us how he came to assume the leadership of the community after his shameful lapse.

1.15c. Among the believers (. . . about one hundred and twenty): The word 'believers' literally means 'brothers'. It is used of brothers of Jesus (1.14), of fellow Christians (6.3), or of fellow Jews (2.29, 37). The crowd includes both men and women. The number 120 is factual; it does not seem to have any symbolic meaning. This information interrupts Peter's speech, so NRSV puts it in parenthesis.

1.16a. The scripture had to be fulfilled: In the NT the term 'scripture' refers to our 'Old Testament'. Most NT writers used a Greek translation of the Old Testament. This is called the Septuagint or simply LXX. (Most Diaspora Jews could not read Hebrew, so the Hebrew Old Testament began to be translated into Greek in the third century BC.)

13

Even before Jesus' time, many psalms were viewed as referring to the coming Messiah. Naturally the early Christians read the Old Testament in the light of their experience of their Messiah/Christ, Jesus of Nazareth, especially his death and resurrection. For Luke, recognizing the risen Jesus requires proper understanding of the scriptural prophecy about his suffering and resurrection (Luke 24.25–27, 32, 44–47). So it is natural that Peter should interpret the enemies of God's anointed or the righteous sufferer in the Psalms as enemies of Jesus. This is what Peter did with Judas in his address.

1.16b. The Holy Spirit through David foretold: This shows how the Early Church viewed the Scripture (our 'Old Testament') as God's word. The Scripture must (Gk, *dei*) be fulfilled (3.21; 9.16; Luke 24.44), since it is God's word which the Holy Spirit spoke through people like David (Acts 2.16; 3.18, 21, 25; 4.25; 15.7; 28.25). So David is called a prophet (2.30; 4.25).

1.17a. He was numbered among us: The description that Judas 'became a guide for those who arrested Jesus' recalls the scene of Jesus' arrest, where Judas was identified as 'one of the twelve' (Luke 22.3, 47–48; Matthew 26.47–50).

1.17b. Allotted his share in this ministry: The Greek word for 'ministry' is *diakonia*, a word which can mean all kinds of service from table service to apostolate. Here it refers to the task of witnessing to the resurrection of Jesus (v. 22).

1.18. (Now this man acquired a field): The parentheses in NRSV indicate that verses 18–19 are not Peter's words but Luke's addition to provide background information to his non-Jewish readers. This is shown by such phrases as 'in their language', i.e. in Aramaic which was the spoken language used by the Jews of Palestine at that time.

Luke's description of Judas' death is somewhat different from the story in Matthew (27.3–10):

1 in Matthew Judas hanged himself, while he 'fell headlong' in Acts;

2 in Matthew the chief priest bought the field with the money which Judas had thrown back, while in Acts Judas himself acquired it.

However, both reports agree on two essential points:

1 that Judas died a tragic death; and

2 that there was a field called Blood Field which was associated with Judas.

Luke's words, 'the reward of his wickedness' find a close parallel in 2 Peter 2.13, 15.

1.19. This became known to all residents in Jerusalem: For the residents of Jerusalem, the circumstances surrounding Jesus' death were common knowledge (Luke 24.18). In fact, Peter declares that they are the chief culprits in Jesus' death (2.22–23, 36; 3.13–15; 4.10).

1.20a. For it is written in the book of Psalms: This continues what Peter began to say in v. 16: 'the scripture had to be fulfilled'.

1.20b. Let his homestead become desolate . . .: This is a quotation from Psalm 69.25 (LXX 68.26) with some modifications. Since the early Christians believed that the Scripture points to Christ, they often took the freedom of modifying details to suit their purpose. In this psalm the poet prays that the dwelling place of his enemies should be deserted. Peter appeals to this passage in order to explain what happened to Judas. It 'had to' (*dei*) happen in that way, since the Scripture had foretold it so.

1.20c. Let another take his position of overseer: Peter now quotes Psalm 109.8 (LXX 108.8). This is a difficult psalm, since here the poet prays for the complete destruction of his enemy: that he may die before his time, another may take his position of leadership, and his family may be completely ruined. Peter understands it to be a prophecy about Judas and presents it as a biblical warrant for the replacement of Judas. Since the Scripture foretold that someone else should take Judas' position, so 'one of these must become a witness with us to his [=Jesus'] resurrection' (v. 22).

1.21. One of the men who have accompanied us: Based on the scriptural prediction, Peter suggests that one of the disciples must (*dei*, v. 21 in Gk) take the place of Judas. Verses 21–22 give the qualifications and the responsibility of the successor. The candidate should be an associate of the Lord and his original followers.

1.22a. From the baptism of John: This is interesting, since it reflects the Johannine tradition that many of his disciples began to follow Jesus immediately after his baptism by John the Baptist (John 1.35–51). The phrase can either mean Jesus' baptism by John or the baptism which John proclaimed and performed. The latter is more likely, since all four Gospels begin their accounts of Jesus' ministry with the story of John's baptism (Acts 10.37; 13.24). This verse shows that the apostles' testimony covers the whole of Jesus' ministry, not just his resurrection.

1.22b. A witness with us to his resurrection: This is the primary task of an apostle (2.32; 3.15; 4.33). Thus he must be someone who has 'accompanied us . . . until the day when he was taken up from us', i.e. an eyewitness of Jesus' resurrection and Ascension. In Jerusalem the death of Jesus was common knowledge; the burden of the apostolic witness was to demonstrate his resurrection.

Interestingly, these qualifications disqualify Paul as an apostle. He was not one of the original followers of Jesus; he did not see the risen Jesus before his Ascension either. Yet Luke later calls Paul and Barnabas 'apostles' (14.4, 14). Then, Luke's purpose here is not to deny Paul's apostleship but to emphasize the continuity between the ministry of Jesus and that of his followers. In a speech attributed to him, Paul acknowledges these qualifications (13.31). Yet he does claim that he has seen the Lord and, therefore, is an apostle (1 Corinthians 9.1; 15.7–8). Not all agreed, of course; hence such recurring problems concerning his apostleship (cf. 2 Corinthians).

1.23. Joseph . . . and Matthias: Neither of them appears elsewhere in the NT. Justus was Joseph's Latin cognomen. He should not be confused with Judas Barsabbas in 15.22. It is also noteworthy that James, the Lord's brother, did not qualify as a candidate.

1.24. Lord, you know everyone's heart: It is not clear to whom their prayer is addressed. God (the Father) is the one who knows everyone's heart (15.8), but it is the Lord Jesus who had chosen his apostles (1.2). The latter seems more likely.

1.25. To take the place . . . to his own place: It seems that Judas' betrayal has motivated his replacement. This verse contains a word play with 'place' (Gk, *topos*): Judas has deserted 'the place in this ministry and apostleship' and gone to 'his own place'. This 'place' can either mean his 'function' (a traitor) or his 'destination' (tragic death and, ultimately, hell). The phrase 'ministry and apostleship' means 'ministry consisting of apostleship' (cf. 1.17).

1.26a. And they cast lots: We should note that the disciples cast lots after due preparations and prayer, much in the spirit of Proverbs 16.33. After this incident we hear no more of casting lots in Acts; the Church rather followed direct guidance of the Holy Spirit (cf. Acts 6.3–6; 13.2–3).

Here again, we detect a word play with 'lot' (Gk, *klēros*): Judas had been 'allotted his share (*klēros*) in this ministry' (v. 17) but failed; now the lot (*klēros*) fell on another who would continue the work Judas had been supposed to do.

 ## Interpretation

The Church in prayer

The disciples now returned to Jerusalem, to the private place in which they were staying. All the apostles appointed by Jesus (1.2) were there, except Judas Iscariot. The shift in the order of the names reflects the different roles they will play in Acts. For example, John, prominent in the following stories (e.g. 3.1, 3, 4, 11; 4.13, 19; 8.14), is listed next to Peter, and Andrew who does not appear in the book has moved to fourth. Women were there too. These had been following Jesus from Galilee (Luke 8.1–3), and were witnesses to the death (23.49), the burial 23.54–56) and the resurrection (24.1–10, 22) of Jesus. The presence of Mary is also noteworthy. Just as the Holy Spirit had come upon her and the power of the Most High had overshadowed her, before she gave birth to the

Messiah (Luke 1.35), so at the time of the Church's birth, she now finds herself among the members of Jesus' spiritual family, waiting once again for the Holy Spirit to come upon her and empower her, now as a disciple of Jesus.

The Church prayed, as they waited for the Holy Spirit. Prayer was one of the many significant threads which bound Jesus and the Church together. Jesus and the Church on their knees show their conviction that history belongs to God's sovereign providence, and that the way of the Church lies in faithful obedience to that providential will of God. Jesus had taught them 'to pray always and not to lose heart' (Luke 18.1), especially for the gift of the Holy Spirit (Luke 11.9–13). This is what the Church was doing now.

The restoration of the Twelve (vv. 15–26)

In a way, this episode interrupts the flow of the narrative from the promise of the Spirit (1.1–11) to its fulfilment (2.1ff.). This makes us feel that we are dealing with something important here, something that has to be settled before the coming of the Spirit. Three points merit special comment.

The replacement of Judas signified the restoration of Israel. In Luke, Jesus had given 'the Twelve' the authority to proclaim the kingdom of God and to heal (9.1–6). He had also conferred on them a kingdom, promising that they would eat and drink at his table in his kingdom and they would sit on thrones judging the twelve tribes of Israel (22.28–30). Now they were the representatives of the eschatological Israel, the renewed people of God. After his suffering and resurrection, Jesus once again taught the apostles about the kingdom of God (Acts 1.5), promising them that they would participate in God's work of restoring the kingdom by becoming his witnesses (1.6–8). Thus, the betrayal of Judas signified more than a personal tragedy; it meant 'the breaking of the fellowship', which endangered the fulfilment of God's work of restoration. So the fellowship of 'the Twelve' had to be restored first, before the process of restoration began in earnest.

This explains the peculiarity of the situation. The Church's concern was not so much to fill the number twelve as to mend the defection caused by one of its members. They did not need someone who could replace Judas but someone who would take the 'place' or 'lot' Judas had had. Thus Luke's real concern does not lie in Matthias himself but in the restoration of the Twelve, a point eloquently illustrated by Matthias' absence from the rest of the book.

The Scripture has to be fulfilled

This episode also illustrates the importance of the Scripture for understanding Jesus and his work in Luke–Acts. In order to justify the replacement of Judas, Peter quotes two separate passages from Psalms with the characteristic *dei*, a word denoting the 'divine necessity' that the Scripture has to be fulfilled. (The word occurs 99 times in the NT, 40 of which are in Luke and Acts.)

For Luke, as for the other NT writers, the Scripture is the book about Christ, a book in which the Holy Spirit foretells the suffering and resurrection of Jesus the Messiah. As the risen Lord declared in the Gospel, 'These are my words that I spoke to you while I was still with you – that everything written about me in the law of Moses, the prophets, and the psalms must (*dei*) be fulfilled' (Luke 24.44). In a way, the Scripture is more important than the parabolic miracle of Lazarus' coming back to life (16.27–32), or even than the physical encounter with the risen Jesus, as is suggested by the Emmaus episode (24.25–27, 31–32). So the risen Jesus 'opened their minds to understand the scriptures' (24.45) and 'interpreted to them the things about himself in all the scriptures' (24.27), declaring, 'You are witnesses of these things' (24.48). Becoming a witness of Jesus' resurrection means testifying to the resurrection promised in the Scriptures and now 'fulfilled among us' (Luke 1.1). By so doing, they will proclaim the heart-warming truth that all history, culminating in the death and resurrection of Jesus, is the result of God's sovereign providence (Acts 2.24–36; 13.27–41).

 STUDY SUGGESTIONS

Word study

1 What is the meaning of the Greek word *homothymadon*?

2 What is the meaning of the term 'Scripture' in the New Testament?

Review of content

3 What are the differences between the lists of apostles in Acts and Luke?

4 What did the Early Church think of Psalms?

5 What is the significance of the election of Matthias?

Bible study

6 Read the following verses in Acts and explain why the disciples were praying.

   (a) 2.42; (b) 6.4, 6; (c) 10.9; (d) 13.3; (e) 28.8.

7 'The scripture had to be fulfilled.'

   (a) Read Luke 16.27–31 and explain why the Scripture is important for our faith.

   (b) Read Luke 24.25–35 and say how the Scripture works in God's forming of our faith.

Discussion and application

8 Both in his Gospel and in Acts, Luke stresses the importance of prayer. Does this still apply to us modern Christians living in a world of science and technology?

9 How important is the Scripture in forming our faith and guiding our life, both individually and as a community? What are the practical implications of the belief that the Scripture is God's word?

Acts 2.1–13

The disciples are filled with the Spirit

 Summary

The disciples are filled with the promised Holy Spirit, and Jews from all around the world hear them declare great deeds of God in inspired languages.

 Notes

2.1a. The day of Pentecost: This Jewish feast (literally 'fiftieth') falls on the 'fiftieth' day after the day following the Passover sabbath (Leviticus 23.15–21). It is also called 'the Feast of Weeks' (Exodus 34.22; Deuteronomy 16.10) or 'the Day of the First Fruits' (Numbers 28.26). This feast is the next great pilgrim feast after Jesus' death at the time of Passover. After winter, sea travel was much easier. So Jerusalem would be filled with pilgrims from all over the world for the feast, as 2.9–11 amply illustrates.

Pentecost was connected with the bestowal of the law in some Jewish traditions, and some scholars relate it to God's bestowal of the Spirit on that day. But Luke does not show any intention of making that point (cf. Ephesians 4.8, where the ascent of Moses is likened to that of Jesus and the gift of the Spirit through him, through a quotation from Psalm 68.18).

The phrase, 'had come' may suggest the idea of fulfilment (so the Greek; cf. 'had fully come', NKJV).

2.1b. All together in one place: This phrase seems to refer to the full 120 people mentioned in 1.15. The precise location of this 'place' is less clear. Are we to imagine all 120 in one house? Or are they now in a different, perhaps more public, place?

Interestingly, Luke frequently depicts all believers as being together, clearly with a view to underscoring the unity of the Church (2.44; 4.24; 5.12).

2.2a. And suddenly from heaven: The suddenness of the event suggests that something supernatural is happening; that the sound was 'from heaven' confirms it.

2.2b. A sound like the rush of a violent wind: In vv. 2–3, Luke tries to convey the supernatural with the help of vivid natural analogies, both auditory (v. 2) and visual (v. 3). Wind is one of the images of theophany, symbolizing divine presence and power (2 Samuel 5.24; 22.16; 1 Kings 19.11; Job 37.9; Psalm 104.4; Ezekiel 13.13). The wind is often connected to the divine Spirit (Ezekiel 37.9–14; John 3.8).

2.3a. Divided tongues, as of fire: This recalls the words of John the Baptist that Jesus would baptize people with fire and the Holy Spirit (Luke 3.16; Acts 1.5). Like wind, fire is also a feature of divine presence (Exodus 3.2; 13.21; 19.16, 18; Isaiah 66.15–16). As in the message of John the Baptist, it is also connected with God's judgement (Luke 3.17; 2 Thessalonians 1.7).

2.3b. And a tongue rested on each of them: The tongue was on each of the assembly. That is, every single one of them ('All of them', v. 4) received the Holy Spirit. Incidentally, the 'tongue' (of fire) is the same word as the 'language' ('tongues', NASB) in the next verse, but the context requires that their meanings are different.

2.4a. Filled with the Holy Spirit: This event fulfils the promise in 1.5. Thus, the 'baptism' of the Holy Spirit and 'being filled' with the Holy Spirit are virtually the same. Luke does not show any intention of distinguishing the two (cf. 11.15–16).

2.4b. And began to speak in other languages: NRSV's translation ('languages') assumes that the tongue spoken here is different from the ecstatic but unintelligible speech in 1 Corinthians 14.1–25. Those who heard the disciples did understand what their 'tongues' meant.

2.4c. As the Spirit gave them ability: The clause literally means: 'as the Spirit was giving them utterance' (NASB). The word 'utterance' here is somewhat unusual, often denoting prophetic speech (LXX 1 Chronicles 25.1; Ezekiel 13.9; Micah 5.12).

2.5. Devout Jews from every nation under heaven living in Jerusalem: Now the scene was no longer private but public: the crowd could hear the disciples. For an obvious reason, Luke's interest falls particularly on the Diaspora Jews, 'Jews from every nation'. The wording ('living') suggests that these were not just temporary visitors but those Jews who had settled in Jerusalem, either to study or to have their end in the holy city. The phrase 'every nation under heaven' underscores the universality of the people represented here, a point impressively confirmed by the long list of names in vv. 9–11. Yet, these were all Jews, and there is a long way to go until the Church would welcome the Gentiles into its community (10.1—11.18).

2.6a. And at this sound the crowd gathered and was bewildered: 'This sound' can either refer to the sound of the Spirit or the sound of the disciples. In view of v. 6b, the latter is more likely. The Greek word behind 'bewildered' appears only in Acts in the NT (2.6; 9.22; 19.32; 21.27, 31). Some interpreters connect it with the 'confusion' of the Babel story, but Luke himself does not press the point.

2.6b. Each . . . in the native language of each: The Spirit was not on the bewildered hearers but on the speakers who had received utterances from the Spirit.

2.7a. Amazed and astonished: Luke reports no less than four times (using three different words) that the people were amazed (vv. 6, 7, 12). This underscores the miraculous nature of the event.

2.7b. Are not all these . . . Galileans?: All the disciples were Galileans speaking the same Galilean dialect. This stands in stark contrast to the diverse origins of the crowd in vv. 8–11.

2.9–10. Parthians . . . Judea . . . visitors from Rome, both Jews and proselytes: The precise logic behind the arrangement of this long list is unclear. The list looks impressive in its variety of nationalities, but many regions important in Acts are curiously missing, such as Syria, Cilicia, Macedonia and Achaia. The inclusion of Judea is puzzling; some suggest that here the 'Judea' should be understood in its widest possible sense. Rome is important, since it is the final destination of Luke's story. It is possible that the visitors from Rome heard the gospel that day and carried it back to Rome to be the founding members of the Roman church (cf. 28.15).

2.10. Both Jews and proselytes: A proselyte was a Gentile converted to Judaism through three rites:

1 circumcision;

2 purificatory self-baptism;

3 the offering of a sacrifice.

Not surprisingly, circumcision was the greatest hurdle to full conversion, and those who wanted to be associated with Judaism without being circumcised were called 'God-fearers' (10.2) or 'worshippers of God' (16.14). Paul's earliest converts came mostly from this rank of Gentiles.

2.11. God's deeds of power: This probably refers to God's great deeds in saving his people (cf. Luke 1.49–55). Hearing the praise of God in foreign languages may have been common during great festival seasons, but now people were hearing such praises in all different languages from the lips of the Galileans!

2.12. 'What does this mean?': Miracles often elicit amazement, and this in turn provides opportunities for proclaiming the gospel (e.g. 3.10–11; 4.9).

2.13. But others sneered: This response is a bit surprising, since the hearers clearly understood the praise uttered by the disciples. This indicates the ecstatic, though intelligible, nature of their speaking in tongues. However, such a mistaken inference would immediately be corrected by Peter in the following speech.

 Interpretation

The coming of the Holy Spirit (2.1–4)

The coming of the Holy Spirit is depicted in four steps: temporal and special circumstances (v. 1); auditory description (v. 2); visionary description (v. 3); the reception of the Spirit and its result (v. 4). The disciples were 'all together in one place' (v. 1). Just as they had been told by the risen Jesus, they stayed in Jerusalem waiting for what the Father had promised (1.5, 8). This note of expectation/fulfilment seems to be reflected in the somewhat strangely phrased 'As the day of Pentecost was being fulfilled' (author's translation).

Luke describes the coming of the Holy Spirit in just three verses, but it creates a vivid impression on the reader's mind with effective use of natural analogies such as wind and fire. Evoking such images as the sound of 'a violent wind' and the display of many-tongued fire, Luke presents the event primarily as a case of *theophany*, God's powerful presence. All the disciples there were filled with this powerful presence of God, as promised by Jesus: 'You will receive power when the Holy Spirit has come upon you' (1.8).

There is an ongoing debate within Christianity concerning the manner of the Holy Spirit's coming and working. Some identify regeneration with the baptism of the Holy Spirit (e.g. Reformed Churches), while others differentiate between the two (Pentecostals). The Holy Spirit is surely essential to being a Christian (19.1–6), but Luke does not show any interest in drawing a dogmatically unified picture of the Spirit's working. For one thing, we are not sure whether the presence of the Holy Spirit is permanent or temporary. While we do not hear of the Holy Spirit's leaving believers, we do hear stories about Peter or the whole Church being filled with the Holy Spirit *again* (4.8, 31). Luke also draws our attention to the numerous occasions where the Holy Spirit guides and empowers the Church in need (Luke 12.12), as is well illustrated by the Stephen story (Acts 6.3, 8–10; 7.55). In some Christian circles there are tendencies to regard the Pentecost incident as unique for its redemptive-historical significance. Yet Luke himself seems more interested in the continuity, rather than the differences, of the Spirit's activity (10.44–47; 11.15–17). Rather than using Luke's account to justify or refute particular doctrines of the Spirit we hold, it would be much wiser to aim to discover what Luke himself tries to say with such a rich and dynamic description of the Holy Spirit.

The Holy Spirit gave the disciples the ability to speak 'in other tongues' or 'in other languages' (NRSV). Scholars differ on what the disciples actually spoke. Some think that they spoke in foreign languages, as NRSV suggests. This is supported by the repeated statement that the crowd heard the disciples 'in the native language of each' (v. 6), 'in our own native language' (v. 8) and 'in our own languages' (v. 11). Others think that they spoke something unintelligible in ecstasy, not foreign languages. The fact that people jibed at the disciples as being drunk supports this.

What happened was really extraordinary. But it was not something that can be written off as mere drunkenness, since those who heard it did recognize that the disciples were declaring great deeds of God. So it must be God's doing, God's giving his own powerful presence to those who had been waiting for it. Therefore, the primary significance of speaking in tongues is evidential, demonstrating God's saving presence among his people. Later these Jewish Christians will recognize God's welcoming presence among the Gentiles by seeing them receiving the Holy Spirit and hearing them speak in tongues (10.46; 19.6).

The response of the crowd (2.5–13)

Now the disciples are in the public eye, though we do not know precisely how such a transition was made. Luke repeatedly underscores the fact that those who heard the disciples were astounded (vv. 6, 7, 12), which is his way of indicating the supernatural nature of the event. God works; people are amazed.

Luke allots no fewer than three verses to the list of countries represented by the crowd. There were people there 'from every nation under heaven' (v. 5). This must have to do with the promise that the disciples, empowered by the Holy Spirit, would be witnesses of Jesus not only in Jerusalem but 'to the ends of the earth' (1.8). Thus, even at the beginning where everything is pretty much Jewish, the note of universality is struck quite clearly.

 STUDY SUGGESTIONS

Word study

1 What feast is the Pentecost in the Old Testament?

2 What is a 'proselyte'?

Review of content

3 What is the main point of Luke's use of vivid natural analogies for the coming of the Holy Spirit?

4 Identify the four steps in Luke's portrayal of the coming of the Holy Spirit.

5 What are the two responses of the crowd to the disciples' speaking in tongues?

6 In Acts what is the primary significance of speaking in tongues?

Bible study

7 Compare different cases of the Holy Spirit's coming (8.14–17; 10.44–48; 11.15–18). What is the significance of receiving the Holy Spirit?

Discussion and application

8 The Holy Spirit brings about the gifts of speaking in tongues both in Acts and in Paul's writings. How are we modern Christians to think of these 'gifts of the Spirit'?

9 Paul emphasizes the Holy Spirit's role of uniting different groups of people in one single body of Christ, but modern Christians are often divided because of their different views of the Holy Spirit (e.g. the debates about the ongoing relevance of 'speaking in tongues' or the 'baptism' of the Holy Spirit). How should we explain this ironic situation? What can we do to mend the gap between different groups of Christians, e.g. between charismatic or Pentecostal Christians and Reformed or Presbyterian Christians?

Acts 2.14–41

Peter's first witness to the risen Jesus

 Summary

Peter powerfully witnesses to the resurrection of Jesus, connecting both the gift of the Spirit and the Scripture to the risen Jesus. A huge number of people came to believe Jesus.

 Notes

2.14a. Peter, standing with the eleven: This is the first instance of fulfilling the promise that the disciples would be Spirit-empowered witnesses of Jesus (1.8; Luke 24.46–49). Peter acted as the spokesperson of the apostles but he was by no means alone (2.37).

2.14b. Raised his voice . . . 'let this be known to you . . . listen to what I say': These rhetorical statements are designed to underscore the importance of the speech.

2.15. These are not drunk: Peter used the mistaken charge of drunkenness as an opportunity for witness. For similar cases, see 4.5–12; 7.1–53; 11.2–18. The point is: 'people drink at night, not in the daytime. It is now only nine o'clock in the morning, so the charge of drunkenness is simply mistaken.' Then Peter proceeded to explain the true nature of the event.

2.16. This is what was spoken through the prophet Joel: This is a bold assertion. What people saw happening before them, far from being drunkenness, was the very fulfilment of God's promise given through the prophet Joel.

2.17. In the last days . . . I will pour out my Spirit upon all flesh: Joel has 'afterwards', but Peter changed it into 'in the last days', heightening the note of eschatological fulfilment. One of the hallmarks of the last days would be God's universal bestowal of his Spirit (cf. Numbers 11.29).

2.18. Even upon my slaves . . . and they shall prophesy: Inclusion of the 'slaves, both men and women' further underlines the universality of the gift. Here Peter added 'and they shall prophesy' to Joel's text to make explicit what is implicit there.

2.19. Portents . . . above and signs . . . below: Peter added 'signs' to the quotation. In Acts 'signs and wonders' typically accompany the Spirit-filled witnesses of the gospel (2.43; 4.16, 22, 30; 5.12; 6.8; 7.36; 14.3; 15.12). In the Old Testament (OT) the phrase is applied to Moses (Deuteronomy 34.10–12; cf. 13.1–3).

2.20. The sun shall be turned to darkness: It is possible to connect this with what happened at the crucifixion (Luke 23.44).

2.21. Everyone who calls on the name of the Lord shall be saved: In Joel, 'the Lord' refers to God but in this Christian context it is applied to the risen Jesus whom God has made 'Lord and Messiah/Christ' (v. 36). Paul also quotes this passage (Romans 10.13). Again, we note a strong note of universality: 'everyone who . . .'

2.22a. That God did through him: God is the real subject. Peter contrasts what God did through Jesus with what people (Jews) did to this Jesus (v. 23). The 'deeds of power, wonders, and signs' connect Jesus both to God's promises in the Scripture and to what the disciples will do in his name, thus underscoring the continuity in God's redemptive history. See the note on v. 19.

2.22b. Among you, as you yourselves know: What Jesus did cannot be disputed, but some would wish to draw a different conclusion about its source (Luke 11.14–22).

2.23. According to the definite plan and foreknowledge of God: God's sovereignty and human culpability stand in stark contrast (also vv. 32, 36). In early parts of Acts the Jews are regularly accused of being the murderers of Jesus (3.13–15; 4.10–11; 5.30; 10.39–40; 13.27–30). In this context, repentance means to repent their sin of handing Jesus over to be killed by the lawless Gentiles. Yet the suffering which they inflicted on Jesus was all part of God's set purpose, as is emphasized again and again (3.18; 4.27–28; Luke 24.26, 44, 46).

2.24a. But God raised him up, having freed him from death: The oppositional conjunction 'but' creates a strong contrast between God's raising Jesus in this verse and 'you crucified and killed' in the previous verse. The 'from death' literally means 'from the pains of death', an expression derived from 'cords of death' (Psalms 18.4; 116.3) and 'cords of Sheol' (Psalm 18.5) in the OT.

2.24b. It was impossible for him to be held in its power: Jesus' resurrection was as much part of God's definite plan foretold in the Scripture as his suffering, a point Peter will soon prove from the Scripture.

2.25–28. I saw the Lord always before me . . .: This is a quotation of the LXX version of Psalm 16.8–11, which is more suitable for the idea of resurrection than the Hebrew text. This passage was probably a piece of OT 'testimony' used by the early Christians to support their belief that

God had raised Jesus. This psalm is attributed to David, but Luke (Peter) interprets it as concerning the resurrection of the Messiah. David was a prophet and by the Spirit of prophecy he spoke for the Messiah.

2.26–27. My flesh will live in hope: It is not clear whether Psalm 16 itself refers to a rescue from untimely death or being shown the ways of life after death. Luke naturally takes it in the latter sense. The flesh of the Messiah will not undergo decomposition, and in the knowledge of that his flesh will 'live' or 'rest' in the hope of resurrection. 'Corruption' (Luke = LXX) makes explicit the idea implied by 'pit' (Hebrew).

2.28. You have made known to me the ways of life: Verse 28 is the positive reversal of vv. 26–27. Here life means more than mere escape from death but joyful existence in God's presence.

2.29. David . . . died . . . and his tomb is with us to this day: David did not write this psalm of resurrection about himself, since he died and still remains buried.

2.30. He was a prophet: David's knowledge of God's oath is expressed in Psalm 132.11.

2.31. He was not abandoned to Hades . . .: This is a fulfilled version of Psalm 16.10 quoted in v. 27. Now the tense is in the past, referring to the resurrection of Jesus the Messiah.

2.32a. This Jesus God raised up: Since God raised Jesus up and he had never done it before, Jesus must be the Messiah that David foretold in his psalm.

2.32b. All of us are witnesses: This recalls earlier statements such as 1.8 and 1.22. Apostles are, more than anything else, witnesses of Jesus (3.15; 4.33; 5.32; 10.41; 13.31).

2.33. He has poured out this that you both see and hear: The coming of the Spirit is the result of Jesus' resurrection and exaltation. Jesus the Messiah, now raised and exalted by God, received the Spirit from the Father and poured it out on people. In this sense he is the one who baptizes people with fire and with the Holy Spirit (1.5; Luke 3.16).

2.34–35. The Lord said to my Lord, 'Sit at my right hand . . .': Once again David spoke about the exaltation of the Messiah. This is a quotation of Psalm 110.1, the one also quoted by Jesus himself (Luke 20.41–44).

2.36. God has made him both Lord and Messiah, this Jesus whom you crucified: Jesus is now in the position of supremacy ('at my right hand'), and thus Lord of the whole universe (Romans 10.9; 1 Corinthians 12.3; Philippians 2.11). Peter's speech concludes with a sharp antithesis between what God did to Jesus and what (Jewish) people did to him. This will become a major point of conflict between the apostles and the Jerusalem leaders (5.28).

2.37. Brothers, what should we do?: Peter's sermon is interrupted as it reaches its climax (cf. 10.44; 17.32; 22.22).

2.38. Repent and be baptized . . . in the name of Jesus Christ: Repentance, a complete change of heart and conduct, has always been an integral part of the Christian gospel since John the Baptist. Somewhat surprisingly, the early Christians continued the rite of (water) baptism 'for the forgiveness of sins' even after Pentecost. But now it is closely linked with the gift of the Holy Spirit. Four elements of conversion listed here (repentance, baptism, forgiveness of sin, reception of the Holy Spirit) are also found elsewhere in Acts (10.44–48; 19.1–6).

2.39. Everyone whom the Lord our God calls to him: The promise extends both in time ('for your children') and space ('for all who are far away').

2.40. From this corrupt generation: In this context this refers to the Jews who reject Jesus (Luke 9.41; 11.29; cf. Deuteronomy 32.5; Psalm 78.8; Philippians 2.15).

 Interpretation

The fulfilment of the promise of the Holy Spirit (2.14–21)

Peter turns the people's jibe into an occasion for witnessing to the resurrection of Jesus. Having dismissed their sneer as mistaken, Peter makes the bold claim that what people see and hear is none other than the fulfilment of God's promise of his Spirit made through the prophet Joel. In the last days, God would give his Spirit to 'all flesh', and those who received it would prophesy. This promise had now begun to be fulfilled when the disciples were filled with the Holy Spirit and began to speak in tongues. This suggests that Luke considers speaking in tongues as a form of prophecy (cf. 19.6).

Peter's quotation of Joel concludes with the promise of salvation: 'Then every one who calls on the name of the Lord shall be saved' (v. 21). This will be connected with Peter's call, 'Save yourselves from this corrupt generation' (v. 40). Before that, however, Peter has to draw people's attention to Jesus of Nazareth, the one who makes this promise meaningful.

Peter witnesses to the resurrection of Jesus (2.22–36)

Granted that the Pentecost experience is the fulfilment of God's ancient promise, what does it have to do with Jesus? So now Peter moves to Jesus, attributing this gift of the Spirit to the risen Jesus. Peter begins with what his audience already knows, i.e. such marvellous deeds God did among them through Jesus of Nazareth (v. 22). Then he draws their attention to what they did to him: 'you crucified and killed'. But there is something they should know about this: the Scripture had already foretold that Jesus must undergo such a fate. Thus, it was 'according to the definite plan and foreknowledge of God' that he was handed over to the Israelites (v. 23). Yet there is more. The Scripture also speaks of his resurrection, and naturally, 'God raised him up' and 'freed him from [the pain of] death' (v. 24). Peter then goes into a scriptural argument on Psalm 16.8–11 (in conjunction with 132.11) to prove the resurrection of the Davidic Messiah. And he applies this scriptural testimony to Jesus: 'This Jesus God raised up, and of that all of us are witnesses' (v. 32). But even this is not all. The same David also has foretold his ascension (vv. 34–35). So he was exalted to the right hand of God, and that explains the true nature of what is happening right now: 'Having received from the Father the promise of the Holy Spirit, he has poured out this that you both see and hear' (v. 33). Therefore, the conclusion is inescapable, and 'the entire house of Israel [should] know with certainty that God has made him both Lord and Messiah, this Jesus whom you crucified' (v. 36).

First converts to the gospel (2.37–41)

We think of Pentecost as the day when the Holy Spirit came. True, but the Holy Spirit did not remain idle. Just as the Spirit empowered the disciples for effective witnessing, the same Spirit also worked in the hearts of those who heard their message: 'they were cut to the heart' and asked the apostles, 'Brothers, what should we do?' (v. 37). So Peter tells them how they can save themselves 'from this corrupt generation': repentance and baptism in the name of Jesus. This will bring forgiveness of their sins, and they will receive the gift of the Holy Spirit just as they see and hear the disciples do (v. 38). Luke reports that three thousand people were added to the number of disciples; such is the power of the Holy Spirit.

We note three additional points. First, we perceive a certain irony in Peter's speech. He keeps striking the note of universality (v. 17, 'all flesh'; v. 21, 'everyone who calls on the name of the Lord'; v. 39, 'everyone whom the Lord our God calls'), but he himself still believes that salvation is only for 'the entire house of Israel' (v. 36). Peter still has some way to go until he finally realizes God's love for the uncircumcised Gentiles (10.44–48).

Second, reading Acts, we cannot help asking about the possible sources of all these speeches reported by Luke. Does he have written accounts in front of him, either Aramaic or Greek? Or has he studied the shape of the earliest sermons and reproduced it in his own way? Or are they purely Luke's own composition, having nothing to do with what Peter or Paul may or may not have said? We can only speculate; inevitably, scholars differ widely in these matters. What we do know is that they are not exact reproductions of actual sermons preached by Peter or Paul; they are summaries of them prepared by Luke. We do not need to doubt that they contain the gist of what was actually said by the apostles, but it is also true that we cannot ignore Luke's role as the author of Acts.

Third, we can also ask about the precise relationship between water baptism and the gift of the Holy Spirit. As far as Acts is concerned, we cannot draw any fixed formula from it. Usually baptism precedes the bestowal of the Holy Spirit, as is the case here, but it can also happen the other way round, as in the cases of Paul and Cornelius (9.17–19; 10.44–48). At times the gift of the Spirit does not necessarily follow the baptism (8.12–16); it often seems to have more to do with the laying on of hands than with baptism (8.17–18; 19.5–6). Overall, Luke does believe that both of them are indispensable in becoming a Christian, but he is not much concerned about the order of the two.

 STUDY SUGGESTIONS

Word study

1 Who does the 'Lord' refer to both in the Joel passage and in Peter's sermon? (vv. 21, 36).

Review of content

2 For what purpose does Peter quote the Joel passage?

3 For what purpose does Peter quote the Psalms passages?

4 To whom does Peter attribute the gift of the Holy Spirit?

Bible study

5 Read Romans 10.9; 1 Corinthians 12.3; Philippians 2.11. What does it mean that the risen Jesus is now our 'Lord'?

6 Read Acts 8.16, 10.44–48 and 19.1–6. Can you identify the four elements of conversion?

Discussion and application

7 Peter accentuates both God's sovereignty and human culpability: the Jews were responsible for the death of Jesus, yet it happened according to the definite plan of God. Is it possible to hold these two convictions together? How do you think this attitude can help us cope with tragic events in our lives?

8 The Holy Spirit is promised to those who repent and are baptized. How does this apply to us modern Christians?

Acts 2.42–47

The fellowship of the believers

 Summary

Luke sketches the dynamic life of the Jerusalem community.

 Notes

2.42. To the apostles' teaching and fellowship, to the breaking of bread and the prayers: These are the four prominent features of the Jerusalem church. The word behind 'they devoted themselves' suggests a steady pattern, not a fad of the moment.

1 Their life was founded on the apostolic teaching. They considered this as the teaching of the Lord mediated through the Spirit-filled apostles. Paul also underscores the importance of the apostolic teaching (Romans 6.17; 16.17; 2 Timothy 4.2; Titus 1.9).

2 They took part in the fellowship (Gk, *koinōnia*, 'sharing'). This fellowship in the Spirit has both vertical (with God) and horizontal (with fellow believers) dimensions. It will express itself in many concrete ways, one of which is sharing their material possessions (see below).

3 They took part in the breaking of the bread. This may either mean ordinary meals or the Lord's Supper which formed part of such regular meals (Luke 22.19; 24.30; cf. 1 Corinthians 11.23–26).

4 They devoted themselves to prayers. This probably means the communal prayers of the Church, similar to the regular Jewish prayers. The importance of prayer in Luke–Acts has already been noted. The picture drawn here looks 'ideal' but that does not mean that it is therefore misleading.

2.43. Wonders and signs: These are harbingers of 'the Lord's great and glorious day' (2.20). These portents were first given by Jesus (2.22), and now by his apostles as the sign of God's Spirit working through them (4.30–31). This engenders awe among people both inside and out (3.10; 5.5, 11, 13; 19.17). It anticipates the miracle story in Acts 3.

2.44–45. All who believed . . . had all things in common: This is a concrete manifestation of the fellowship. For Luke our attitude towards material possessions is one of the most important tests of our faith (6.1–6; 11.28–29; 20.33–35; 24.17; Luke 19.8).

2.46. Together in the temple . . . broke bread at home: The believers continued to meet in the Temple for prayer and witness (Luke 24.53). But Luke does not tell us how much they were involved in the temple services. On the other hand, they 'broke bread . . . and ate their food' at home, i.e. they had their fellowship meals at various houses. The 'house' was the most important space for the Early Church: apostolic teaching, daily fellowship, prayer and worship (5.42; 8.3; 11.14; 16.15, 31–32; 18.8; 20.20). The 'glad and generous hearts' also looks back to their willingness to share their possessions.

2.47a. The goodwill of all the people: The initial attitude to the gospel was quite favourable even among those who did not accept the gospel. No hint of tension is visible yet.

2.47b. Day by day the Lord added to their number: Luke frequently refers to the dynamic growth of the Church (6.7; 9.31; 11.1–21; 12.12; 14.1).

 Interpretation

Life together in the power of the Holy Spirit

This is the first of those sketches of the Early Church Luke provides in the course of his account (4.32–35; 5.12–16; 9.31). A few things merit special comments. First, the apostolic teaching played a key role in the establishment of the Church (4.2, 18; 5.21, 25, 28, 42). So the apostles continued the 'teaching' ministry their Lord had begun (1.1). Eventually, these teachings were collected in the NT, and it is only natural that this book has now become the foundation of the Church.

Second, the frequent division between the evangelistic *kerygma* ('proclamation') and the ethical *didache* ('teaching') should not be pressed too hard. We may distinguish the two for the sake of convenience, but in practice they can never be separated from each other, any more than faith and obedience can occur without each other. The early Christians called the gospel 'the Way' to walk, not a set of doctrines to believe intellectually (9.2 and in many other places).

Third, the Earliest Church shared everything in common, and that was the direct result of their receiving the Holy Spirit. Such an ideal state did not last long, but the fact still remains that our attitude towards material possessions is a crucial barometer for our spiritual condition, a point amply illustrated by such stories as the message of John the Baptist (Luke 3.10–14), the folly of a rich farmer (12.13–21), the rich man and Lazarus

(16.19–30), and the story of Zacchaeus who repents of his sin by redistributing his money (19.1–10). The gospel is for the poor (6.20), and there is no spiritualizing it, 'for where your treasure is, there your heart will be also' (12.34).

Fourth, we should also remember that this summary follows Peter's powerful witness to the gospel. The 'ideal' society drawn here is a very concrete, real community of those who have come to believe Jesus as their Messiah and Lord and live a new life in the power of the Spirit. Such is the power of the gospel, and this is one dimension of the 'certainty' or 'truth' of the gospel that Luke wants his Theophilus to be convinced of. The details of this ideal society cannot be reproduced here and now, but the Church is still guided by the same Spirit who empowered the earliest followers of Jesus. So we keep asking: how can we show the power of the gospel in our own life settings?

 STUDY SUGGESTIONS

Word study

1 What does the 'breaking of bread' signify? (Luke 22.19; 24.30; 1 Corinthians 11.23–26).

Review of content

2 What are the four major elements in the life of the Jerusalem church?

3 What was the most important manifestation of 'fellowship'?

4 The believers continued to meet in the Temple. What was the purpose of it?

Bible study

5 Read 4.2, 18; 5.21, 25, 28, 42 and Ephesians 2.19–20. What can we learn about the importance of the apostolic teaching in the Early Church?

Discussion and application

6 In the Jerusalem church one of the most important expressions of the power of the gospel was 'having all things in common'. How do you think you can apply this to your church?

Acts 3.1–26

The name of Jesus heals a crippled beggar

 Summary

Peter heals a crippled beggar at the Temple, which provides another chance to proclaim the risen Jesus as the promised Messiah and saviour of Israel.

 Notes

3.1. Peter and John were going up to the temple: In Acts John appears to be a (somewhat shadowy) companion of Peter (3.4, 11; 4.13, 19; 8.14). There were two daily services at the Temple, one after dawn and the other at three o'clock in the afternoon.

3.2. The Beautiful Gate: This name does not occur anywhere else. Various identifications have been made but there is no way of knowing it for sure.

3.4. Peter looked intently: This shows a definite intention on Peter's part. The crippled man responded to this with a fixed gaze of expectation (v. 5).

3.6. What I have . . . in the name of Jesus Christ of Nazareth: Peter did not have money but he had something much better, namely, the name of Jesus Christ. This name healed this person not because it was magical but because it was (and still is) authoritative and powerful. Naturally, the 'name of Jesus' plays an important role in the stories of Acts 3 and 4 (3.6, 16; 4.10, 12, 17, 18, 30). We also note the interchange between 'name' and 'power' in 4.7.

3.8. Jumping up, he stood and began to walk . . . walking and leaping: Luke's vivid, even repetitious, description underscores that the man was completely cured. The language here reflects Isaiah 35.6. Cripples were not allowed into the Temple (2 Samuel 5.8). Thus, his entering the Temple further stresses that the healing was complete.

3.9. All the people saw: The result of the healing was known to all in the temple court, and Peter and John found themselves in the middle of an astounded crowd (v. 11).

3.11. All the people: Luke frequently refers to Israel as 'the people' (3.9; 4.10; 5.34, etc.).

Solomon's Portico: This ran along the eastern side of the outer court of the Temple. It is also called 'Solomon's Colonnade' (NIV).

3.12. Why do you stare at us, as though . . .: As in 2.14–15 Peter began by correcting the mistaken perception of the crowd.

3.13a. The God . . . has glorified his servant Jesus: Like the gift of the Spirit, the cure of the cripple is also explained as the result of Jesus' exaltation. The language here alludes to the Servant Song in Isaiah 52.13—53.12: 'My servant . . . will be exalted' (cf. 8.32). The liturgical 'the God of Abraham . . . the God of our ancestors' also connects God's work in Jesus with God's work in Israel's history, striking a strong note of continuity.

3.13b–15a. Whom you handed over . . . you killed the Author of life: As in 2.22–23 and 10.39–40, God's act of glorifying Jesus is sharply contrasted with Israel's rejection of him. The absurdity of their behaviour is carefully underlined:

1 Pilate, a Gentile who did not know God, wanted to release him (Luke 23.13–25);

2 Jesus, whom they rejected, is the God-appointed 'Holy and Righteous One' (Acts 2.27; 7.52; 22.14);

3 they let live a murderer (Luke 23.18–19) but killed the Author of life!

3.15a. The author of life: The word 'author' (Gk, *archēgos*, also rendered 'pioneer' or 'forerunner') is used here and in 5.31. Hebrews also uses it twice (2.10; 12.2). Jesus is the pioneer who has opened up the way of salvation, so that others may follow suit. Salvation has both vicarious (substitutional) and participatory dimensions.

3.15b. Whom God raised from the dead: Peter's argument takes yet another turn: now Israel's rejection of Jesus stands in sharp antithesis to God's act of raising him up. Of course, the apostles are witnesses to that.

3.16a. By faith in his name, his name itself: This brings out the truth behind Peter's appeal to Jesus' name in v. 6. Just as the Holy Spirit was given by the exalted Jesus, so this act of healing was done by the name of the exalted Jesus. We can also say that the man has been healed 'by faith in his name', since it is 'the faith [working] through him'.

3.16b. Whom you see and know: Luke underscores the public nature of the healing. As in the case of Pentecost, Peter's argument is an explanation of what has actually happened 'in the presence of all of you', something 'you see and know'.

3.17. Acted in ignorance: This verse brings out what is implicit in 2.23. Such ignorance leaves room for mercy. Of the ignorance of the rulers, see 4.25–29. In 13.27–29 Paul specifies it as the ignorance of Scripture.

3.18. In this way God fulfilled: Israel did a terrible thing in ignorance, but that was God's way of fulfilling 'what he had foretold' in the Scripture, namely, the counter-intuitive necessity that the Messiah must suffer.

3.19. Repent . . . turn to God: Doubling synonyms strengthens the force of the call.

3.20–21. Times of refreshing: This could refer to moments of relief during the eschatological distress of the present time, or to the final restoration as the 'universal restoration' in v. 21. The plural 'times' renders the former more likely but the context favours the latter. The 'restoration of all things' (NASB) recalls the prophecy in Malachi 3. In this passage, God promises that he 'will send' Elijah, who will 'restore' the heart of father to son and the heart of a man to his neighbour (Luke 1.16–17). Luke looks to the time when Jesus the Messiah will come and restore God's world (cf. Ephesians 1.10).

3.22–23. God will raise a prophet like me: Well before the Christian era, Deuteronomy 18.15–20 had been taken to refer to a specific 'prophet like Moses'. For Christians this referred to Jesus: Israel must listen to him, or they will be destroyed.

3.24–25a. All the prophets . . . predicted these days: Not just Moses (law) but all the prophets also foretold the coming of Jesus.

3.25b. Descendants . . . of the covenant: This means those who have received a place in the covenant.

3.26. God raised up his servant: God's raising up Jesus mostly refers to his resurrection. But here, as in v. 22, it means his incarnation: God raised him on to the stage of history.

 Interpretation

Healing of a lame man (3.1–10)

This episode is a concrete illustration of the 'wonders and signs' done by the apostles (2.43). The narrative follows the same pattern as in the Pentecost episode:

1 something miraculous or extraordinary happens;

2 the miracle attracts the people's attention;

3 Peter begins his witness.

The apostles display the power of the risen Jesus

This episode demonstrates the power of Jesus working through his apostles. Peter appealed to the name of Jesus, and the healing was both immediate and perfect. Calling on the name of Jesus, the apostles were doing exactly the same thing that Jesus himself had done. This powerful name, that is, the name of the 'author of life', is what the apostles possessed and gave to those who needed it. The apostles were no less powerful for their lack of 'silver or gold', since they had something more valuable, something that could 'save' people in the most comprehensive sense of the word.

God works among the people

Throughout Acts, Luke emphasizes the public nature of the miracle. The apostles did things 'among the people' (5.12). The healed person accompanied Peter and John into the Temple, thereby astounding people by the shocking contrast between his 'before' and his 'after'. The intrigued crowd gathered around the apostles; the stage was set for carrying out what they were called to do: to tell people about Jesus of Nazareth. The Earliest Church was no ghetto isolated from the rest of the world, a lamp hidden 'under a bushel' (KJV), but a lamp 'on the lampstand' (NASB) and a 'city built on a hill', a community of witness, the community that seeks to go out and proclaim the risen Jesus as the Lord and Messiah (Matthew 5.14–16).

Israel's guilt and the call for repentance

In his sermon Peter accused the people relentlessly of killing Jesus the Author of life. Yet he did so only to make them understand what God had done and open up before them the way to repentance and forgiveness: 'Repent, therefore, and turn to God!' That the people were wrong about Jesus has become unmistakable by the power of the risen Jesus working through the Spirit-filled apostles. Now that God had shown them the true identity of Jesus of Nazareth, they had to respond to the apostles' call, either under the promise of blessing or the curse of exclusion.

Israel in God's redemptive history

The Israelites were the descendants of the prophets who had predicted Jesus the Messiah; they were also children of the covenant God had made with their ancestors. So they were bound to the prophecies about Jesus: they had to listen to him! That was all the more so, since they occupied a special place in God's redemptive history. God promised Abraham, 'In your descendants all the families of the earth shall be blessed.' So Israel should be the God-appointed agent of blessing for the rest of the world. That is why God sent Jesus first to them 'to bless you by turning each of you from your wicked ways'. But they fell short of living up to such a privileged responsibility, as the following stories of persecution show. This failure would become all the more evident, as the gospel expanded itself beyond the borders of the Jewish Palestine (cf. 7.51–53; 13.46; 28.25–28).

STUDY SUGGESTIONS

Word study

1 Read 3.9; 4.10; 5.34. Who does 'the people' refer to in these verses?

2 Jesus is called 'author of life' in Acts 3.15. What does the title convey about the work of Jesus?

Review of content

3 What narrative pattern can we find in both the Pentecost episode and the healing of the cripple?

4 To what does Peter attribute the cure of the cripple?

5 What was the ultimate result of the ignorance of Israel?

Bible study

6 Does healing always require faith? Read the following passages and answer the question.

   (a) Luke 5.18–24; **(b)** Luke 8.46–48; **(c)** Luke 18.35–43; **(d)** Acts 3.2–6; **(e)** Acts 14.8–10.

7 Jesus is identified as 'a prophet like Moses'. According to Deuteronomy 18.15–20, what is the role of this prophet?

Discussion and application

8 The apostles are witnesses, and thus Luke frequently underscores the public nature of miracles. What do you think are the ways in which we can make our faith more relevant and beneficial to those outside the Church?

9 In God's purpose, Israel should have been an agent of God's blessing for the rest of the world. As the New Israel, what can we Christians do to mediate God's blessing to others?

10 What are possible ways of displaying the power of the risen Jesus through our lives?

Theological essay 1

Mission and healing in Acts

EMMANUEL ANIM

Introduction

In the book of Acts a band of faithful leaders spread the message of the gospel across the Roman Empire. This courageous group of believers preached, taught and healed the sick and the afflicted wherever they felt led by the Spirit of Christ.

In performing signs and wonders in the name of Jesus, the apostles demonstrated that the risen Lord was active in his Church and in the world as God's accredited messenger. The account in Acts ultimately demonstrates that Christ himself is present in his Church by his Spirit, and this is confirmed by the acts of signs and wonders such as healing performed in his name. Thus healing has a role in mission.

Healing as part of salvation history

Central to the message of the Bible is salvation. God is revealed as the author of salvation. The Jewish people understood salvation as freedom from limitations. Deliverance becomes a divine intervention rescuing us from the power of sin or from danger (Jeremiah 15.20), bringing about the healing of sickness (Isaiah 38.20) or release from captivity (Psalm 14.7).

Although the nation of Israel in the Old Testament believed that suffering was part of human history and experience, they were deeply convinced of the connection between personal sin and sickness (Genesis 32.32; Exodus 15.26; Leviticus 26.14–16; Numbers 12.9–16). This latter conviction gave people little sympathy for the sick and the afflicted, as such sufferings were considered to be judgement from God (Deuteronomy 32.39).

However, the Jews also believed that God could cure sickness, and for this reason he was known to them as Jehovah Rapha, 'I am the Lord, your healer' (cf. Psalm 103.3). Similarly, provision of health was seen as a gift of God granted to the obedient Jews (Exodus 15.26).

Jesus picks up the theme of sin and sickness in his own ministry and in his teachings about the kingdom of God but also indicates that sickness is not always the consequence of sin. The kingdom is where 'God is still at work in his creation and in history to redeem the world unto himself'. It is his intervention in the affairs of nations and in all of nature. For Luke, salvation is, above all, something that realizes itself in this life (Luke 4.21; 19.9; 23.43). This includes the termination of poverty, the healing of broken hearts and the recovery of sight for the blind (Luke 4.16–18). At the heart of the kingdom of God is the Church, the people of God on earth. Through the Church, God proclaims the good news of his kingdom, and Christ stands at the centre of this process.

Mission and healing: reflections from Africa

The matter of health and healing has relevance to the world view of all peoples. In Africa, as in the case of the Jews, health is not just the absence of sickness and disease but the presence of peace, harmony and prosperity in one's life. It means one is in harmony with nature and the cosmic world. As in the Hebrew tradition, most traditional Africans make a connection between sin and sickness. Chronic diseases are sometimes seen as a sign of God's judgement on the afflicted; so is barrenness or infertility. Jews believed that the gift of children or the lack of them indicated God's blessing or curse (Exodus 23.26; Deuteronomy 7.14). In Africa, it is believed that the 'violation of morals leads to a severing of the established relationship between God and his creatures, and between the living and the departed ancestors'. The consequences of this may be illness, impotence (loss of power) or infertility.

For the traditional African, health is harmony between the spiritual and physical body. Sickness is seen as an imbalance in the divine order, and healing is a means or process of restoring such harmony.

As a result of this belief, people who are sick try to find out the cause of the sickness – the diagnosis relates not to the sickness or the ailment but to the 'spiritual' cause behind the sickness. Once this is ascertained, the solution will be sought. If the source of sickness is identified to be God or the gods, the question will be: what did the person, or his/her family, do wrong?

If the sickness is traced to an individual, then the approach will be to find out if there was a quarrel between that individual and someone else, or within their families, and whether the other person has pronounced a curse or gone to ask a witch doctor or fetish priest(ess) to cause the gods to punish the sufferer.

Some believe that people may deserve a curse if they have been in the wrong and failed to admit it. Such a curse, it is said, can be removed only by confession and pacifying the spirits or by going to a stronger or higher spirit to avert the curse or sickness. It is against this religious orientation that African Christians read their Bibles and respond to the gospel. In modern Africa, most people deal with their health needs through hospitals and clinics, and only if their health problems persist do they work their way backwards through the spiritualist and Pentecostal churches and then to the traditional healing communities or shrines. Prophets and pastors are consulted while the services of the skilled or specialists such as medicine men, diviners and mediums may also be sought. This phenomenon has, however, become more pronounced in recent times. In some cases traditional healers have assumed ecclesiastical positions and function at both levels without feeling they are betraying any principle. Indeed, the Pentecostal movement, in its tapping into African spirituality, has made a significant contribution to Christian mission by making divine healing a central part of pastoral care.

Sin, suffering and healing

Identifying appropriate healing patterns in African Christianity has always been a complex issue. Among the Pentecostals and the charismatics,

41

healing functions as a validation of the pastor's or prophet's divine calling. The process of healing usually involves active participation by the sufferer. Some conditions may require the minister to ask about the sufferer's history, including any previous attempts to seek a remedy at a traditional shrine. In such a case, the process begins with confession, which may be led by the minister and followed by a prayer for deliverance, all said in the name of Jesus. The name of the sickness is often called out loud and cast out in the name of Jesus. If the sufferer is not a Christian, he or she is first led to say a sinner's prayer and made to accept Jesus Christ as his or her Lord and Saviour. The sick person may then be anointed with oil after prayers have been said.

In other cases, the minister will simply pray a prayer of faith in the hope that God will activate healing in the name of Jesus. This latter approach is not always appreciated by the sufferer, as the following case study reveals:

A middle-aged woman, Ama, confessed to her pastor that before she became a Christian she considered herself barren because she had no children after many years of marriage. As an African, she risked losing her marriage through not having children. Ama and her loving husband approached a medicine man, who performed some rituals and promised that the couple would have children. The condition attached was that, every year, Ama should visit the shrine and make sacrifices to the gods who had given her children.

Ama had a child and therefore kept her side of the covenant by making sacrifices at the shrine every year. After her second child was born, Ama stopped visiting the shrine. Her first child became seriously ill and later died. Not too long afterwards, her second child also started getting sick and Ama feared the worst. Ama went to the shrine to enquire why the child had died. The medium explained to her that she had failed in her promise to bring annual sacrifices to the gods.

Ama knew that, now that she had become a Christian, she could not continue to visit the shrine with sacrifices. She wanted her pastor's opinion on what to do.

The pastor prayed with Ama and assured her with Scripture that Jesus was greater than the gods and would protect her, and that she need not visit the shrine to make sacrifices. The child was also prayed for. After some time, Ama complained to other members of the congregation that the pastor had not done much about her problem. 'He just prayed!'

It came to light that Ama had expected the pastor's prayers to be accompanied by some ritual, such as the burning of any fetish she had been given at the shrine and perhaps anointing her and the remaining children as an assurance of a complete break with the past and its consequences. Such an act was necessary to activate her faith for healing and the deliverance of her family.

Ritual sacrifices are very much a part of the African religious outlook and world view, and may enable an understanding and appreciation of Christ, who underwent a sacrificial ritual not only as propitiation for our sins but also as a means to our healing. Sacrifices are linked not only to healing and the protection of the individual and the community but also to prosperity, good health, long life and the cleansing of pollution. Sin is considered a spiritual and moral pollution which has particular consequences. The majority of African people hold the view that God and the gods are concerned with the moral life of humankind. There is no belief that people are punished in the hereafter for what they did wrong in this present life. The punishment for sin is experienced in this life and therefore misfortunes are often interpreted as indicating that the victim has broken some moral or ritual law against God, the spirits, the elders or other members of society. However, the belief is also held that some members of society, such as magicians, sorcerers, witches and diviners, are able to cause harm or bring sickness to other human beings for diabolical reasons.

In the African context, sacrifices involve the shedding of the blood of human beings, animals or birds, while offerings do not involve blood but concern the giving of all other things, such as foodstuffs, water, wine, milk and honey. Sacrifice is the point where the visible and the invisible worlds meet. It is humankind's attempt to project itself into the spirit or the invisible world. At that point one may be assured of God's intervention or blessing in a particular situation.

At the traditional shrines, performance of a healing ceremony usually involves some form of sacrifice. It may be the slaying of a cow, a sheep, a fowl, a pigeon or in some extreme cases a human being. The shedding of such blood is intended to appease the ancestors and the gods who act on behalf of God the Supreme Being. The belief is that the shedding of blood brings about the preservation of another, be it an individual or a group in a community. It also averts disaster, misfortune or loss of power. The nature of the object of sacrifice depends upon the severity of the sickness or misfortune or the sin that has been committed.

Once healing has taken place, the supplicant or the one healed is obliged to give an offering of (a) specified item(s) to the oracle as a sign of submission and recognition of divine grace. In this regard, sacrifices and offerings become a form of worship of a higher moral and spiritual authority. This is the covenant Ama was expected to keep, having been cured of her infertility. Her children are now a constant reminder of the power that made her whole, a gift which she must reciprocate by her annual thanksgiving offering.

The essence of sacrifice with reference to healing and forgiveness of sin is extensively discussed in the book of Hebrews. The OT sacrifices had ritual significance but they were also types foreshadowing what was yet to come, the sacrifice of Christ. Jesus is identified in Isaiah as the suffering servant (Isaiah 52—53), who is to be the sacrificial lamb for the guilt of others (Isaiah 53.10). The need to repeat various sacrifices suggests that they were inadequate to remove sin, and were incapable of granting human beings entrance into the Holy of Holies. The rending of the veil came only with the death of Christ (Mark 15.37—38; Hebrews 10.20).

Mission and healing: reflections from the book of Acts

In his Gospel, Luke focused on the mission of the historical Jesus as one who forgives sin and heals the sick, emphasizing both his humanity and his divinity. Acts brings to our attention what the ascended Christ was still his doing in his Church by works of healing and miracles empowered by his Spirit.

The power to heal and perform miracles, for Luke, was a demonstration that the power of God in Christ was still at work, since such healings and miracles could be done only in Jesus' name. So, when Peter heals a crippled beggar at the gate called Beautiful in the company of John on their way to worship at the Temple (Acts 3.1–10), for Peter and John the miracle is not so much that a sick man has been healed as that the opportunity has been provided to make an undeniable statement that Jesus is Lord. This comes through in the sermon that follows:

> The God of Abraham, the God of Isaac, and the God of Jacob, the God of our ancestors has glorified his servant Jesus . . . you killed the Author of life, whom God raised from the dead. To this we are witnesses. And by faith in his name, his name itself has made this man strong, whom you see and know; and the faith that is through Jesus has given him this perfect health in the presence of all of you.
>
> (Acts 3.13–17)

For Peter and John, the opportunity to heal was an opportunity to tell the story. In this regard, healing and mission belong together for the single purpose of declaring Jesus as Lord and Saviour.

Healing also functioned prophetically. The healings confirmed Peter and Paul as successful healers and accredited messengers, Peter to the Jews, Paul to the Gentiles. Healing confirmed their apostolic status as they in turn validated the status of Jesus (Acts 2.22; 10.38). The latter was an affirmation of the continuation of Jesus' earthly ministry, entrusted to the apostles in the proclamation of salvation, as it had been in the ministry of Jesus.

Healing in Acts: lessons for the contemporary Church

It may be difficult to discover a healing pattern which the contemporary Church must always follow. However, the use of the name of Jesus, faith and prayer appear as important categories in the healing process (Acts 4.12; 5.41; 9.16; 15.26; 21.13). The name and person of Jesus Christ is a source of power, under whose authority healing is performed. This notion points more to the authenticity of Jesus' ministry and claim of messiahship than to relieving the suffering victim.

In John, we realize that the sufferings of the man born blind had nothing to do with the victim's moral or spiritual behaviour or pathological imbalance but were purely for the glory of God. Jesus uses this situation in order to announce his kingdom and authority (John 9.1–3). Here, the whole healing process is subject to the beneficent outworking of God's sovereignty. Jesus makes the point that not all sickness is the result of personal sin. This suggests that although religious traditions and world views may be important in understanding people groups and their response to God and the supernatural, it is also the case that these views may not always be accurate.

The healing activities of the apostles in Acts tended to underscore the authority of Jesus in whose name healing was effected, rather than relief for the victim. Fewer records of healing activities are recorded in Acts than in the Gospels but, where they appear, they mention the power and presence of the risen Christ and suggest that he is the Son of God. This gives legitimacy and credence to the believers' own ministry and demonstrates that the risen Christ is still active in his mission, which is now entrusted to believers.

Healing comes by direct command. There are a number of cases where healing is effected by a direct command from Jesus, or by the apostles who exercised healing power in the name of Jesus. The man who was lame from birth and begging daily for alms at the gate called Beautiful received his healing at the simple command of Peter and John (Acts 3.1–10).

In Acts 8.32–35, a simple command from Peter was all that it took to restore the health of Aeneas at Lydda. What is significant in this healing process is the name of Jesus, the one who heals. The effect of the healing was that the people of Lydda and Sharon gave their lives to the Saviour and healer, Jesus Christ of Nazareth.

In some instances, healing is connected with a touch or the laying of hands on the sick. Saul (Paul) receives a touch from Ananias, who lays his hands on Paul in order to restore his sight after the Damascus experience (Acts 9.17–19).

Faith is mentioned on two occasions, in Acts 3.16 and 14.9. The healing of the paralysed man took place not because he expected it but because Peter anticipated God would achieve a restorative miracle; by commanding the man to stand up, Peter was responding in faith to that affirmation (cf. Acts 9.32–35). The lesson for the Church here is that believers should look to God for guidance as to his will when praying for people and be prepared for his gift of faith in the context of their prayer.

Prayer plays a significant role in the healing ministry as well as in the performance of miracles. Peter could only pray in faith when confronted with the dead body of Tabitha (Acts 9.36–43). By prayer, the supplicant acknowledges the presence and power of God in activating his will, both on behalf of the sufferer and in response to the commission of God. Thus prayer functions not only as a means to bring one's request to God but also as an opportunity to hear from God that the risen Christ is still active in his mission, which is now entrusted to believers.

Conclusion

Our common understanding of healing of the human person in which the medical doctor takes care of the physical body and the Church or priest looks after the soul may be based on a fragmented view. God in his sovereign wisdom has placed healing agents in our environment; and has given wisdom and skill to people such as doctors and traditional healers who may employ their abilities for the purpose of healing (Mark 2.17; Luke 4.23), but such people may not have answers to the problems of sin and guilt. From a missiological perspective, we should understand healing more holistically. This idea of healing will encompass the whole person: physically, spiritually, socially, psychologically and emotionally. Thus the Church must respond not only to physical illness or disease but also to the emotional and spiritual imbalances that come as the result of sin and guilt.

In this regard, the Church must talk about healing on the basis of redemption, provided by God through Jesus Christ. Healing on the basis of redemption brings forgiveness of sin, reconciliation with God and renewal of all human relationships, a demonstration that God is still at work in his world today.

Acts 4.1–31

Peter and John before the Sanhedrin

 Summary

Peter and John confidently bear witness to the resurrection of Jesus before the threatening Sanhedrin.

 Notes

4.1. While . . . speaking to the people: Peter was appealing for the repentance of the people, when the apostles' opponents confronted them.

The priests, the captain of the temple, and the Sadducees: These hostile 'leaders' or 'rulers' stand in contrast to 'the people' who respond to the apostles' preaching favourably (vv. 2, 4). The Sadducees, chiefly associated with aristocracy and temple priesthood, appear as major foils for the Christian message, because they did not believe in the resurrection of the dead (4.2; 23.6–10; Luke 20.27). The captain of the Temple was just below the high priest in rank, and in charge of maintaining order in the temple precinct.

4.2. In Jesus there is the resurrection of the dead: This is a succinct summary of the apostles' preaching. A more detailed statement occurs in 26.23.

4.3. For it was already evening: The arrest happened much later than the three o'clock prayer (3.1).

4.4. They numbered about five thousand: The number is even greater than that of the Pentecost converts. This sets up a sharp contrast with the hostile behaviour of the leaders.

4.5. Their rulers, elders, and scribes: The 'rulers' is a general term, while 'elders' and 'scribes' are specific groups in the Jewish council of Sanhedrin (v. 15).

4.6. Annas . . . Caiaphas: They are also mentioned together in Luke 3.2. Annas was a former high priest (AD 6–15) and the father-in-law of Caiaphas, who was currently holding the office (AD 18–36). John and Alexander are otherwise unknown.

4.7. By what power or . . . name: The question functions as a perfect introduction to Peter's speech that follows. Some distinguish 'power' (source) and 'name' (authority) but they are probably synonymous here; Luke is concerned to show how powerful the name of Jesus is.

4.8. Filled with the Holy Spirit: This recalls Jesus' promise in Luke 12.11–12. It is not Peter who speaks but the Holy Spirit talking through Peter. This is Luke's favourite characterization of major figures in his account (2.4; 4.31; 6.3, 5; 7.55; 9.17; 11.24; 13.9; Luke 1.15, 41, 67; 4.1).

4.9a. A good deed: Peter seems to be saying: Is it right to question someone who has done a good thing such as healing a sick man?

4.9b. How this man has been healed: The 'healed' literally means 'saved'. It refers to the healing of the man (v. 10) but the use of this particular verb seems deliberate (see v. 12).

4.10a. To all the people of Israel: Peter's words are no longer a defence but a proclamation to 'all of Israel'. See 3.16.

4.10b. Whom you crucified, whom God raised: Again Israel's response and God's action are contrasted, as in 2.36; 3.15.

4.11. Stone that was rejected by you: In the Gospels Jesus applies Psalm 118.22 (LXX 117.22) to the leaders (Luke 20.17, at the conclusion of the parable of the vineyard; Matthew 21.42; cf. 1 Peter 2.7). There they perceive it as specifically addressed to them. Here Luke makes it even clearer by adding 'by you' to the quoted text. Here the 'cornerstone' refers to the stone essential for the building. Its concrete meaning is explained in the following verse.

4.12. Salvation in no one else: The sentence is a bit awkward, but the point could not be clearer: salvation is available only in the name of Jesus. Here we see the comprehensive nature of salvation: physical, social and spiritual (13.26; 16.17).

4.13a. The boldness of Peter and John: Luke considers 'boldness' in proclaiming the gospel as the hallmark of the Spirit-filled apostles (2.29; 4.29–31; 9.27–28; 18.26; 28.31; cf. Ephesians 6.19).

4.13b. Uneducated and ordinary: The epithet points to the fact that they lack professional training as teachers. It underlines the power of Peter's Spirit-filled proclamation.

4.14. They had nothing to say in opposition: The leaders themselves confess to it in v. 16, 'We cannot deny it'. This fulfils Jesus' promise in Luke 21.15.

4.16. A notable sign: Most translations notwithstanding, a better rendering would be: 'A sign is known', as the *Revised New Korean Standard Version* has it. The word *gnōston* appears to be a predicate ('known'), not attributive ('notable').

4.17–18. They . . . ordered them not to speak: The rulers oppose the apostles, even when the evidence speaks volumes.

4.19. Listen to you rather than to God: This recalls the famous words of Socrates: 'I shall obey the god rather than you, and . . . I shall never give up philosophy' (*Apology*, 29D).

4.20. What we have seen and heard: The apostles have seen and heard 'all that Jesus did and taught' (1.1).

4.21. Because of the people: It was not God but the fear of the people that guided the behaviour, as was the case with their attitude toward Jesus (Luke 19.48; 20.6, 19, 26; 21.38; 22.2). They obeyed people rather than God.

4.22. More than forty years old: The person's age underscores the remarkable nature of the healing (9.33; Luke 8.43; 13.11).

4.23. To their friends: The phrase literally means 'to their own'. It is unclear whether the phrase refers to the rest of the apostles or to the community as a whole, though the latter seems more likely.

4.24a. Sovereign Lord: This epithet (Gk, *despotēs*) is translated 'Master' in Luke 2.29. The word is different from the more usual 'Lord' (Gk, *kyrios*).

4.24b. Who has made the heaven and the earth: This is an important ingredient of biblical faith (e.g. Genesis 14.19; Exodus 20.11; Psalm 146.6; Isaiah 37.16; Acts 14.15; 17.24).

4.25a. It is you who said by the Holy Spirit: The Early Church believed that the Scripture (our 'Old Testament') is God's word spoken through human agents.

4.25b. Why did the Gentiles . . . and the peoples: Acts 4.25b–26 is a citation of Psalm 2.1–2, which had been interpreted as a messianic prophecy before the Christian era. The early Christians took it to be a prophecy about the suffering of Jesus the Messiah. According to v. 27, the 'Gentiles' are Romans, and the 'peoples' refers to Israel (it is plural, but the same plural is used for Israel in v. 27). For this type of *pesher* interpretation, the Qumran community provides excellent examples.

4.26a. The kings . . . the rulers: 'The kings' are represented by Herod Antipas, tetrarch of Galilee and Peraea. In Luke, he questioned Jesus by Pilate's courtesy (23.7–12). The 'rulers' are represented by Pontius Pilate.

4.26b. Against his Messiah: Luke takes 'his anointed one' in the sense of 'his Messiah', i.e. Jesus.

4.27. Against your holy servant Jesus: The Greek term *pais* (also in 3.13, 26; 4.20) means either child or servant. In view of Psalm 2.7, not quoted here but quoted in 13.33, it is better to read 'your holy child'.

4.28. Your hand . . . had predestined: The Gentiles and Israel conspired together against God and his Messiah, but they did so only because God had planned it so (3.17–18).

4.29a. Look at their threats: This recalls the 'threat' of Sanhedrin in v. 17. Now the rulers' gathering against Jesus is extended to their 'gathering' (v. 5) against the apostles. The term 'servants' (Gk, *doulos*) here translates a word different from that in vv. 25 and 27.

4.29b. To speak your word with all boldness: This prayer is immediately granted in 4.31.

4.30. To heal, and signs and wonders: The healing refers to the healing miracle at the start of the story.

4.31. The place . . . was shaken: This signifies a theophany, God's empowering presence. Filled with God's powerful Spirit, they proclaim the name of Jesus 'with boldness'.

 Interpretation

The opposition of the Sadducees

The apostles' message was focused on the resurrection of Jesus (1.22; 2.24–32; 3.15; 4.10). It is no wonder, therefore, that the Sadducees emerged as the chief opponents of the apostles, since they did not believe in resurrection. But this was not just a conflict between rival theories. From the first, the apostles' proclamation of Jesus' resurrection was accompanied by remarkable pieces of evidence which everybody could 'see and hear'. Yet the double-minded leaders refused to believe it, even though they could not deny the reality of the power working through the apostles. Instead they tried to keep the message from spreading by gagging the mouths of the apostles. Their only concern was to maintain the status quo and their vested interest in it. This forms a stark contrast to the simple faith of the five thousand people who 'heard the word' and 'believed' (4.4).

The boldness of the apostles

Unlike the political manoeuvring of the leaders, the apostles' voice was loud and clear: 'let it be known to all of you' (v. 10); 'Whether it is right in God's sight to listen to you rather than to God, you must judge, for we cannot keep from speaking about what we have seen and heard' (vv. 19–20). They might be 'uneducated and ordinary', but their boldness was such that it amazed the leaders who questioned them (v. 13). Peter, the representative of the apostles, was filled with the Holy Spirit as he spoke, and that explains his boldness. He was no longer the Peter who denied Jesus three times (Luke 22.54–62). The Holy Spirit had come upon him; he had received power from on high; he had become a witness of the risen Jesus. Now nobody could resist him (Luke 21.15).

The gospel as an event

However, their boldness also had to do with the 'signs and wonders' Jesus performed through the apostles. Strictly speaking, it was the miracles, and not the apostles' words, that reduced the leaders to embarrassment. Once again, Peter's speech began as an explanation of the 'signs and wonders' which had just happened before the people. This is only natural, since that was God's way of testifying to Jesus, namely, by 'doing great powers, wonders, and signs through him' (2.22). Now the apostles were following his suit, testifying to the risen Jesus by words of mouth and deeds of hands. If the Holy Spirit had not come and empowered the apostles, no story could have been written about them. If the lame man had not been healed, there would have been nothing to proclaim. As Paul aptly puts it, if Christ had not been raised from the dead, both apostolic proclamation and faith itself would have been in vain (1 Corinthians 15.14–15, 17). So the Early Church prayed not only for boldness in their testimony but also for wonders and signs to be performed through their words and the Lord's hand (Acts 4.29–30).

Everything is in God's hand

We can also see that the Church's belief in God's sovereign providence was at work behind its undaunted witness to Jesus. People might plot against God and his Messiah, but they were merely doing what God had already planned; all their plotting and scheming became pointless with the resurrection of Jesus. This belief shone more brightly in the face of heavy threats. The Early Church knew that God worked through Jesus; they were also convinced that the same God was still working through them. So they had no reason to fear any human threats and every reason to obey God even at the cost of life.

The Revd Yangwon Son, a Korean pastor, devoted his life to serving those with Hansen's disease. His two sons were brutally murdered by a young Communist during the Korean War. Though grief-stricken, at his sons' funeral he read a prayer in which he named ten reasons why he was grateful to God for the tragedy. Later he even rescued the killer of his sons from execution and adopted him as his own son. This moving story is a good illustration of what it means to believe in God's sovereignty. Not surprisingly, the story continues to be an unceasing source of inspiration for both Christians and non-Christians alike.

 STUDY SUGGESTIONS

Word study

1 What is the meaning of 'salvation' (4.12; 13.26; 16.17)?

2 What is the meaning of 'uneducated and ordinary'?

Review of content

3 Why did the Sadducees become the chief opponents of the Christian message?

4 How does Peter contrast what Israel did to Jesus and what God did to him?

5 What is the purpose of mentioning the age of the cured cripple?

Bible study

6 Read the following passages:

(a) 2.36; **(b)** 3.15; **(c)** 4.10.

What common theme can we find in these verses?

7 Read the following passages and say what role Psalm 118.22 plays in them:

(a) Matthew 21.42; **(b)** 1 Peter 2.7.

Discussion and application

8 The apostles were witnesses of Jesus' resurrection. According to Paul too, saving faith means faith in the God who 'gives life to the dead and calls into existence the things that do not exist' (Romans 4.17; 10.9–10) and the God who raised Jesus from the dead (Galatians 1.1). What difference does this resurrection faith make to the way we think and behave?

Acts 4.32—5.16

The Church overcomes a danger from within

 Summary

Satan has Ananias and Sapphira test the Holy Spirit by lying to the apostle Peter but fails. The holy unity of the Church is maintained and the authority of the apostles shines through.

 Notes

4.32. The whole group . . . were of one heart and soul, and no one claimed private ownership . . . everything . . . in common: Verses 32–37 form the second summary of the community life (see 2.43–47). Here sharing of possessions stands out as the most important expression of the unity of the community. Unlike the Qumran community, the sharing of possessions was completely voluntary. Luke's picture must have reminded his contemporary readers of the Hellenistic ideal of friendship that 'friends have all things in common' (e.g. Plato, *Republic*, 449C), but it also recalls Jesus' teachings about renouncing possessions (Luke 12.33; 14.33; 18.22). In context, this summary forms a background for the stories of Barnabas, and of Ananias and Sapphira.

4.33. The apostles gave their testimony to the resurrection: A reference to the apostles' powerful testimony may seem oddly placed. But Luke's idea seems to be that the harmonious life of the Church is a direct result of proclaiming the name of Jesus, showing that indeed God's powerful grace was upon the community.

4.34. There was not a needy person among them: For Jewish leaders this recalls the promise in Deuteronomy 15.4. The richer members voluntarily sold their possessions and offered the money for the needy in the Church. They did not do so all at once but as need arose. This is not a case of 'communism' but a Spirit-guided community of love.

4.35. At the apostles' feet: The apostles were considered authoritative, and they were in charge of the distribution of the money (4.37; 5.2). The phrase also suggests that some sort of system had been set up for charity work.

4.36–37. Barnabas . . . 'son of encouragement': Here Luke introduces an important figure to his account. It is not clear how the name Barnabas is interpreted as 'son of encouragement', but it certainly is a perfect characterization of his role in Acts. He acts as a mediator between the newly converted Paul and the apostles, thereby enabling and encouraging Paul's ministry.

5.1. But a man named Ananias: The story begins with a strong adversative 'but', forming a sharp contrast to the story of Barnabas.

5.2. With his wife's knowledge, he kept back some of the proceeds: Also note 'with the consent of his wife Sapphira' in v. 1; this is a case of conspiracy. His 'keeping back' (a rare Greek word, *nosphizō*) strongly recalls the story of Achan who 'kept back' (*nosphizō*) some of the booty that had been banned (*herem*) by God (Joshua 7.1). Superficially, Ananias' behaviour resembles that of Barnabas (4.37), except that he kept back some of the money for himself.

5.3–4. Why . . . Satan . . . lie to the Holy Spirit . . . lie . . . to God: The problem is lying. This is no mere case of human lapse; it is a spiritual war in which Satan tried to demolish the unity of the Spirit-formed community (cf. Luke 4.1–2). This does not, however, take away human culpability.

5.5. He fell down and died: After the announcement of Peter, this is an act of God's judgement (Numbers 16.28–35; 2 Kings 2.24; 2 Chronicles 26.16–21).

5.7. Not knowing what had happened: This forms a revealing contrast to her previous knowledge of her husband's doing (v. 2).

5.9. Put the Spirit of the Lord to the test: Lying to the Holy Spirit and God was also putting the Spirit of the Lord to the test. Satan in the form of Ananias and Sapphira was testing the Spirit represented by Peter.

5.10. She fell down at his feet: They mimicked Barnabas' Spirit-guided act of laying his money at the feet of the apostles (4.37; 5.2). Now they themselves fell at the feet of the apostles, a chilling reminder of the seriousness of their wilful behaviour.

5.11. Great fear seized the whole church: See the same comment about Ananias' death in v. 5. God's presence was felt through the power of the apostles, here in the form of chilling judgement (2.43; 5.5; 9.31; 19.17). This is the first instance of the word 'church' (Gk, *ekklēsia*) in Acts.

5.12. Many signs and wonders: Luke repeatedly underscores the power exhibited by the Spirit-filled apostles (2.43; 4.30). For 'Solomon's Portico' see note on 3.11.

5.13–14. None . . . dare to join them . . . more than ever believers were added: This may seem contradictory, but in real life it is not difficult to think of such situations in which people feel both respectful fear and irresistible attraction at the same time. 'To join' here does not need to mean 'join the community'; it rather refers to people's attitude to the apostles, especially after the death of the couple.

5.15. Peter's shadow might fall: This gives an apt illustration of Peter's powerfulness. The phrase recalls Jesus' garment (Luke 8.44) and Paul's handkerchief (19.12).

 Interpretation

Releasing the grip of greed

Money is important for living in complex societies. For that reason it can easily turn into an object of human greed. But in the Spirit-guided community, money and material possessions become a means of enjoying and sharing God's life-giving and life-sustaining grace, since believers have learned that what they have is not their own but what they have received from God. A commentator puts it this way: 'The power which broke the bonds of death at Easter, shattered the divisions of speech at Pentecost, and empowered one who was lame now releases the tight grip of private property.' Experiencing and following God's generosity is one of the clearest marks of an authentic Christian community.

The sad case of Ananias and Sapphira

There are not only attacks from outside but also threats from within. We modern readers are often obsessed with the idea of ownership, but the point of this story is not ownership but believers' attitude toward material possessions as an indicator of our relationship with God. Thus, the core of the problem is not that the couple held back some of the money but that they followed their greed and lied to the Spirit-filled apostle and, therefore, to God.

Holiness of the Church

Some find the severity of the punishment offensive. But such modern sensibility should not keep us from perceiving the clear lesson of the passage. Failure to remove the leaven of evil may result in ruining the whole Church. Peter confronted the greedy deceit of the two, so that the 'life together' of the community might not be damaged. As Paul makes clear, the holiness of the Church is never to be compromised (1 Corinthians 3.16–17). God takes our sins seriously; so should we. For that reason it is crucial to exercise proper church discipline. It does not seem accidental that Luke uses the word 'church' in this passage for the first time (Acts 5.11). Love does not mean blurring the line between good and evil.

Peter's shadow

Despite people's expectation, we know that Peter's shadow itself did not heal; God himself did. But sometimes God does not seem much troubled by people's superstitious ignorance as long as their hearts are humble. On the other hand, he shows deep displeasure at the wilful desire to control his sovereign grace, as the case of Simon the Magus aptly illustrates (8.9–25). It is often not easy to distinguish between persistent faith and greedy desire, and that is the reason why the Bible keeps telling the believers to examine and test their hearts.

 STUDY SUGGESTIONS

Word study

1 According to Luke, what is the meaning of the name Barnabas?

Review of content

2 What role can material possessions play in the Spirit-filled community?

3 How does Ananias' behaviour resemble the act of Barnabas? And what is the difference between the two?

4 How does Luke summarize the attitude of outsiders toward the Church after the incident of Ananias and Sapphira?

Bible study

5 Read the following passages:

(a) Numbers 16.28–35; (b) 2 Kings 2.24; (c) 2 Chronicles 26.16–21.

In the light of these passages, how are we to understand the death of Ananias and Sapphira?

Discussion and application

6 Read Luke 8.44, Acts 5.15 and 19.12 and discuss how genuine faith differs from superstition.

7 The Church is God's dwelling place, and therefore it should be holy. What are the potential ways in which we might hamper its holiness?

8 To what extent can we view the death of the couple as God's punishment? In one place Paul also seems to take the many cases of sickness and death as God's disciplinary punishment (1 Corinthians 11.30). Can we also follow these examples? Or do we not run the danger of mistaking innocent suffering for God's punishment? For example, some Christian ministers claimed that HIV & AIDS was God's punishment for homosexuals. Were they mistaken or not? If they were, what is the problem with such a view?

Theological essay 2

Communal sharing and poverty

THE REVD DR ANDREA ZAKI STEPHANOUS

Among the defining characteristics of the Early Church in Acts were the breaking of bread, prayer and communal sharing. These materials and their theological significance relate to the life, death and resurrection of Jesus Christ. The connections between the resurrection of Christ and the concept of communal sharing are key elements of the Christian commitment to community.

Many early Christians came from situations of poverty. They faced unemployment and economic sanctions placed upon them by the state that shaped their Christian life and identity. The practice of spiritual oneness was expressed in the sharing of goods. The central message expressed in Acts 2.42–47 and 4.32–35 forms the basis of the theological connection between the resurrected Christ expressed in eschatology and the fellowship identified as the act of breaking bread combined with prayer. This sacred meal represents the resurrected Christ, as well as alluding to the isolation and poverty experienced by early Christians. This correlation of resurrection and fellowship guided the Early Church in its adaptation of communal sharing as a means of overcoming the difficulties of poverty.

Peace and stability begin when all individuals are given opportunity for personal growth; when people are seen as people and not labelled by race, nationality, religion or gender. We believe that God created all people equal, but that injustice and the misdistribution of resources has created poverty and oppression. To challenge such a situation, we need to remobilize our resources and focus them to create a better future, that is, to make the kingdom of God a present reality.

The concept of the kingdom of God is central to our understanding of the challenge of communal sharing in the face of overwhelming poverty. Down the ages numerous interpretations of the kingdom have been given. The interpretation of the kingdom of God that is closest to that found in Acts reflects the prophetic messages of messianic hope. The prophets foresaw a day when God's Messiah would come to pour out the Spirit in a new way (Joel 2.28–29), and restore God's people as a visible community living in right relationship with God, and in harmony with neighbour and earth. In this vision, the kingdom of God is the salvific proclamation of the word of God and also God's present healing of the sick and the oppressed. The kingdom, therefore, includes both salvation and social action.

This holistic conception of the kingdom of God is crucial for our understanding of the communal sharing seen in the New Testament. The Early Church practised this holistic conception of the kingdom and reorganized itself in a creative way to respond to the needs of the community as well as to the challenges of poverty. As seen in Acts 4.32–37, the group of assembled believers felt the presence of the Holy Spirit and were compelled to share all that they had with one another until none among them was needy. Thus, through the action of the Holy Spirit and by discipleship, they developed new economic relationships. All this contributed to the birth of the Church, where evangelism and social action were combined to fulfil Christ's holistic mission.

I believe that the communal sharing described in Acts is a model for spiritual revival and social transformation in the twenty-first century. In the complex world of today, we talk of sinful structures, bad governance, economic repression, human oppression, the clash of cultures, religious tensions and personal corruption. Communal sharing addresses all these concerns by encouraging personal repentance and contextual transformation. It makes no distinction between evangelism and social change.

Communal sharing that challenges poverty is based on the process of action and reflection. The community of believers examines the root causes of each problem and decides collectively on the neccessary action. The process of action and reflection is accompanied by investing in people who can identify problems, analyse causes and find solutions. Such a process leads to the mobilization of resources, new confidence and improved competence in a variety of areas of interest. This process of communal sharing requires a theology to underpin it.

A theology of transparency, co-existence and involvement

In the complexity of today's context it is important to establish theological models for developing a response of communal sharing that can challenge poverty. Based on the concept of the kingdom of God as both current reality and future hope, the following theological models may offer ways forward.

Jesus acted in different ways to accomplish his mission on earth. In one context we can see social change and spiritual teaching going together, creating a holistic gospel for the whole person (Luke 5.12–14). In Matthew 5.3–11, Jesus preached only for repentance. In a third context we see social transformation that is independent of spiritual teaching; Christ changed the conditions of people regardless of their faith and commitment (Luke 17.12–19). All these differing models of mission were practised by the Early Church.

The Church today needs to reflect on these models and apply each strategy with transparency, integrity and cultural sensitivity. First, when working with people to build awareness and share a vision of social change, transparency is vital. Without a relationship of trust established through transparency, the mission cannot be effective. Transparency is achieved through the gifts of the Holy Spirit – wisdom, understanding, knowledge, counsel, fortitude, piety and fear of the Lord; and through the fruits of the Spirit – love, joy, peace, patience, goodness, friendliness, faithfulness, gentleness and self-control.

Second, through Jesus' interaction with Gentiles he forced the Jews to think outside their own exclusive community and broaden their perceptions and their hearts. Paul's insistence that Gentiles need not become Jews to become Christians was also an indication of openness and a vision that went beyond traditional thinking. The account of the Good Samaritan (Luke 10) can be used to increase this understanding of co-existence. The story challenges us to define who our neighbour is. It provides a basis for peaceful and supportive co-existence between different churches and different faiths and cultures. Communal sharing must go beyond church boundaries and contribute to a community of equals regardless of faith, ethnicity, race or gender.

Third, the Church in the New Testament is called to go into the world. It is called to heal, reconcile and bind up wounds; to minister to the needs of the poor, the sick, the lonely and the powerless; to struggle to free people from sin, fear, oppression and hunger; and to provide justice. The Church is called to give of itself and its substance to the service of those who suffer, and to share with Christ in establishing a just, peaceful and loving rule in the world. And if the Christian faith is to be put into practice, this will have social, political and economic implications. The Church today needs to speak the language of the people. Theology must be understandable and relevant to men and women in the street. The Church must critically read the word of God, and relate its message to the current context in order to put theology into practice. Now, in our reflection-for-action, we turn to communal sharing.

Communal sharing

Half of the world's population faces critical issues of poverty in one way or another. Poverty means death: physical and cultural death. The destruction of individuals and people groups, cultures and traditions, and the repressive methods used by those in power, all contribute to poverty. In the face of this crisis, what role can the Church adopt to challenge this situation created by sin and sinful actions? The Church needs to be prophetically faithful to Christ who declares that he sided with the poor and oppressed. The book of Acts highlights the work of the Early Church and its emphasis on communal sharing (Acts 2.42–47). The foundation of the Early Church is characterized by a spirit of acceptance and shared poverty; Gentiles, widows, the sick and the poor are all accepted.

Disadvantaged and deprived persons deserve the opportunity to develop themselves and to live in dignity. Such persons live in the worst socioeconomic conditions. They are silent in their plight. Should they be given only the monetary resources needed to rise out of poverty, they would have a tendency to remain resentful towards society and despised by society. Having stood alone in their poverty, they would also tend to stand alone in plenty. The first point of challenging poverty is to provide disadvantaged persons with a supportive community and the skills that are necessary to create progress. People are the best resources for challenging poverty today.

Church leaders must be able to lead the community in overcoming poverty. To reach this point, they should be representative of its groups, which collectively represent society. Leadership must seek to help the community realize its own vision, dreams and goals, rather than imposing the leaders' own will on the community. With this kind of leadership the Church can maintain the process of participation that is necessary to challenge poverty and create a community of equals.

Second, the Church must recognize and speak out about the many problems that exist within society. Leadership plays an important role in facilitating this process, by focusing awareness on the problems, addressing the problems at every level of society, and motivating society to solve its problems. This in turn leads to a process of empowering people to face poverty at different levels.

In addition, a community of believers must be able to carry out the Church's decisions. Through the decision-making process the community will learn to overcome differences and conflict in order to establish cooperation. These connections start at the grassroots level and work their way through greater society. Let us take the programmes of the Coptic Evangelical Organization for Social Services (CEOSS – a Christian non-governmental organization) as examples for the role of Christian organizations in communal sharing. Through the CEOSS Building the Capacity of Church Leaders programme, which organizes workshops dedicated to providing conflict resolution training, church leaders are introduced to practical methods of implementing transparency and open dialogue in their congregations. These changes within the church governing system both provide an example to the surrounding community and encourage members to employ these practices within their own businesses and workplaces. With just a few key members receiving training and learning new ideas, an entire community can be changed by the influence and sharing of this newly acquired knowledge.

Enabling communal sharing

One can argue that there are three aspects to communal sharing. The first is that of social services, where education, healthcare, and agricultural and economic development are delivered to rural and urban communities facing poverty. The method for delivering these services has changed in recent decades. Past efforts focused on a centralized, top-down approach in which larger governing bodies controlled the method and amount of aid the grassroots poor received and did not grant the poor an active voice in the programmes being carried out. The provision of services to the poor now entails a more participatory approach, in which the local people both identify their needs and contribute to the solution of their problems. This shift in methodology considers the participation of people at the grassroots level as a vital component of social development. It is undeniable that this approach has been accompanied by cultural change as well. However, these changes are often limited to local-level programming. Communal sharing can be defined as a social change that occurs through promoting new thoughts within a specific social structure, with the aim of increasing personal incomes and improving the standard of living by increasing production and improving control.

One example of this type of communal sharing is the development of models of micro-enterprise community banking and insurance schemes, which emphasize the interdependence of individuals within the community. These activities most often entail the community members pooling together what income they can spare each month and then proceeding to loan the money to a member who will purchase equipment for a small business. As income is generated the loan will be repaid and other community members will be able to take advantage of a similar loan. This grassroots approach to generating income for poor families not only addresses the monetary needs of the individuals involved, but also creates interdependency within the community and genuine support for individuals to succeed in their endeavour.

Through the Small and Micro-Enterprise programmes in Egypt, the lives of many poor women have been completely transformed. Small loans have enabled them to improve their living standards and given them greater dignity.

The second model of communal sharing is based on capacity-building. The aim of this model is to re-engineer the current structure of Church and society to promote social development. Capacity-building in civil society organizations and churches will enhance democracy and create a new generation of leaders who believe in pluralism and diversity. Just as the disciples began to increase their numbers in order to serve more communities and spread the message of Christ (Acts 6.1–7), the emergence of new types of leaders at different levels of church and civil society will lead to the restructuring of the social elite and challenge the current social structure. Capacity-building involves social, economic, political and cultural issues, all of which must be dealt with in order to create new structures that have a more holistic agenda. In this context, capacity-building within the Church and civil society is a tool for social change.

In many conflict-prone areas of the world, CEOSS has begun to provide conflict management for community leaders, conducting workshops and seminars that address issues of conflict within the society and equip individuals with the necessary training to transform conflict successfully at grassroots level. The increased capacity of key individuals to deal effectively with conflict before it escalates has had a profound effect not only on direct participants, but also on the families, friends and neighbours of these individuals. The local capacity for peacefully dealing with conflict has unquestionably improved, and the knowledge gained by a small number of individuals has been passed to other community members, resulting in a more peaceable community for the majority. The example can be cited of a church leader who completed a conflict resolution workshop through the CEOSS Building the Capacity of Church Leaders programme. As a member of his township's board dealing with citizen complaints, he was able to use the negotiation and communication skills he learned in the workshop to defuse a land dispute conflict. His negotiation benefited both the parties involved in the conflict and also the entire community, because the land was eventually used to build a school for village children.

The third aspect of communal sharing is advocacy and networking for social restructuring. As Christ told the Pharisee in Luke 14.1–14, the greatest blessing you can receive comes when you share your wealth with others and invite them to become equals with you. Advocacy and networking among civil society organizations and churches will strengthen the role of civil society and will promote the agenda of these organizations in efficient and effective ways. Advocacy in areas of co-existence, equality, justice, human rights and citizenship will force the state to put these issues on its agenda. Advocacy will promote social change from the grassroots to the highest governing structures. Networking will maximize the efforts of civil society organizations at national and international levels. As the field of conflict resolution within Egypt is still relatively small, many workshop participants in CEOSS programming have commented on the importance, not only of the skills being learned, but also of the connections being made with like-minded individuals from churches and organizations throughout Egypt. These connections serve as resources for knowledge and experience, as well as support for the programmes individuals are undertaking within their communities.

In order to create social change on a wider scale, ideas and resources must be shared between individuals and communities to facilitate change from the bottom up. Networking provides a chance for individuals to share their experiences and inspire new ideas and beliefs, as can be seen in intercultural dialogues that aim to create understanding and dispel preconceived notions of 'the other'. Advocacy can bring about change simply by creating awareness of the issues. Very often the voices of the poor go unheard, but when groups join together to present one clear and unified message, those previously voiceless can become a powerful catalyst for social change. Such a change can influence the structures and functions of society.

Each model of communal sharing mentioned above relies on transforming the ideas and beliefs both of the individual and of the community. We must recognize that for long-term sustainable change to take place, such change must be embraced at the grassroots level. Sustainable social restructuring that transforms society's political, economic and ecological systems and relations must not only be embraced but also created by society. Restructuring will fail if it is forced through via top-down devices that fail to include the individual. Reduction in family size, for example, may be of long-term benefit to families and communities. However, the traditional importance of having a large family and its impact on well-being need to be understood and challenged at grassroots level if change is to occur.

Social restructuring brings about societal changes with the following priorities:

1 Changes in social values, which catalyse restructuring at different levels.

2 Institutional change, which includes political changes such as shifting from a dictatorship to a democracy, and economic changes such as moving from a central economy to a free market.

3 Changes in the positions of individuals in a specific social context, which brings changes within that context.

4 Changes in the attitudes and the skills of individuals, resulting in a context for restructuring in which they are able to exercise power.

Conclusion

In Acts, the experience of Christ's resurrection changed his followers' conception of the kingdom in many ways. Now the 'age to come' is present and the kingdom of God is nearer. The eschatological hope has become part of the challenge of the current reality. In Christ the principles of heaven were incarnated, and in his being he brought both the future and the age to come into the present. Through Jesus, God invaded history and brought himself to us. In the same way Jesus invaded our hearts and in human history continues to bring to us the fullness of the age to come; which will be fulfilled through the liberation of the oppressed, the feeding of the hungry, the loving of the unlovable, and the conversion of sinners who accept Christ as Lord. This is what is meant by communal sharing. It is the holistic mission of the Church. One can agree with Gustavo Gutiérrez that 'there is no authentic evangelization that is not accompanied by action on behalf of the poor' (1984, p. 44). If poverty means death, the followers of Christ are witnesses to life. As stated earlier, it is personal sin as well as social sin that results in poverty. Thus, the only way in which to challenge this situation is through a gospel that transforms both our own life and the situation in which we live.

We conclude that the power of the resurrected Christ, who can inspire his followers to see people as people and believe in equality for all, is the basis for communal sharing. As exemplified so many times in the book of Acts, members of the Early Church challenged poverty by sharing their possessions and urged others to do the same. Christ's own teachings in Luke continually urge those who have wealth to humble themselves and share with those who are not so fortunate. In today's complex context, Christ's biblical models of communal sharing are essential if we are to eradicate poverty and defend human dignity.

 Reference

Gutiérrez, Gustavo, *We Drink from Our Own Wells*, Maryknoll, NY: Orbis Books, 1984.

Acts 5.17–42

The apostles before the Sanhedrin

 Summary

Now all the apostles stand before the full assembly of the Sanhedrin under the threat of death, but they continue to proclaim the message of life with great boldness.

 Notes

5.17. Filled with jealousy: As jealousy is often connected with an urge to kill in Greek literature, Luke also connects it with persecution (7.9; 17.5).

5.19. Angel of the Lord: The similar episode in 12.6–11 describes Peter's escape in more detail. In Acts the angel appears four more times (7.30–38; 8.26; 12.7–10, 23). The word 'angel' can simply mean 'messenger', but in the Bible it typically means a divine agent, whether human or not. The main point is, however, that God's sovereign power lay behind this miracle. Interestingly, the Sanhedrin failed to mention this when they questioned the apostles.

5.20. The whole message about this life: This uncommon expression recalls the epithet, 'Author of life' (3.14).

5.21. The council and the whole body: NIV translates 'Sanhedrin – the full assembly', rightly taking the two words as appositional. Now the whole Jewish leadership paraded its pomp, only to be humiliated on a grander scale.

5.24. When the captain of the temple and the chief priests heard: The captain of the Temple was in charge of keeping the prisoners in custody, and the chief priests were Sadducees who first instigated the council to arrest the apostles (v. 17).

5.25. In the temple and teaching the people: Now they were back to the situation before their first arrest (3.11; 4.1–2); the leaders were plotting 'in vain' (4.25).

5.26. For they were afraid: This verse recalls Jesus in Jerusalem (Luke 20.19; 22.2). Once again, we note the widely different attitudes of the leaders and of the people toward the apostles.

5.28a. You have filled Jerusalem with your teaching: The high priest, as president of the council, indicted the apostles, but his word sounded like a virtual acknowledgement of their defeat. Their previous order in 4.18 had not worked.

5.28b. To bring this man's blood on us: This biblical expression means to lay blame for a death (Genesis 4.10–11; 2 Samuel 1.16, etc.; cf. Luke 11.50–51). In response to this charge, Peter levels the same criticism even more explicitly (v. 30).

5.29. We must obey God rather than any human authority: The Sanhedrin reiterated the same prohibition and Peter repeated the same reply (4.18–19). Yet the tone was now much stronger than before (not a question but a flat announcement).

5.30. The God of our ancestors: In his defence, Peter provoked the Sanhedrin by doing exactly what it had prohibited: speaking in the name of Jesus! The phrase 'hanging him on a tree' (10.39; 13.29) is derived from Deuteronomy 21.23 (Galatians 3.13; 1 Peter 2.24).

5.31. Leader and Saviour: The term 'Leader' is rendered 'Author' in 3.15. For the epithet 'Saviour' see Luke 2.11 and Acts 13.23. Peter was still limiting repentance and forgiveness to Israel. But compare this with the Cornelius episode, especially the concluding response of the Jewish Christians in 11.18.

5.33. Enraged . . . wanted to kill: The word 'enraged' means 'torn apart' or 'ripped asunder' in heart. Luke uses the same word to describe the Sanhedrin's response to Stephen's speech (7.54).

5.34. A Pharisee . . . named Gamaliel: This is Gamaliel I (the Elder), later identified as Paul's teacher (22.3). The description, 'respected by all the people' further puts the Sanhedrin on the opposite side from the people. It is unclear whether Luke's portrayal of Gamaliel is favourable or not, but this verse does seem to reveal a favourable view of him.

5.36. Theudas . . . Judas the Galilean: Both of them are leaders of unsuccessful revolutionary movements. Here we meet a thorny problem about the historical accuracy of Luke's report. The problem is twofold:

1 Josephus, a noted Jewish historian, also mentions these two but puts Judas before Theudas;

2 Josephus connects Theudas with the prefecture of Crispius Fadus (AD 45–46), well after the time of the present episode.

Different solutions have been proffered but, historically speaking, no definite conclusion is possible. Either one of them is wrong or they refer to different figures of the same name. Gamaliel's choice of these two reveals that he viewed Jesus' followers in a similar way (see Interpretation).

5.38–39. Let them alone . . . if it is of God: Gamaliel's advice reflected the Pharisaic belief in divine providence. But if he had really been open-minded, he should have believed the gospel by now, since he had already seen irrefutable evidence of its power.

5.41–42. They rejoiced: Jesus had already taught them what to do in a situation like this (Luke 6.22–23). The dynamic picture in v. 42 shows how futile the Sanhedrin's attempt was. This makes Gamaliel's word in vv. 38–39 an ironic prophecy.

 # Interpretation

The threat continues

The second arrest of the apostles by the Sanhedrin repeats the major themes present in the first (4.1–22); we cannot miss the growing tension between the apostles and their opponents.

(a) This time, not just Peter and John (4.1) but the apostles as a whole are arrested and questioned (5.18).

(b) The same Sadducean group takes the initiative (4.1; 5.17), but it is now the full assembly of Sanhedrin, including the Pharisees, that question the apostles (5.21).

(c) The charges and punishment are also much stronger. Instead of mere verbal threat (4.18), the apostles are now under the threat of death from the enraged Sanhedrin (5.33); later on, they are actually flogged (5.40).

(d) Accordingly, the apostles are firmer and more resolute, as the change in Peter's tone indicates (4.19; 5.29).

So we can see a clear irony running through the story. The leaders use all their power to subdue the apostles, but the attempt proves to be 'in vain'. At the conclusion of the episode, we find the apostles doing exactly the same thing they had been doing at the time of their arrest: proclaiming Jesus in the Temple (4.1; 5.12, 17, 42).

Gamaliel

Here we meet the intriguing figure, Gamaliel. He was a renowned teacher of the law, highly respected by all the people. Yet there is ambiguity in Luke's portrayal of him. On the surface, he appears to be a 'nice guy' who comes to the defence of the apostles by dissuading the Sanhedrin from putting them to death. Yet, his choice of two failed revolts suggests that he viewed Jesus' followers in a similar way: 'Their leader is already dead, and so they will soon die away. Why pollute ourselves by touching what will die away anyway?' His belief in divine providence sounds just right, but it soon becomes suspect, once we remember that this is also a member of the Sanhedrin which had earlier condemned Jesus to death. Even now he has more than enough evidence for the divine origin of the apostles' activity, but he refuses to acknowledge it, just as the Sadducees had done earlier (4.13–16). He feared the possibility of their 'fighting against God' but he agreed anyway to have the apostles flogged and order them not to speak in the name of Jesus. What a fine way of 'letting them alone'! He is surely much less hostile to the apostles than the Sadducees, but his sober advice about 'this plan (Gk, *boulē*) or this undertaking' turns out to be an example of the Pharisees and the teachers of the law rejecting 'God's plan' (*boulē*, Luke 7.30).

 STUDY SUGGESTIONS

Review of content

1 What was the motivation behind the Sanhedrin's persecution of the apostles?

2 What were the two titles Peter used to describe Jesus in his answer to the Sanhedrin?

3 In what ways does the present episode intensify the tone of the previous one?

4 Gamaliel chose two failed revolutionaries to back up his position. What does his choice tell us about his view of the Christian movement?

Bible study

5 In addition to 5.19, read also the following passages where the angel appears:

(a) 7.30–38; (b) 8.26; (c) 12.7–10, 23.

What does the angel signify in Acts?

Discussion and application

6 How sober is Gamaliel's advice (5.38–39)? Or can such a 'disinterested' attitude be a way of evading what we should do?

Acts 6.1–15

A new leadership emerges

 Summary

The Church chooses seven new leaders to serve the Church. Through their leadership, the Church now prepares itself to take a revolutionary step beyond Jerusalem.

 Notes

6.1a. The disciples were increasing: This is the first occurrence of the term 'disciple' in Acts (6.2, 7; 9.36; 11.26; 19.1–4). The term is virtually synonymous with the name 'Christian'. The problem was the result of the rapid growth of the Church, not a symptom of its waning.

6.1b. Hellenists . . . Hebrews: This is not an ethnic but a linguistic and cultural distinction. The term 'Hellenists' (Gk, *hellēnistēs*) means 'Greek-speaking people': either 'Greek-speaking Jews' (here and 9.29) or 'Greek-speaking Gentiles' (11.29). Probably the Greek-speaking Jews were mostly from the Diaspora (2.7–12; 4.36; 6.9). By the same token, the 'Hebrews' refers to 'Aramaic-speaking people'. So there was an inevitable linguistic and cultural barrier among the Jews of the time, a fact of life which the Early Church could not avoid. In this particular text, the Hellenists were disciples drawn from the Greek-speaking synagogues in Jerusalem (6.9). It is almost certain that they formed their own Greek-speaking house groups within the Church.

6.1c. Their widows were being neglected in the daily distribution of food: Under the strain of rapid growth, the linguistic and cultural difference finally spilled over into 'the daily distribution of food'. Most women did not have economic independence, especially the immigrants. The 'daily distribution' literally means 'the daily service' (Gk, *diakonia*; cf. 'deacon'). The same word is used in vv. 2 and 4.

6.2. Neglect the word of God . . . to wait at tables: The term 'the Twelve' is used only here in Acts (Luke 6.13; 1 Corinthians 15.5). 'To wait on tables' refers to the administration of the relief fund. The apostles found the situation too much for them to handle on their own. Interestingly, the apostles found their neglect of the word more problematic than their ineffective administration.

6.3. Seven . . . to this task: The seven leaders were selected for the administration of the fund, but Luke will soon draw quite a different picture of them.

6.4. Serving the word: Luke uses the same Greek word (*diakonia*) both here and in v. 2: 'ministry of the table' and 'ministry of the word'. There are different 'ministries', but they are all acts of 'serving' the same Lord (1 Corinthians 12.5).

6.5. Stephen, a man full of faith and the Holy Spirit: All the seven seem to have been leading figures among the Hellenists. Only Stephen has a special introduction. This will soon be confirmed by the following story of his powerful witness. Philip will also play an important role in chapter 8, but for the rest Luke does not say anything further. Nicolaus is specified as a proselyte, that is, a Gentile who had converted to Judaism before his coming to faith. Some early traditions associate him with 'the Nicolaitans' in Revelation 2.6, 15, but there is no evidence for such identification.

6.6. The apostles . . . laid their hands on them: In Acts this rite is associated with the gift of the Holy Spirit (8.17, 19; 19.6), healing (9.12, 17; 28.8), and commissioning for ministry (13.3). In the Old Testament, it is used for the purpose of bestowing blessing (Genesis 48.13–20), sacrificial identification (Leviticus 1.4; 3.2, etc.), or ordination of the priest (Numbers 8.10). The present passage recalls most strongly the transfer of leadership from Moses to Joshua (Numbers 27.18–23).

6.7a. The word of God continued to spread: Luke is fond of inserting short notices into his narrative to show the Church's steady growth even in the face of threats and hardships (2.41, 47; 4.4; 5.14; 9.31; 11.21; 12.24; 16.5; 19.20).

6.7b. A great many priests became obedient: Unlike the wealthy chief-priestly families, most of the ordinary priests seem to have been economically marginalized. Think of Zechariah, the father of John the Baptist (Luke 1.5–6). Intriguingly, Luke reports a large-scale conversion of priests just before Stephen's criticism of the Temple in Acts 7. Luke does not tell us what role these priests played in the Church.

6.8. Stephen . . . did great wonders and signs: Stephen looked not much different from other Spirit-filled apostles. Luke repeatedly underscores Stephen's virtue; his death becomes all the more appalling for that (6.5, 10, 15; 7.55–60).

6.9. The synagogue of the Freedmen . . . Cyrenians, Alexandrians: Freedmen were former slaves. Archaeological data confirms the existence of such synagogues in Jerusalem. Luke's sentence here is not easy to interpret. Some take this to mean one synagogue attended by different groups (so NRSV). Others suggest two synagogues: one group from Africa (Cyrene and Alexandria) and another group from Asia Minor (Cilicia and Asia). Despite such ambiguity, Luke's point is clear: Stephen is attacked by fellow Diaspora Jews.

6.11. Against Moses and God: That is, against the law of Moses and God's Temple. This charge becomes explicit in vv. 13–14. It is not accidental that such charges were brought against Stephen who has a Diaspora background.

6.12. They stirred up the people: Unlike earlier episodes, 'the people' were now allied with the leaders against the Church (cf. 2.47; 4.1–2). This is only natural, since the charges were now about such sensitive issues as the law and the Temple. In this verse, the scene changes into one of a formal hearing before the Sanhedrin.

6.13–14. Jesus . . . will destroy this place and will change the customs that Moses handed on to us: Ironically this false testimony contains a grain of truth in it, as Stephen's speech will soon show. The same charges had been made against Jesus. Unlike other Gospel writers (Mark 14.58; 15.29; Matthew 26.61), however, Luke omits these accusations in his account of the trial of Jesus and introduces it in the new context of the Early Church's evangelism.

6.15. Like the face of an angel: The glow of Stephen's face recalls the shining of Moses' face (Exodus 34.29–30). It implies that he now stands in the presence of God. It anticipates the vision at the time of his death (7.55–56).

 ## Interpretation

Acts 6—7 is often called 'Acts of Stephen'. Within Acts these chapters serve as a bridge concluding the story of the earliest community in Jerusalem and at the same time setting the stage for the spread of the gospel beyond Jerusalem.

Balancing the leadership structure

The rapid growth of the Church created problems within it which might threaten its unity. Complaints were voiced, measures taken. The community in Jerusalem was multicultural from the first, and unbalanced leadership from the Galilean apostles soon showed its limitations. So the community tried to restore the unity by choosing seven new leaders from the relatively disenfranchised Hellenist group and commissioning them to the administration of the fund. With this measure the leadership structure now reflected more adequately the actual cultural and linguistic makeup of the community.

The Church prepares for the changing situations

But the Church's decision meant much more than mere leadership balance. To our surprise, we hear nothing of their administrative effort. Instead, Luke tells us how Stephen and Philip, representing the seven, proclaimed the gospel with power. Luke portrays Stephen virtually as an apostle, the apostle for the Diaspora Jews (6.8–9). And his death and the subsequent persecution triggered the uncontrollable spread of the gospel. In Acts 8 Philip also evangelizes the Samaritans and the Ethiopian eunuch, and Luke rightly calls him an 'evangelist' (21.8). So by divine providence, the Church's effort to resolve its administrative problem becomes an unexpected way of fulfilling Jesus' promise that they will be his witnesses not only in Jerusalem but also 'in all Judea and Samaria, and to the ends of the earth' (1.8).

In line with this cultural and geographical transition, we also note that such issues as the Temple and the law newly emerge as tension points between the Church and its opponents. Luke underscores this by repeating the charge no less than three times (vv. 11, 13, 14). As noted earlier, Luke omits these issues in his account of Jesus' trials, and introduces them here for the first time, as the Church was about to move to non-Jewish and more multicultural environments. No doubt, these are issues touching the question of Jewish identity: who are the people of God? This is the question the Jews and the Church will have to struggle with in the following stories (Acts 10—11, 15).

 STUDY SUGGESTIONS

Word study

1 What is another name given to Christians?

2 How is the word *diakonia* used in Acts 6 (vv. 2, 4)?

Review of content

3 Explain the meaning of the 'Hellenists' and the 'Hebrews'.

4 For what purpose did the early Christians lay hands on other Christians?

5 What were the main charges brought against Stephen?

6 Why were the people now allied with the leaders against the Church?

Bible study

7 Read Mark 7.1–7 and Matthew 15.3–6. In light of these passages, how 'false' or 'true' were the accusations made in Acts 6.14?

Discussion and application

8 What can we learn from the way the Jerusalem church handled its conflict?

9 The Church elected the 'seven' initially for an administrative purpose. Yet many of them ended up being more active in evangelism than in administration, thereby helping to spread the gospel further to the Greek-speaking Jews. What can we learn from this unexpected turn of events?

Stephen's speech

 Summary

Stephen criticizes the Jews' obsession with the Temple and their rejection of Jesus, predicted by the prophets, and becomes the first martyr in Christian history.

 Notes

7.2. The God of glory appeared . . . in Mesopotamia: 'The God of glory' occurs in Psalm 29.3 and anticipates 'the glory of God' in Acts 7.55. According to Genesis 11.3—12.5, Abraham was already in Haran when God appeared to him. Luke's point is that God could appear even in a Gentile land.

7.3. Leave your country: This is Genesis 12.1.

7.5. He did not give . . . but promised to give: Abraham moved to the promised land of Canaan without actually possessing it, but believing in God's promise which was yet to be realized (cf. Hebrews 11.8-10, 13-16). Stephen used words from such verses as Genesis 13.15; 17.8; 48.4. This also underscores the point that God's presence does not depend on the possession of the land.

7.6. Resident aliens in a country belonging to others: This verse is dependent on Genesis 15.3-4.

7.7. I will judge . . . they shall come out and worship me: This verse comes from Genesis 15.14 and Exodus 3.12. Here 'in this place' refers to the land of Canaan, not the Temple as in Acts 6.13-14. God did his part, but Israel did not worship him but idols instead (vv. 39-43).

7.8. Abraham . . . Isaac . . . Jacob . . . the twelve patriarchs: Stephen passes by Isaac and Jacob and moves quickly to Joseph. See Genesis 21.1-4 (Isaac's circumcision); 25.26 (birth of Jacob); 29.31—30.24 (birth of the patriarchs) for the background.

7.9-10. The patriarchs . . . but God: Joseph was carried out of Canaan (Genesis 37.11, 18-36) but God's presence followed him (Genesis 39—41).

Stephen also contrasts the patriarchs' mistreatment of Joseph and Pharaoh's exalting him.

7.11–16. A famine throughout Egypt: These verses retell Genesis 41.53—50.26. Exodus 1.6 also notes the death of Joseph and his brothers. The 'seventy-five' is from the Septuagint (the Greek OT). In the Hebrew OT the number is seventy (Genesis 46.27). According to Genesis 50.13, Jacob was not buried in Shechem but Hebron, in a tomb purchased by Abraham. But it was not Abraham but Jacob who bought the tomb in Shechem (33.19). So Stephen's account is somewhat different from the story in Genesis; he seems to be telescoping two separate purchase stories.

7.17–19. The promise . . . made to Abraham: This refers to the promise quoted in v. 7. These verses reflect Exodus 1.7–10.

7.20–22. Moses was born . . . See Exodus 2.2–10.

7.22. Powerful in his words and deeds: The Bible says nothing about Moses' education, but Luke's description of Moses resembles that of Jesus (Luke 2.52; 24.19). Stephen himself is also portrayed in similar terms (Acts 6.5, 8, 10).

7.23–29. When he was forty years old: These verses come from Exodus 2.11–22, where Moses fled to Midian for fear of Pharaoh's anger.

7.25. Understand . . . but . . . not understand: This is Stephen's addition, designed to accentuate the theme of rejection through ignorance found in the stories of Joseph, Moses and Jesus (v. 13; 3.17; cf. Luke 24.21).

7.30–34. The place . . . is holy ground: God's presence makes even the Gentile ground holy. God's glory is not limited to 'this holy place' as Stephen's opponents would have it (6.13).

7.35. This Moses . . . rejected . . . sent as both ruler and liberator: Here we see the pattern Luke also discerns in Jesus: rejected by humans, vindicated by God, and sent again in greater power (2.23, 36; 10.39). Note the similar identifications in vv. 37 and 38.

7.36–37. Wonders and signs: Moses performed wonders and signs, and Moses predicted that God would raise up a prophet like him (Deuteronomy 18.15). So God sent Jesus performing great 'powers, wonders and signs' through him (Acts 2.22), as well as the apostles who spoke in his name. That Moses carried out his ministry in Gentile territories also underscores Stephen's criticism of the Jewish preoccupation with 'this holy place'.

7.38. He received living oracles to give to us: Some connect this pattern to Jesus' receiving and pouring out of the Spirit (2.33).

7.39–42. They pushed him aside: These verses are based on Exodus 32. For the second time the ancestors rejected the God-sent Moses; instead, they 'revelled in the works of their hands'. This act of idolatry is soon connected to their obsession with the Temple, a house 'made of human hands' (v. 48).

7.42. God turned away from them: Or 'God turned them away' (transitive). Their turning away from God was met by God's turning them back to their depravity (Romans 1.24, 26, 28).

7.42–43. Did you offer . . . : This is a citation of Amos 5.25–27. They went into exile because they worshipped idols instead of God, a staple criticism of the post-exilic prophets.

7.44–45. The tent of testimony: This is contrasted to the tent of Moloch in v. 43. This verse is based on Exodus 33.7; 25.8–9 and Joshua 3.14–17.

7.46. For the house of Jacob: We can also read 'for the God of Jacob' as the footnote in NRSV indicates. If authentic, this forms a strong contrast: they built a house for God but God does not dwell in houses made with human hands.

7.47–48. Solomon . . . built . . . Yet the Most High does not dwell: The contrast strongly implies that building the Temple was misguided from the first. The idea that God does not dwell in houses made by humans is already present in 1 Kings 8.27–30, but Luke's intention seems more radical than that, especially in view of the same phrase applied to the pagan temples (Acts 17.24).

7.49–50. Heaven is my throne . . . : This is a quotation of Isaiah 66.1–2.

7.51. Stiff-necked . . . uncircumcised in heart and ears: These are biblical expressions applied to Israel in the wilderness (Exodus 33.3, 5; Deuteronomy 10.16; Jeremiah 6.10). The 'opposing the Holy Spirit' is derived from Isaiah 63.10. It recalls the episode of Ananias and Sapphira who tested the Holy Spirit (Acts 5.1–11) and Jesus' words about the unforgivable sin of blaspheming against the Holy Spirit (Luke 12.10).

7.52. Your ancestors . . . and now you: The present Israel's betraying and murdering of Jesus is aligned with ancient Israel's persecution of the prophets (2.23; 3.14–15; 4.10; 5.30). Jesus has already made the same point in Luke 11.47–51.

7.53a. The law as ordained by angels: The idea, not explicit in the OT, is also found in Galatians 3.19 and Hebrews 2.2.

7.53b. Yet you have not kept it: This is a staple menu in the early Christian criticism of Judaism (Luke 3.7–9; 11.42; Matthew 23.3; Romans 2; Galatians 6.12–13). They did not keep the law, at least the more important parts of it (Matthew 23.23), putting on a show of external piety.

7.54. Ground their teeth: See Luke 13.28; Job 16.9. They responded to Peter's charge with heart-stricken remorse; now they are enraged by

Stephen's accusation. Does the issue of Jewish identity have anything to do with this change?

7.55. But filled with the Holy Spirit: We note a sharp contrast between the people and Stephen.

7.56. Jesus standing at the right hand of God: This recalls Jesus' words at the time of his trial (Luke 22.69; cf. Psalm 110.1; Daniel 7.13). Also see Acts 2.33, 35.

7.58. They dragged him out of the city: Stoning was to be done outside the city (Leviticus 24.14; Numbers 15.35–36). Here we meet Saul for the first time. He is the hero of the second half of the story, but now he comes into the picture as a persecutor of the gospel.

7.59–60. Receive my spirit . . . do not hold this sin against them: Stephen's death closely conforms to that of Jesus in the Gospel of Luke: his last words are those of Jesus on the cross (23.46, 34).

8.1a. Saul approved: This sets the stage for the subsequent persecutions of the Church both in Jerusalem (8.1b–3) and beyond (9.1–2). Paul uses the same word 'approved' in his recounting of this incident (26.10).

 # Interpretation

Stephen's speech, the longest one in Acts, is his defence before the Sanhedrin. It takes the form of rehearsing the stories of a few prominent figures in Israel's history: Abraham (7.2–8); Joseph (7.9–16); Moses (7.17–45); David and Solomon (7.46–50). The speech concludes with a scathing criticism of the audience (7.51–53). The large space allotted to Moses is natural, since the points at issue are the Temple and the law. To this Luke adds the story of Stephen's martyrdom (7.54—8.1a). On the whole Luke makes two crucial points:

1 the Temple is ultimately irrelevant, even mistaken;

2 not Christians but the Israelites are law-breakers, since they reject Jesus, the promised prophet, like Moses.

God's unbound presence and the Temple

Stephen's speech is a reinterpretation of Israel's history, a familiar way of making a point (Joshua 24.2–13; Nehemiah 9.6–37; Psalms 78; 105; 135). For Stephen, this was essentially the history of God's revelation (Acts 7.30, 35, 44). Significantly, Stephen included himself within this history of revelation (vv. 55, 56), and that explains why his view of history should be different from that of the unbelieving Jewish colleagues.

Following Stephen's retelling of the stories of Abraham and Joseph, we cannot miss his main point: God's presence and his providence are not limited to 'this holy place' (6.13). God's glory was revealed in such places as Mesopotamia (v. 2), Haran (vv. 2, 4), Egypt (16 times in all), Midian (v. 29), Mount Sinai (vv. 30, 38), the Red Sea (v. 36); namely, in places outside Palestine. On the other hand, Canaan is described as a place to which Abraham 'moved' (v. 4), where the inheritance was yet to be given (v. 5) and the land of 'great suffering' (v. 11). God appeared to Moses on Mount Sinai, and that made the place 'holy ground' (v. 33).

Stephen's argument reaches its climax in his discussion of the Temple: Solomon built a house for God, but God does not dwell in houses made by human hands (v. 48; 1 Kings 8.27; 2 Chronicles 6.18). Taken at face value, the point is that building the Temple was a mistake from the first. God is the One who dwells in the house made by his own hand (Acts 7. 49). Thus, blind obsession with the human-made Temple amounts to idolatry, that is, worshipping what is made by humans instead of God himself who has made all (vv. 41, 50). Instead, they had to 'obey the Holy Spirit' working through the apostles and now through Stephen. But they keep rejecting the offer of repentance and salvation in the name of Jesus. So Stephen calls his attackers 'stiff-necked' and 'uncircumcised in heart and ears' (v. 51).

Stephen's speech remains crucial for modern Christians too. We believe that God is now present among us in his Spirit through Jesus Christ, making us God's holy temple (1 Corinthians 3.16–17; 2 Corinthians 6.16–18; Ephesians 2.21–22; Hebrews 3.6; 1 Peter 2.4–10). We are God's temple, not because God is bound to us, but because he has decided to show his loving glory to us through Jesus Christ and we have decided to live out this grace by reflecting his glory in our lives, individually and communally. Forgetting that will be lapsing into the same mistake that Israel had made before the benefit of Christ.

The law-breaking Israel

When it comes to the issue of the law, Stephen turns the tables on his accusers. History shows that Israel, 'your ancestors', repeatedly rejected Moses and the law he had given them (Acts 7.35, 38–39). Now their descendants are rejecting Jesus, the very prophet like Moses who had been predicted by Moses himself. The ancestors killed those who foretold the coming of the Righteous One, while the present Israel have become his betrayers and murderers (v. 52). So the conclusion is inevitable: 'You are the ones that received the law . . . yet you have not kept it' (v. 53).

Discrepancies in the Bible

Reading Stephen's speech, we notice that what Stephen says does not always match the data in the OT. And we may wonder how the inspired Scripture contains such discrepancies. But we have to remember the simple but important fact that God has decided to communicate with us through human authors. More importantly, we also need to pay attention to the genre of the writing we are reading. The Bible contains many 'historical' works such as the four Gospels and Acts, but the purpose of those writings is not to provide snapshot-like reports on Jesus or the Early Church. These are more like portraits: truthful yet with their own distinctive theological and pastoral accents. Undue preoccupation with trivial differences may blind us to the main messages of the text.

? STUDY SUGGESTIONS

Review of content

1 What are the differences between the description of events in Genesis and Stephen's speech?

2 What is the parallel pattern visible in both Moses and Jesus as the saviour of the people?

3 What is Stephen's main answer to the charge concerning the Temple?

4 What is Stephen's main answer to the charge of breaking the law?

Bible study

5 In light of the following passages what can we say about God's principle of choosing his instrument?

(a) Acts 7.22; (b) Luke 1.68–80; (c) Luke 2.29–32, 40, 52; (d) Acts 6.5, 8, 10.

6 Read the following passages. How are we to understand such references to God's turning away from his people?

(a) Acts 7.42; (b) Deuteronomy 32.21; (c) Romans 1.24, 26, 28.

7 Read the following passages, which speak of the circumcision of heart. What does such circumcision signify?

(a) Exodus 33.3, 5; (b) Deuteronomy 10.16; (c) Jeremiah 6.10; (d) Romans 2.29.

8 Read the following passages. What was the main criticism the early Christians made against contemporary Judaism?

(a) Acts 7.53; (b) Luke 3.7–9; (c) Matthew 23.3; (d) Romans 2; (e) Galatians 6.12–13.

Discussion and application

9 Think of how Jesus and Stephen faced their deaths. What can we learn from these examples about the way we are to treat our persecutors?

10 We are now the temple of God, 'not because God is bound to us but because he had decided to show his loving glory to us through Jesus Christ and because we have decided to live out this grace by reflecting his glory in our lives, both individually and communally' (p. 77). What are the concrete ways in which we can reflect God's loving glory in our everyday lives?

11 In light of several discrepancies between stories from the Old Testament and Stephen's speech, how are we to understand the inspiration of the Scripture?

12 For the Israelites, recounting their history was an important way of forming their identity as God's people (Joshua 24.2–13; Nehemiah 9.6–37; Psalms 78; 105; 106; 135). How can we modern Christians utilize this insight in forming our identity as God's people?

Acts 8.1b–40

Witnessing in all Judea and Samaria

 Summary

The scattered believers carry the gospel along with them to Judea and Samaria. Philip evangelizes Samaria and the Ethiopian eunuch in the Judean wilderness.

 Notes

8.1b. All except the apostles: This seems somewhat hyperbolic, since the Jerusalem church still remained after this persecution (9.31; 11.2, 22). The major target was probably the Hellenist Christians, who will play major roles in subsequent chapters. The fact that believers were scattered from Jerusalem to Judea and Samaria strikes a note of anticipation rather than despair (1.8).

8.3. But Saul was ravaging the church: We note a strong contrast between the devout men who buried Stephen and Saul. To 'ravage' is a strong word. Paul himself says he tried to 'destroy' the church (Galatians 1.13; cf. Acts 9.21).

8.4. Those who were scattered . . . proclaiming the word: This explains the real significance of the scattering mentioned in v. 1. The verb 'to proclaim' (Gk, *euangelizomai*) means 'to preach the good news' (v. 12).

8.5. To the city of Samaria: This is Philip of the seven. Like Stephen, he too is described as a powerful preacher of the gospel (21.8). The rest of the chapter is an 'Acts of Philip'. Considering the animosity between Jews and Samaritans (Luke 9.51–56; 10.29–37; John 4.1–42), this move constitutes a significant development in the spread of the gospel. Samaria usually means the whole region, but 'the city of Samaria' probably refers to either Sechem or Sebaste.

8.6a. The crowd listened eagerly: The term 'listened eagerly' occurs twice more (vv. 10, 11).

8.6b. Hearing and seeing: The crowd heard what he proclaimed and saw the signs he performed. Here Philip looked like the Spirit-filled Peter: bold speech combined with powerful signs. Initially, it was the miracles that drew people's attention to the gospel.

8.7. For unclean spirits . . . came out: This recalls the ministry of Jesus (Luke 4.33, 36; 6.18; 7.21; 8.2, etc). This anticipates the clash between Simon and Peter. For Luke, magic represents the demonic power which fights against the kingdom of God (8.20; 13.10; 19.13–20).

8.9. A certain man named Simon: Verses 9–11 provide a flashback to the time before Philip's arrival. Simon 'practised magic' and called himself 'great', that is, 'the power of God that is called Great' (v. 10). For Luke this attitude is Satanic, deserving due punishment (12.21–23). It sets up a nice contrast to Peter who refuses to take the credit for the healing miracle he performed (3.12), and anticipates Simon's later behaviour. In later Christian writings Simon is portrayed as the originator of the Gnostic heresies and chief adversary of Peter (e.g. Acts of Peter).

8.10–11. All of them . . . listened to him eagerly: There is a superficial similarity between magic and the gospel. The multitude of followers does not always prove the authenticity of the message.

8.12. The kingdom of God and the name of Jesus Christ: The 'Christ' is the Greek form of the Hebrew 'Messiah': 'the anointed'. So this verse elaborates on Philip's proclaiming 'the Messiah' (v. 5).

8.13. Simon himself believed: Simon, who had amazed people and enjoyed the people's acclamation, was himself amazed by the 'signs and great miracles' done by Philip.

8.14–18. Peter and John laid their hands on them, and they received the Holy Spirit: This raises a number of thorny theological questions. Why did the Holy Spirit not follow their confession and baptism? Does it mean that their conversion was incomplete or inauthentic? Does the gift of the Spirit need the imposition of the apostolic hands? As we have noted earlier, the manner of the Spirit's coming varies widely in Acts, and we cannot give definite answers to these questions, though there are many who pick and choose the cases which suit their purpose and ignore others. We should not forget that God is free to work in his own way, not according to our own theological programmes.

8.19. Give me also this power: Simon craved for the 'power' (in Greek, 'authority') to impart the Holy Spirit ('anyone on whom I lay my hands') and offered money to buy it from Peter, the master of magic. He did not realize that the Holy Spirit is God's free gift, which cannot be bought with money or concocted by any human means. God gives it; we receive it. The same goes for the 'ability' to mediate the Holy Spirit, as given to Peter and John. Neither money nor a money-oriented person has any 'part or share in this' (v. 21).

8.20. May your silver perish with you: Money often poses the greatest hurdle to genuine faith (1.18; 5.1–11; 16.16–18; 19.24–27).

8.22. Repent . . . if possible . . . be forgiven: A chance of repentance is offered, probably because Simon acted as he did out of ignorance. This may explain the severity of punishment inflicted on Ananias and Sapphira who lied to Peter wilfully. Yet Peter expresses his doubt, knowing the inveterate habit of Simon's heart.

8.23. The gall of bitterness and the chains of wickedness: The two words for 'gall' and 'bitterness' occur together in Deuteronomy 29.17 (LXX), depicting the consequences of idolatry.

8.24. Pray for me: We do not know how genuine Simon's penitence was, as we do not know if the elder son went into the house with his father in Jesus' parable (Luke 15.28).

8.25. Proclaiming the good news to many villages of the Samaritans: In evangelizing Samaria, the Jerusalem apostles did a lot more than just praying and laying their hands on the already converted believers.

8.26. An angel of the Lord: Philip acts at God's unexpected bidding. For Luke the angel of the Lord is virtually the same as the Spirit of the Lord (vv. 29, 39). The point is: God himself is guiding the progress of the gospel.

8.27. An Ethiopian eunuch: That this person is from a 'far away' land recalls the promise in 2.39. Here Ethiopia refers to the region south of Egypt (Ezekiel 29.10), known as the land of Cush (Genesis 2.13). Candace is a title (like the Egyptian Pharaoh), not a personal name. In Acts the Ethiopian eunuch is the first Gentile converted to Christianity, foreshadowing the full-fledged Gentile mission in later chapters. His worshipping in Jerusalem and reading the Isaiah scroll suggest that he was a 'God-fearer', a Gentile attracted to Judaism without being circumcised. (A castrated person was barred from full participation in Judaism.)

8.30. Heard him reading the prophet Isaiah: In ancient days it was customary to read aloud. There is a nice word play in Philip's question: 'Do you understand (*ginōskō*) what you are reading (*ana-ginōskō*)?'

8.32–33. Like a sheep he was led to the slaughter . . . : The quoted passage is Isaiah 53.7–8. The idea of the 'suffering servant' based on this and other Isaiah passages had a great influence on the early Christians' understanding of Jesus (John 12.38; 1 Peter 2.21–25; Romans 10.16).

8.34–35. About whom, may I ask . . . Then Philip began to speak: This is the best question that an evangelist could possibly hope for from an enquirer. Philip's proclaiming Jesus from the Scripture recalls the risen Jesus who explained from the Scripture 'things about himself' to his disciples (Luke 24.25–27, 44–47).

8.36–38. What is to prevent me . . .?: The same verb 'prevent' is used in relation to the conversion of Cornelius (10.47; 11.17). The Western text has verse 37: 'And said, "If you believe with all your heart, you may." And he replied, "I believe that Jesus Christ is the Son of God."' See the textual note on this verse in NRSV.

Most modern translations put verse 37 in the footnote (but see KJV or NKJV). The verse is found in some manuscripts, but it is not part of the original text of Acts but a later addition reflecting the baptismal practices of a later period.

From the earliest period, 'baptism by immersion' was the normal practice, but different modes of baptism began to develop fairly early, most probably due to the limited availability of baptizing water. *Didache* (also known as *Teaching of the Twelve Apostles*), an early Christian document written during the 90s of the first century, advises that if possible, baptism should be performed in 'living (= running) water', but different kinds of water can also be used: still water when there is no river nearby; warm water when the water is too cold. One could also 'pour out water on the head three times' when water supply was limited (*Didache* 7.1–3).

8.39. On his way rejoicing: Philip's sudden disappearance from the rejoicing eunuch recalls the sudden disappearance of the risen Jesus from the heart-burning disciples at Emmaus (Luke 24.31–32). For Luke, joy marks the presence of the Holy Spirit (Acts 5.41; 8.8).

8.40. At Azotus . . . to Caesarea: The story ends with Philip moving along the coastline toward Caesarea. There he will meet Paul in a later chapter (21.8).

 Interpretation

Persecution and expansion (8.1–3)

Stephen's death triggered a severe persecution. Luke says that all except the apostles fled Jerusalem, but still its major target must have been the Hellenists like Stephen. So they had to flee, and that must have threatened the very existence of the community in Jerusalem. But Luke is not worried. He is not so much concerned about persecution itself as its consequences: the scattered believers went everywhere, proclaiming the gospel throughout Judea and Samaria. Persecution, far from destroying the Church, turned out to be a paradoxical way of expanding it. Just as the Jewish leaders' persecution had come to naught, so did the persecution of the Hellenists by people like Saul, since it only helped them to spread the gospel even further, this time beyond the border of Jerusalem (1.8). Once again, it was a vain thing to try to persecute the Church, since in reality the opponents of the gospel were unwittingly performing what God himself had planned (4.25–26). We can find a modern example of this in China where the number of believers is fast-growing despite the systematic oppression of the Communist government.

Meeting Saul

We have already met Saul in the context of Stephen's death (7.58; 8.1). Luke refers to him once again in 8.3, before he recounts the evangelization of Samaria. Here what we see is a fierce opponent of the gospel who was 'ravaging the church'. He entered 'house after house', and dragged off not only men but also women in order to throw them into prison. But this would not last long. As we will learn in Acts 9, his present rage was nothing more than a last-ditch effort to 'kick against the goads' (26.14) before finally submitting to the authority of the risen Jesus. After that he himself would follow in the footsteps of Stephen.

Philip evangelizes Samaria (8.4–25)

These 'Acts of Philip' provide an example of the summary statement in v. 3. The story of Samaria looks peculiar in two respects:

1   the delay of the Spirit; and

2   the intriguing figure of Simon the magician.

Philip's ministry in Samaria was no less powerful than that of either Peter or Stephen. He proclaimed the same word about the kingdom of God; he also performed miracles and amazed people there, even Simon the magician. So the Samaritans believed and were baptized, no doubt, in the name of Jesus. Yet the Holy Spirit did not come upon them. It was only when Peter and John laid their hands on them that they received the Holy Spirit. Why? Most interpreters believe that it has to do with the fact that most Jews despised Samaritans. The delay of the Spirit may have been embarrassing to Philip. But it must have been wonderful that the Samaritans received the Holy Spirit through the mediation of Peter and John, the apostles par excellence. That alone must clear any lingering doubts about the status of Samaritan converts within the believing community, allowing them full fellowship with other 'Jewish' Christians. So this story did for Samaria what Peter's eating with Cornelius was to do for the Gentiles as a whole: apostolic recognition and acceptance of those who had been 'far away'.

In this story Simon represents the demonic force opposing the kingdom of God at a critical juncture of the Church's history. In a way the whole story of Luke–Acts can be read in terms of an ongoing conflict between God and the Satan who tries to thwart his purpose. This incident is yet another manifestation of such deep-rooted spiritual warfare. Later we will read about a remarkably similar confrontation at another juncture of the gospel history, i.e. at the beginning of the Gentile mission by Paul and Barnabas (13.4–12).

Acts of the Spirit

Philip's mission with the Ethiopian eunuch was done by the initiative of the Holy Spirit (vv. 26, 29, 39). The same Spirit sends Peter to Cornelius (10.19; 11.12), orders the church in Antioch to set apart Barnabas and

Paul for the Gentile mission (13.4), directs Paul's path toward Macedonia (16.6, 7), tells Paul that he will proclaim the gospel in Rome (23.11). The advance of the gospel is made by the will and guidance of the Spirit, and not by human decision or will. The power to tear down existing walls and expand the frontier of the gospel does not come from human wisdom but from the Holy Spirit. What we discover in the 'acts' of such powerful witnesses as Peter, Stephen, Philip and Paul is the working of the Holy Spirit through such human agents (1.8). This is the 'certainty' or the 'truth' of the Christian gospel which Luke wants us to realize. For the kingdom of God is not about mere words but about power (1 Corinthians 4.20).

Magic

Considering magic as 'primitive' is very much mistaken, since it continues to be in vogue all around the world, including most civilized countries such as the USA. Many moderns resort to various kinds of magical practices such as astrology or tarot cards. They do so not to find out the right path to walk but mainly to have their own wishes granted. We can even 'practise Christian faith' out of such motives, as Simon did in the present episode. We should keep reminding ourselves: we have the Lord to serve, not a servant to lord it over.

 STUDY SUGGESTIONS

Word study

1 What does the word 'magic' represent in Acts?

2 What does 'Ethiopia' refer to in the Bible?

Review of content

3 Who was the major target of the persecution after Stephen's death?

4 What was the consequence of the scattering of the believers?

5 What are the two peculiarities in the story of the Samaritan mission?

6 What was the resultant benefit of the delay of the Holy Spirit in Samaria?

Bible study

7 Read Luke 9.51–56; 10.29–37; John 4.1–42. In view of the relationship between the Jews and Samaritans of the day, what was the significance of Philip's mission?

8 Name a few passages in the Bible which speak of Christians rejoicing even in unlikely situations. What is the ground for such joy?

Discussion and application

9 Can you think of any practices around you which are comparable to the 'magic' of Simon?

10 Simon's mistake was trying to have control over God's power for his own purpose. Can you think of similar ways of turning God's gift into a means of realizing unholy desires (Matthew 7.21–23)?

11 Philip and Peter were swift in perceiving the meaning of God's giving the Holy Spirit to the Gentiles and then in giving up their old prejudices. Can you think of cases in which we tend to hold to our old habits or misguided convictions even when God's will clearly appears to run in the other direction?

12 Persecution of the Church turned out to be 'a blessing in disguise' for the spread of the gospel (Philippians 1.12–18). What can we learn from this about the way we look at the events in our lives?

Acts 9.1–30

The conversion of Saul

 Summary

Jesus appears to Saul and calls him as the instrument for the Gentile mission. Paul begins to proclaim Jesus in Damascus and then gets to know the disciples in Jerusalem.

 Notes

9.1–2. Still breathing threats and murder: This expands the earlier report in 8.3. The gospel kept spreading under the guidance of the Spirit, but Saul still opposed the Holy Spirit by persecuting Jesus' followers (7.51–52). Saul was portrayed as in league with the high priest, the chief opponent of the Jerusalem church (9.14; 22.5). So Luke underscores that the Jewish leadership continued to be involved in persecution beyond Jerusalem.

9.2a. Synagogues at Damascus: Damascus was the most important city in Syria with a large Jewish population. Paul's trip to Damascus assumes that the gospel has reached the region well beyond Judea and Samaria. This reminds us that Luke's reports in Acts are fairly selective.

9.2b. The Way: Luke alone uses the term to refer to the Christian gospel (19.9, 23; 22.4; 24.14, 22). For the early Christians the gospel was a way to walk and not just an idea to acknowledge. Also note similar expressions such as the 'way of salvation' (16.17), 'the Way of God' (18.26).

9.3. A light from heaven: This is a sign of theophany (e.g. Exodus 19.16; 2 Samuel 22.15; Luke 9.29; 10.18; 17.24; 24.4), as is falling to the ground in v. 4 (Ezekiel 1.28; Daniel 10.9).

9.4. Why do you persecute me?: The risen Jesus had been active through his followers. Now he acted directly, telling Saul that persecuting Jesus' followers was persecuting Jesus himself (Luke 10.16). The double calling, 'Saul, Saul' recalls the way God calls people in the OT (Genesis 22.11; 46.2; Exodus 3.4; 1 Samuel 3.4).

9.5. Who are you, Lord?: The 'Lord' may be simply deferential, but with the heavenly light shining around him, Saul must have felt that he was in the presence of a deity.

9.6. You will be told: In v. 10 a certain Ananias comes into the picture to help him out. Now Saul could not act on his own but should be told by others what to do.

9.7. They heard the voice: This differs from the account in 22.6–16 and 26.14. See notes there.

9.8–9. He could see nothing: Saul's blindness seems symbolic (Luke 2.30; 4.18; 24.16, 31; Acts 13.11; 28.27). Compare this blind Saul with the murder-breathing Saul in v. 3.

9.10. Ananias . . . in a vision: Luke calls him a 'disciple'. For 'Here, I am, Lord', see Genesis 22.1; 1 Samuel 3.6, 8.

9.11a. The street called Straight . . . a man of Tarsus: This was a long, straight street that ran through the city. Saul's birthplace is here mentioned for the first time (9.30; 21.39).

9.11b–12. Praying . . . in a vision: Prayer is often connected with visions (10.9–11; Luke 1.10; 3.21; 9.28). Guiding both Saul and Ananias through visions resembles 10.1–16 (Peter and Cornelius).

9.13–14. But Ananias answered: His reluctance was only natural; it foreshadows the fear of the disciples in Jerusalem (9.26–27). Here Luke begins to use the word 'saints', i.e. 'the holy' (vv. 32, 41).

9.15. Gentiles and kings and . . . Israel: Indeed later on Saul/Paul would speak to Gentiles (17.22–31), kings (26.2–32) and Israel (13.16–41; 22.1–2). Paul himself considered his calling as exclusively for the Gentiles (Galatians 1.15–16; Romans 11.13).

9.16. He must suffer: The phrase 'must (Gk, *dei*) suffer' denotes divine necessity (1.16, 22). Saul had been inflicting suffering on those who called on Jesus' name; now he was chosen to suffer for the sake of Jesus' name.

9.17. Laid his hands on Saul: The imposition of hands here was associated both with healing of sight and the gift of the Holy Spirit. Interestingly, the actual coming of the Spirit is not described; Luke does not show much concern about the manner of the Spirit's coming. The phrase 'who appeared to you' is the language of the resurrection appearances (1 Corinthians 15.5–8).

9.20. Immediately he began to proclaim Jesus . . . the Son of God: This fulfils Jesus' prediction in 9.15. As in Damascus, Saul regularly started his mission by preaching in the synagogues (13.5; 14.1; 17.1–2, 10; 18.4, 19; 19.8). Surprisingly, only here in Acts is Jesus explicitly called 'the Son of God' (cf. 13.33; Luke 22.70). Here it seems to be a correlate of the 'Messiah' (v. 22).

9.21. All . . . were amazed: In Acts, amazement often denotes a miracle. Such a complete transformation could not be explained in human terms. Paul himself called it God's grace. People's words here recall Ananias' words in vv. 13–14. In Galatians, Paul reports that believers in Judea also said the same thing (1.23).

9.22. Saul became increasingly more powerful: Interestingly, Paul describes his own ministry in the same way (Philippians 4.13; 1 Timothy 1.12; 2 Timothy 4.17). Here Luke begins to use the term 'Jews' (*ioudaios*) to refer to the non-believing Jews.

9.23. After some time: This literally means 'after many days'. We do not know how long but in Galatians Paul says three years (1.17–18).

9.23–25. The Jews plotted to kill him: In 2 Corinthians 11.32–33 Paul attributes this attempt to the governor under King Aretas. Compare 'lowering him in a basket' with Paul's phrase that he was 'let down in a basket through the wall' (11.33). This incident begins to fulfil Jesus' prediction about his suffering in 9.16. 'His disciples' in v. 25 is somewhat surprising, considering the short period of Saul's ministry in Damascus. Or it may be that Luke gives us a very brief account of a much longer story.

9.26. For they did not believe: Like Ananias, the disciples in Jerusalem were also sceptical about Saul's abrupt change.

9.27. Barnabas . . . brought him to the apostles: For Saul, Barnabas is surely a 'son of encouragement' (4.36), an effective mediator between him and the apostles. Yet, we find considerable tension between Luke's description and Paul's own report that he did not see any other apostles except Peter (Galatians 1.17–18).

9.28. He went in and out among them: Luke's report here is difficult to reconcile with Paul's own report that he was 'unknown by sight to the churches of Judea that are in Christ' (Galatians 1.22). This difference has to do with each author's intention: Luke wants to underscore the unity of Paul and the Jerusalem apostles, but Paul tries to stress his independence by distancing himself from them.

9.29. With the Hellenists: Here Saul took up the place of Stephen, and found himself under the threat of death from the same group he himself had once belonged to. So Saul began to experience suffering for the sake of Jesus' name.

9.30–31. Sent him off to Tarsus: Saul went back to his birthplace and stayed there until Barnabas would seek him out (11.25–26).

9.31. The church throughout Judea, Galilee, and Samaria: See 6.5 for a similar report on the growth of the church. The mention of Galilee is unexpected, since Luke says nothing about it in Acts. Once again, the selectivity of his account becomes unmistakable.

9.32. Peter . . . in Lydda: Lydda was located on the Plain of Sharon between Jerusalem and Joppa (v. 35). Luke does not tell us how this town was evangelized.

9.33–34. 'Jesus Christ heals you' . . . and immediately: The report is less dramatic than before but the point is the same: it was Jesus who gave the healing; Peter was just a mediating instrument of Christ's power.

9.35. All . . . saw . . . and turned to the Lord: Here too, healing provided an impetus to a large-scale conversion. Also see the statement in v. 42.

9.36a. A disciple . . . Tabitha . . . Dorcas: This is the only occurrence of the feminine noun for 'disciple' (*mathētria*) in the NT. Tabitha is the Aramaic word for gazelle, which is Dorcas in Greek.

9.36b. Devoted to good works and acts of charity: This resembles Luke's portrayal of Cornelius (10.2).

9.37–41. She became ill and died: Interpreters note the remarkable resemblance between this episode and Jesus' raising of the little girl in Luke 8.49–56: the two messengers, the weeping bystanders, the exclusion of outsiders, call to rise, taking by the hand. In both cases, the call must sound strikingly similar in Aramaic: *'Talitha, cumi'* (Little girl, get up!) and *'Tabitha, cumi'* (Tabitha, get up!).

9.42. This became known throughout Joppa, and many believed: As with the healing of Aeneas, here too the healing functioned as an impetus to belief. People believed in Jesus, not Peter, knowing that the power came from Jesus and not from Peter.

9.43. He stayed in Joppa: This sets the stage for the following story about Cornelius.

 Interpretation

Saul meets the risen Jesus

Saul's conversion or calling was one of the most important consequences of the death of Stephen. This event is recounted three times in
Acts (22.3–21; 26.4–23), and that shows the importance of this event.
The story of his conversion begins with Saul the persecutor. That has the
effect of underscoring God's initiative in it: such a drastic transformation
could not be explained in human terms. Paul himself was acutely aware
of his past as a persecutor of the Church (1 Corinthians 15.9; Galatians
1.13, 23; Philippians 3.6; 1 Timothy 1.13), and declares repeatedly that
his conversion/call was nothing but a miracle of pure grace, the grace

powerful enough to bring about such a dramatic change in his life (1 Corinthians 15.10).

In a dramatic experience of theophany, Saul saw the risen Jesus in his heavenly glory (vv. 3–6, 17, 27; 22.14; 26.16). Paul himself says that he saw the glory of God shining in the face of Christ (2 Corinthians 4.6). Of course, he did not know him at first, but this heavenly presence identified himself as Jesus (of Nazareth), the Lord of the Christians he had been persecuting. In the presence of the risen Jesus, Paul made two discoveries:

1 the Christians were right after all; indeed Jesus was raised and exalted; and

2 Jesus identifies himself with his followers; persecuting the church, Paul had been persecuting Jesus himself.

Then Jesus told him what to do. Jesus' order to enter the city was surely ironical: authorized by the high priest, Saul had planned to go there to persecute those who called on Jesus' name; now Jesus sends him there, but this time to proclaim the name of Jesus. Once again, his plotting against God will prove futile, since it was in fact a mysterious way of fulfilling it. He still entered Damascus as originally planned, but he did so as a different person.

The mediation of Ananias

The visionary conversation between Ananias and Jesus is also revealing. Ananias was afraid that Saul came here 'to bind all who invoke your name' (v. 14), but Jesus now told him that he was 'an instrument whom I have chosen to bring my name' before everybody (v. 15), so much so that he would even suffer greatly 'for the sake of my name' (v. 16). These predictions of Jesus immediately found their fulfilment in Paul's obedient discharge of his mission in Damascus and Jerusalem: proclaiming Jesus (vv. 20, 22, 28) and suffering for it (vv. 23–25, 29–30). This inevitable combination of proclamation and suffering would be something Paul had to learn to endure throughout his life.

We also note that this crucial revelation was given to Ananias, and not to Saul himself. He was still in the dark even after meeting the risen Jesus, and someone else in the community had to come and help him to complete the conversion process with baptism and receiving the Holy Spirit. Later on we also discover that the Spirit gave an order to the church, and not to Paul or Barnabas individually, that they should set apart the two for a special mission (13.2).

Grace in power

Paul says in 1 Corinthians that God's grace was not given him in vain. That became clear even in his activity in Damascus and Jerusalem: 'Saul became increasingly more powerful and confounded the Jews who lived in Damascus' (v. 22); 'Barnabas . . . described for them how . . . in Damascus he had spoken boldly in the name of Jesus' (v. 27); so 'he went in and out among them in Jerusalem, speaking boldly in the name of the Lord' (v. 28). Such was the power of God's grace, and thus it is no wonder that Paul has come to define the gospel of Christ as the 'power of God' who gives salvation to all who believe (Romans 1.16; 1 Corinthians 1.18, 24; 2.1–5).

Peter in Judea

As Paul returns to his home town, Luke turns his attention to Peter once more. But he was no longer based in Jerusalem but moved about through different parts of Judea: from Lydda to Joppa, and then from there to Caesarea, the place of Cornelius. So with these two stories, Luke prepares us for the following story in Acts 10 and 11.

In this passage Luke further emphasizes the great power working through Peter: he not only healed a sick person, he even brought a dead person back to life. And wherever he went, this powerful manifestation of Jesus' power provided an impetus to the effective evangelization of the region (vv. 35, 42). So, with a refreshed confidence in Peter as the apostle of Jesus, we read the story of his encounter with Cornelius, a Gentile par excellence.

 STUDY SUGGESTIONS

Word study

1   What is the idea behind the epithet, 'the saints' (9.14, 32, 41; 1 Corinthians 6.9–11; 1 Thessalonians 4.3)?

Review of content

2   Why did the early Christians call the gospel 'the Way'?

3   What were the discoveries Paul made at his encounter with the risen Jesus?

4   What are the three groups of people Paul was called to proclaim the gospel to?

5   Luke's picture of Paul in Jerusalem is somewhat different from Paul's own account. How can we explain such a difference?

6   What was the major result of Peter's powerful healing ministry?

Bible study

7   Read the following passages. Why does Paul call his apostleship 'grace'?

   (a) 1 Corinthians 15.9–10; **(b)** Galatians 1.11–15, 23; Philippians 3.6; 1 Timothy 1.12–17.

8 Read Acts 9.36 and 10.2. Is it possible to find a connection between God's grace and human faithfulness?

Discussion and application

9 The service of Barnabas was indispensable for a person like Saul. Can you think of anyone around you who is comparable to Barnabas?

10 We have noted above the communal nature of Saul's calling. How does this help us to build a more biblical view of God's calling?

Acts 10.1—11.18

Opening the door:
Peter and Cornelius

 Summary

Peter preaches the gospel to a Gentile household, and God gives them the Holy Spirit. The Jewish Christians realize that salvation is for both Jews and Gentiles.

 Notes

10.1. In Caesarea . . . a man named Cornelius, a centurion of the Italian Cohort: This is Caesarea Maritima. This coastal city was named after Caesar and famous for Herod the Great's magnificent building projects. It was the headquarters of the Roman government of Judea, and thus its population was mostly Gentile. A 'centurion' was an officer in charge of 100 soldiers. The Italian Cohort was a unit of the Roman army. Some think Cornelius was retired, since there is no evidence for the troop's presence in Caesarea around that time.

10.2. A devout man who feared God: Though a Gentile, his life was exemplary to Jewish eyes. Luke frequently refers to those Gentiles who 'fear God' or worship God (13.16, 26; 16.14; 18.7). But it remains disputed whether there was a distinct group called 'God-fearers', namely, those who attended the synagogues and tried to live by the rules of Jewish Torah without becoming circumcised proselytes. Prayer and almsgiving were staple components of Jewish piety (Matthew 6.2–6).

Luke underscores the uprightness of Cornelius' piety by repeating his generous almsgiving and prayer no less than three times (vv. 2, 4, 31; cf. v. 22). His salvation was surely the result of God's grace, but it is also true that God had paid attention to his uprightness. As Paul would put it, he was an internal Jew, though externally he was not (cf. Romans 2.28–29).

10.3. About three o'clock: This is the time for sacrifice and prayer (3.1). He was praying when he had a vision (v. 30). For Luke, the 'angel' of the Lord seems functionally identical with the Holy Spirit (v. 19; cf. 'a holy angel', v. 22).

10.4a. What is it, Lord?: His response of fear implies that he felt a divine presence.

10.4b. A memorial before God: A 'memorial before God' means a 'memorial offering' brought before God; Cornelius' righteousness is likened to a cereal offering. Psalm 112 tells us how God treats a righteous person. The odour of the cereal offering rises to God's presence, so that he remembers the person offering the sacrifice (Leviticus 2.2, 9, 16). Cornelius rightly took it as a promise of salvation (Acts 11.14).

10.8. He sent them to Joppa: On hearing the angel's order, Cornelius went into action without hesitation. Luke emphasizes his unreserved obedience.

10.9. Peter went up on the roof to pray: Now the spotlight moves to Joppa. Peter's vision also happened during a prayer. The roof, flat and accessible from an outdoor stairway, was a perfect place for prayer (2 Kings 23.12; Nehemiah 8.16).

10.10. He became hungry: This provides a foil for the command, 'Kill and eat' (v. 13). Peter's vision was a trance (Gk, *ekstasis*), and thus somewhat different from that of Cornelius.

10.11. The heaven opened: This is a sign of God's presence or revelation (Psalm 78.23; Isaiah 24.18; Luke 3.21).

10.12–13. All kinds of four-footed creatures and reptiles and birds of the air: This follows the standard categorization of animals in the OT (Genesis 1.24; 6.20; cf. Romans 1.23). The picture is that of both clean and unclean animals all mixed up.

10.14. I have never eaten anything . . . profane or unclean: Peter's refusal is very strong. The Jews had a very strict sense of what to eat and what not to eat. See Ezekiel 4.14 for a similar attitude.

10.15. What God has made clean, you must not call profane: The point of the heavenly voice is that Peter must now ignore the cherished distinction between clean and unclean. This recalls the words of Jesus and Mark's interpretation of it (Mark 7.15; 7.19). The true significance of this declaration is yet to be discovered.

10.17. Peter was greatly puzzled about . . . the vision . . . suddenly: The wording implies a providential hand. Peter must have made a connection between his vision and the sudden appearance of the guests.

10.19. The Spirit said to him: The Spirit directly told Peter to go into action, but we may assume that his previous vision helped him discern what the Spirit wanted.

10.20. Go with them . . . for I have sent them: So after all, the angel who had appeared to Cornelius was not different from the Spirit. Here everything happened under the direction of the Spirit.

10.23. Some of the believers from Joppa: These six 'men of circumcision' will function as Peter's witnesses (11.12).

10.24. His relatives and close friends: Cornelius had gathered them for he was expecting a message of salvation for his entire household (11.14).

10.25–26. Cornelius . . . worshipped him: Cornelius' gesture and Peter's rejoinder indicates Cornelius' sense that he was under God's direction. His humility recalls that of the other centurion in the Gospel (Luke 7.6).

10.28a. It is unlawful for a Jew to associate with or to visit a Gentile: In post-biblical Judaism, the uncircumcised Gentiles were considered as unholy, and beyond hope of salvation. And eating with a Gentile ran the risk of defilement, since they could never be certain that the food had been prepared according to the regulations of the law (Leviticus 17.10, 11, 14). Especially under the Gentile oppression the attitude of most Jews toward the Gentiles was very harsh. The word Peter used here is 'of another race', which is a much gentler way of referring to a Gentile.

10.28b. But God has shown me that I should not call anyone profane or unclean: Here Peter realizes the meaning of his vision. The Spirit's direction to go 'without hesitation' (v. 20) in fact means to go 'without making any distinction'. He is yet to realize its full implication for the salvation of the Gentiles, but a significant step has now been taken.

10.29. May I ask why you sent for me?: This question invites Cornelius's account of his vision, which will put Peter in the picture.

10.32. Send therefore to Joppa: The causal connection is explicitly stated. God allowed Cornelius a chance to hear the gospel, because of his upright piety.

10.33. All that the Lord has commanded you to say: Once again Cornelius shows his sense of divine guidance: God is going to say something to him through Peter.

10.34a. Then Peter began to speak: The phrase literally means 'opened his mouth'. This expression often indicates the importance of the subject.

10.34b. God shows no partiality: The idea is traditional (Deuteronomy 10.17; 2 Chronicles 19.7; Job 34.19; Malachi 2.9), but Jews of the first century only applied this within the Jewish boundary. Now Peter is surprised to find that this familiar belief does mean what it says: a person's acceptance with God does not depend on external conditions such as nationality but on the internal disposition of the heart.

10.35. In every nation anyone who fears him and does what is right is acceptable to him: This is the true criterion of acceptance with God. As Paul makes it clear, God's impartiality means that he is not concerned about how a person looks but what that person does in his life (Romans 2.6–11). This is a very important point to remember in order to avoid the dangerous lapse into 'cheap grace' (cf. Psalm 15.1-2). So Christ the Saviour is at the same time the 'judge of the living and the dead' (v. 42).

10.36a. Preaching peace by Jesus Christ: Here 'peace' is virtually synonymous with 'salvation'. But in the context of the relationship between Jews and Gentiles it also includes a more specific sense of peace between the two (Ephesians 2.1-15).

10.36b. Lord of all: Here the expression refers to Jesus (2.36). Jesus is the Lord, not only of Jews but also of Gentiles. So everyone who calls on the name of Jesus will be saved (2.21; cf. Romans 10.12).

10.37. That message spread throughout Judea: Scholars note that Peter's summary of the ministry of Jesus resembles the outline of the Gospel of Mark (beginning after John's baptism; focus on the healing ministry).

10.38. God anointed Jesus . . . with the Holy Spirit and with power: Jesus is the Messiah in the sense that he had been anointed by God with the Holy Spirit. This was the source of his doing good and healing all the oppressed. In other words, 'God was with him' (Genesis 21.20, 22; Isaiah 58.11).

10.39, 41. We are witnesses. The apostles' witness includes both Jesus' earthly ministry and God's raising him up on the third day. The risen Jesus' appearance to the limited number of witnesses recalls 1.2-3.

10.41. Who ate and drank with him: Eating and drinking proves Jesus' bodily resurrection. In the context of Peter's eating with a Gentile, the expression seems more poignant.

10.42. He commanded us to preach: Normally, 'the people' refers to the Jews, but here it seems better to take it more inclusively (1.8; Luke 24.47-48).

10.43. All the prophets testify: The Scripture testifies that everyone who believes in Jesus will receive forgiveness of sins, namely, not only Jews but also Gentiles.

10.44. The Holy Spirit fell upon all who heard the word: The outpouring of the Spirit was unexpected ('still'). God's giving the Holy Spirit constitutes definitive evidence for God's acceptance of the Gentiles. Peter was saying, 'Everyone who believes', when the Spirit came 'upon all who heard the word'. Can it be merely accidental?

10.45. The circumcised . . . were astounded: God keeps surprising people. Just as the people were astounded by the giving of the Holy Spirit at Pentecost (2.12), now the Jewish Christians were astounded by God's doing the same to the Gentiles.

10.46. Speaking in tongues and extolling God: The Spirit-filled disciples did the same at Pentecost (2.4, 11). So the Jewish Christians recognized the fact: 'These people have received the Holy Spirit just as we have' (v. 47; 11.15).

10.47. Can anyone withhold . . . water? The gift of the Spirit means that the Gentiles have been saved; so there is no point in refusing baptism. This rhetorical question recalls that of the Ethiopian eunuch: 'What is to prevent (*kōluō*) me from being baptized?' (8.36). Peter will repeat the same question in his defence: 'Who was I that I could hinder (*kōluō*) God?' (11.17). This shows that Peter has now fully understood the meaning of his vision. Here the order of water baptism and the gift of the Spirit is reversed, but Luke does not seem to be troubled by that at all.

10.48. They invited him to stay: This gesture completes the tearing down of theological and social barriers between Jews and Gentiles. In the meantime the news reached Jerusalem.

11.2–3. Circumcised believers: All Jewish Christian men are circumcised. Luke uses this expression to contrast them with 'uncircumcised men' like Cornelius. The criticism focuses on Peter's social interaction with Gentiles.

11.4. Peter began to explain: The whole section of vv. 4–17 recapitulates the incident in chapter 10.

11.12. The Spirit told me . . . not to make a distinction: This combines 10.20 and 10.34. It was not Peter's own inference but the Spirit's instruction, though the two do not necessarily exclude each other.

11.14. A message by which you . . . will be saved: Peter's message is explicitly explained as the message of salvation. This episode is not just about social interaction of Jews and Gentiles but about the salvation of Gentiles. The so-called 'new perspective on Paul' tends to neglect this important point to bring out the social dimension of the Jew–Gentile conflict.

11.16. You will be baptized with the Holy Spirit: This recalls 1.5 and Luke 3.16. It practically puts this incident on a par with the Jews' receiving the Spirit at Pentecost.

11.17. Who was I that I could hinder God? See note on 10.47. Luke keeps accentuating the divine initiative in the progress of the gospel.

11.18. Then God has given even to the Gentiles the repentance that leads to life: This recalls the earlier statements in 2.38; 5.31 and 26.20. Now the Church explicitly acknowledges the fact that God has fully opened the door of salvation for the Gentiles. God takes the initiative and the Church follows in his footsteps, cautiously but faithfully.

 Interpretation

This long section divides into several scenes:

1   Caesarea: Cornelius' vision (1–8);

2   Joppa: Peter's vision and the Gentile guests (9–23a);

3 Caesarea: the Gentiles believe (23b–48);

4 Judea: the Church opens the door to the Gentiles (11.1-18).

The Church opens its door to the Gentiles

Luke considers this incident as the symbolic beginning of the Gentile mission, since it is the first case in which the issue of Gentile mission is consciously raised. We have already seen the evangelization of Samaria and the conversion of the Ethiopian eunuch, but it is only here that the Church raises a question about the propriety of receiving Gentiles. In that sense this story forms one of the most critical moments in the movement of the Church's mission. However, the Church's decision to accept the Gentiles is not the end of the story. Having opened its door to the Gentiles, the Church continues to debate the necessity of circumcision for the converted Gentiles, as we will see in Acts 15.

Divine initiative and the Church's obedience

As in the conversion of Saul, it is the visions that both prompt and sustain the whole story. The story begins with the visions of Cornelius (10.3-8) and of Peter (10.9-16). It is also sustained by repeated retelling of these visions by Cornelius' servants (10.21-23), and by Cornelius himself (10.30-33). God also intervenes directly at crucial moments, by directing Peter to go to the house of Cornelius (10.19-20) and, most importantly, by bestowing the Holy Spirit on the Gentile audience (10.44-46). Throughout the story both Cornelius and Peter recognize this very clearly. Thus this story makes one thing unmistakable: it is God himself who made the Church open its door toward the Gentiles; it was not the Church's decision but God's. God took the initiative, and the Church simply obeyed it (10.47-48; 11.17-18).

However, under the circumstances the Church's courage to obey God's direction is admirable. Peter did not hesitate to allow the Gentiles to be baptized when he saw the Holy Spirit come upon them. The church in Jerusalem also acknowledged God's decision immediately. In Acts, this simple and courageous obedience forms a nice contrast to the attitude of the Sanhedrin who saw the undeniable evidence for God's work but ignored it to retain their vested interest.

This leaves an important point to ponder for modern Christians about discerning the evidence of God's work and the courage to obey him at any cost. The Church continues to find itself in new situations and facing new problems. Yet we sometimes want to do things on our own and fail to discern the real actor of the scene, God himself. At other times we try to obscure the clear manifestation of God's Spirit with certain doctrines or traditions of our own. So we need a Spirit-filled balance here: a clear vision to see God working among us and the courage to follow it. Careful discernment is crucial and so is the courage to obey it, once we have found where God is going.

Good works and God's grace

The story of Cornelius also touches on a time-honoured question about divine grace and human work. No one denies that divine grace is the ground of salvation, but people differ about the value of human works in God's work of salvation. Cornelius had to be saved by hearing the message of Jesus Christ proclaimed by Peter, but Luke also makes it clear that God made this happen, because he had honoured the sincere piety of Cornelius. So we learn from this story that God's grace does not work in a way that cancels out or devalues human work. The Bible keeps telling us that the real danger is not the effort to develop sincere piety but the attempt to concoct a form of piety without power, the power of life that comes from above, i.e. from our faith in Jesus Christ.

Jews and Gentiles in the New Testament

The gospel grew in Jewish soil and extended itself toward the Gentiles. The Church decided to open its door, but the process was never easy, especially for the devout Jews who cherished their traditions. It was not just a matter of maintaining their vested interests as God's chosen people. There were also difficult theological problems about God's election and divine sincerity with his chosen people (Romans 9—11). One decision could not solve all the problems and silence all differing opinions. Conflicts were unavoidable, and the Church had to spend much of its energy in dealing with this critical issue, as is amply illustrated by Paul's Letters such as Galatians, Romans and Philippians.

As modern readers of the New Testament we need to keep this 'social context' in mind: the question of the relationship between Jews and Gentiles constitutes one of the most important factors in understanding the life of the Earliest Church. This is one of the most important contributions of the 'new perspective on Paul'. Our desire to hear God's word for us today often tends to blind us to the concrete historical context of the NT itself, but that only moves us further from the message of the Scriptures.

 STUDY SUGGESTIONS

Word study

1 What does 'three o'clock' signify?

2 What significance does it have that Peter proclaimed Jesus as the one who preached 'peace' at the house of Cornelius?

Review of content

3 Why does Luke underscore Cornelius' uprightness?

4 What was the meaning of Peter's vision?

5   What was the significance of the Holy Spirit for the Gentiles?

6   What conclusion did the Judean church draw after they heard Peter's account?

7   What is one of the most important contributions of the 'new perspective' on Paul?

Bible study

8   Read Mark 7.15 and 7.19 together with Acts 10.15 and 10.34–35. What does it mean that Jesus is 'our peace' (Ephesians 2.14–18)?

9   Read the following passages. What do these verses tell us about God's nature?

(a) Romans 2.6–11; (b) Ephesians 6.9; (c) Colossians 3.25; (d) James 2.1; (e) 1 Peter 1.17.

Discussion and application

10   Believing Jesus means abolishing all kinds of barriers between different groups of people. What kinds of discrimination do we still find in our lives and what can we do to overcome such an anti-gospel disposition?

11   'The real danger is not the effort to develop sincere piety but the attempt to concoct a form of piety without power . . . that comes from above' (p. 100). Do you agree with this statement? If you do, what is your reason?

Acts 11.19–30

The church in Antioch

 Summary

The gospel rapidly spreads to Gentiles and a church of both Jews and Gentiles is formed in Antioch. The church in Antioch maintains a strong bond with the Jerusalem church.

 Notes

11.19. Those who were scattered . . . Phoenicia, Cyprus and Antioch: This takes up the story in 8.1 and 8.4. Luke now follows these 'scattered' northward to Phoenicia (such as Ptolemais, Tyre, Sidon; cf. 21.3, 7; 27.3). Some sailed to Cyprus, others moved further north to Antioch on the River Orontes, the capital city of the Roman province of Syria. It had a large and strong Jewish community, and many Gentiles there were attracted to Judaism.

11.20. Men of Cyprus and Cyrene . . . spoke to the Hellenists: In this particular context the word 'Hellenists' must include the Greek-speaking Gentiles (cf. 6.1). These 'men of Cyprus and Cyrene' were those who fled Jerusalem (6.1–6; 8.1). So it was through these Hellenist Christians that the Gentile mission began in earnest. We may say that this extension of the gospel beyond the Jews marked one of the most critical developments in the history of the Church. In the context of Acts, the Cornelius incident functions as the theological legitimization of it.

11.21. The hand of the Lord was with them: God's hand signifies God's powerful presence (4.30). For the expression 'to turn to the Lord' see Luke 1.16–17; Acts 3.19; 9.35; 14.15; 15.19, etc. The English word 'conversion' comes from the Latin for 'to turn to the Lord' (cf. 1 Thessalonians 1.9).

11.22. The church in Jerusalem . . . sent Barnabas: As with Samaria (8.14) and Cornelius (11.1–3), the Jerusalem church investigates these new developments. This time, however, the church did not send Peter but Barnabas, a Greek-speaking Jew from Cyprus, reflecting the changing climate of the Church's mission.

11.23. He came and saw the grace of God: Like the church in Jerusalem (2.42–47), the church in Antioch also displayed visible signs of God's grace for Barnabas to see. This 'son of encouragement' saw that their faith was authentic, and encouraged them 'to remain faithful to the Lord with steadfast devotion'. Gospel is a 'word' to hear, but a word that works, the word of the living God (1 Thessalonians 2.13).

11.24. Full of the Holy Spirit and of faith: This recalls Luke's description of Stephen (6.5). So Barnabas' ministry in Antioch was as powerful as any.

11.25–26a. Barnabas went to Tarsus to look for Saul: Saul had been sent to Tarsus by the Jerusalem church after the conflict with the Hellenists (9.30). Barnabas went there to find him. The Greek implies that the search was not easy. Just as the apostle taught the Jerusalem church (2.42), Barnabas and Saul taught the Antioch church for a whole year. This ministry formed the basis for their missionary activities.

11.26b. First called 'Christians': The name means 'followers of Christ'. It was given by others (cf. 26.28; 1 Peter 4.16), which indicates that by this time Christians in Antioch had formed a distinctive group of people. The term may well have been a pejorative joke but the believers took it with humble pride.

11.27. Prophets came down from Jerusalem: For similar references, see 13.1; 21.10. Paul lists prophecy as one of the spiritual gifts and the foundation of the Church (1 Corinthians 12.28–29; 14.29, 32, 37; Ephesians 2.20; 3.5; 4.11), and Jesus also speaks of the charismatic prophets (Matthew 7.15, 22). Agabus appears one more time in 21.10. Claudius was emperor in AD 41–54. He is the one who expelled Jews from Rome in AD 40 (18.2).

11.29. Each would send relief to . . . Judea: The Greek for 'relief' (*diakonia*) can be used for all kinds of 'ministry' or 'service' in the church (see notes on 6.1). The same term will be used in 12.25. Luke accentuates the practical dimension of spirituality. The Spirit-filled Jerusalem church did its best to help its poorer members, so the church in Antioch did their best to help the poorer members in the Jerusalem church.

11.30. To the elders by Barnabas and Saul: Luke has used the term 'elders' exclusively for the antagonistic Jewish leaders (4.5, 8, 23; 6.12; Luke 7.3, 9.22; 20.1). Now he begins to use the term for the elders in the church (14.23; 15.2, 4, 6, 22, 23; 16.4; 20.17; 21.18). Some identify this visit with that recorded in Galatians 2.1–10, while others identify the latter with the meeting in Acts 15.

 Interpretation

A community of both Jews and Gentiles

This section deals with the emergence of the church in Antioch. Luke has so far described the conversion of Saul, the hero of Gentile mission (Acts 9), the opening of Gentile mission by Peter and its recognition by the Jerusalem church (Acts 10—11). Now Luke tells us how the Gentile mission gained momentum.

As in Samaria and other parts of Judea, the main players were the Hellenist Christians. Initially, they spoke the word 'to no one except Jews' (11.19), since the gospel was considered as 'the message . . . sent to the people of Israel' (10.36; Luke 1.16, 33, 54–55, 68–79). Yet, the good news could not be held in check for ever, and some of the Hellenists began to proclaim the word to the Gentiles. It was surely a bold and innovative move, but God's hand was with them, and their effort proved fruitful (11.21). This was how the church in Antioch began. Once again, the Jerusalem church sent Barnabas to look into this new development, but the condition of these Gentile believers was even better than that of the Samaritan converts. Barnabas simply saw God's grace upon them, and encouraged them to continue what they had been doing.

According to the typical pattern, we would expect Barnabas to return to Jerusalem after his mission. Yet, the situation took a different course here. Being a Cypriot Jew himself, he was the perfect person to serve the church there, the church of both Jews and Greeks. Another important step he took was to bring Saul to Antioch as his co-worker. So once again Barnabas acted as Paul's patron. For both of them this ministry together provided a crucial preparation for their work as missionaries, as we will read in the rest of the book of Acts.

Luke also tells us that in Antioch believers were first called 'Christians', namely, Christ-followers. Believers were perceived as a distinct group of people, and their identity was defined by Christ (Messiah) whom they also called 'Lord'. In a way, the whole of Acts is about the name of Jesus, and now his name has also become the name of his followers. For modern believers, the term 'Christians' seems to have lost much of its original force and become a virtual synonym of 'church-goers'. The name can change, but our identity as 'Christ-followers' (or 'Christ-smellers' as Paul would put it, 2 Corinthians 2.14) is not something to be compromised. We need to ask: how well are we doing in making people know Christ the Lord? What are the ways for us to do this?

The Gentile Christians' relief effort for the poor saints in Judea is also notable. It took an important place in Paul's work with the Gentiles. For Paul it was an expression of gratitude on the part of the Gentile Christians toward the Jewish Christians for sharing the gospel. For that reason, it signified the spiritual unity of the Jewish and Gentile Christians. Paul's concern about the relief project is well reflected in such passages as 1 Corinthians 16.1–4 and 2 Corinthians 8—9.

STUDY SUGGESTIONS

Word study

1 What does 'elder' mean in the following passages?

   (a) Acts 4.5, 8, 23; Luke 7.3; 9.22; 20.1;

   (b) Acts 14.23; 15.2, 4, 6, 22, 23; 16.4; 20.17; 21.18.

Review of content

2 Why did the Jewish Christians first speak the word only to the Jews?

3 What does 'Hellenist' mean in 11.20?

4 Why was speaking the word to the Gentiles so important?

5 Why did the church in Jerusalem send Barnabas rather than Peter to Antioch?

Bible study

6 Read the following passages. What were the roles of the prophets in the Early Church?

   (a) Acts 13.1; 21.10;

   (b) 1 Corinthians 12.28–29; 14.29, 32, 37; Ephesians 2.20; 3.5; 4.11;

   (c) Matthew 7.15, 22.

Discussion and application

7 Once again in 11.25–26 Barnabas acted as a spiritual sponsor for Paul by making him his co-minister of the church in Antioch. What can we learn from people like him?

8 In Antioch the believers were first called 'Christians', i.e. Christ-followers. So Christians are known by their following of Christ or for enabling others to know Christ. What are the ways of letting Christ be known to others in our everyday life?

9 What can we learn about Christian fellowship from the relief effort of the Gentile believers for the poor Judean Christians?

Acts 12.1–25

Herod persecutes the Church

 Summary

Herod persecutes the Church by putting James to death and imprisoning Peter. But God rescues Peter and strikes Herod for his disobedient arrogance.

 Notes

12.1. King Herod: This is Herod Agrippa I, grandson of Herod the Great and his Hasmonaean queen Mariamne. Around the time of his death (AD 44) he controlled most of Palestine. Agrippa was more popular with the Jews than many others in his family, partly because of his descent from the Jewish Hasmonaean family. Naturally, he was anxious to retain their goodwill. Three of his children appear later in Acts: Herod Agrippa II and his widowed sister Bernice (25.13), and Drusilla, now wife of Felix (24.24).

12.2. James, the brother of John: This is one of the Twelve (1.13; Luke 5.10; 6.14; 9.54). This suggests that the other apostles were also very active in their ministry, though Luke does not tell us anything about it.

12.3a. It pleased the Jews: Now the resistance came from 'the Jews' in general rather than certain parties within the Jewish community. It is possible that the Jewish antipathy had something to do with the apostles' association with the Gentiles.

12.3b. The festival of Unleavened Bread: Peter's arrest at this feast recalls the arrest of Jesus (Luke 22.1, 7).

12.4. Four squads of soldiers: They took turns, one for each watch of the night.

12.5. The church prayed fervently: Peter looks helpless, but the church at prayer strikes an expectant note (4.31; 16.25).

12.6. Bound with two chains . . . sleeping between two soldiers: Peter was bound with two soldiers, one on each side. The wonder of escape becomes all the greater, since it seems practically impossible.

12.7. An angel of the Lord: Angels often serve as the agent of God's rescue operation. The accompanying light also suggests divine presence (9.3; 26.13; Luke 2.9).

12.10. It opened for them of its own accord: Some liken this to the rolling away of the stone on the first Easter morning. The dream-like quality of the story also underscores the divine initiative in this rescue operation.

12.11. Peter came to himself: Peter came to himself, as the angel had suddenly left. In this verse too the power of Herod and the hostile intention of the Jews are combined (12.3).

12.12a. Mary the mother of John . . . Mark: John is his Jewish name and Mark (Marcus) is Roman. He was a member of the first missionary journey of Barnabas and Saul, but later provided the cause of the split between Paul and Barnabas (12.25; 13.13; 15.36–41. Also see Colossians 4.10; 2 Timothy 4.11; Philemon 24; 1 Peter 5.13). Later church tradition considers him as the author of the Gospel of Mark.

12.12b. Many . . . were praying: So prayer brackets the whole episode of Peter's rescue (vv. 5, 12). The implication is clear: prayer is the power that enabled Peter's rescue.

12.14. She was so overjoyed: She forgot to open the door for sheer joy, just as the disciples did not believe in Jesus 'for their joy' (Luke 24.41).

12.15. You are out of your mind . . . It is his angel: She 'announced' the news to the believers, but they said: 'You are crazy.' The scene recalls the empty tomb story: the women 'announced' the news to the eleven, but they thought it to be mere nonsense (Luke 24.11). The idea of a guardian angel is also found in Matthew 18.10. A commentator, Luke Johnson, puts this rather humorous situation in this way: 'an angel gets Peter out of Herod's cell but Peter himself cannot get through the locked gate to the Christian household because he is mistaken for an angel!'

12.16. They saw him and were amazed: This is the typical response to a miraculous work done by God.

12.17a. James: This is 'James the brother of the Lord'. After Stephen's death and the dispersion of the Hellenists, he was emerging as one of the leaders of the Jerusalem church. He presided over the Jerusalem Council in Acts 15, and Paul reported to him on arriving in Jerusalem (21.18). Paul calls him, Peter and John 'pillars' (Galatians 2.9).

12.17b. Then he left and went to another place: We do not know where Peter went, but he left Jerusalem safely.

12.18. No small commotion: See the same expression in 19.23. Luke is fond of the rhetorical device called litotes (understatement), a way of emphasizing one thing by negating the opposite. The phrase 'no small' is found in many other places in Acts (15.2; 17.4, 12; 19.23, 24). We also remember the famous 'no mean city' (21.39, KJV).

12.20. Herod was angry with . . . Tyre and Sidon: The nature of the trouble is not known. Since these cities depended heavily on Galilean wheat (cf. 1 Kings 5.9), they had to regain Herod's favour as soon as possible.

12.21–23. On an appointed day Herod: According to the Jewish historian Josephus, people addressed Herod as a god and he did not reject the title. Immediately he saw an owl which reminded him of earlier predictions about his death. He soon succumbed to severe abdominal pain and died five days later. So Josephus and Luke agree that Herod was punished by God for accepting blasphemous adulation.

12.24. The word of God continued to advance: This is one of Luke's summary statements (2.42–47; 5.14; 6.7; 9.31; 11.21; 16.5; 19.20). Herod, the persecutor of the church, was struck by God, but the church did not stop growing.

12.25. Return to Jerusalem: Most reliable manuscripts have 'to Jerusalem' or 'in Jerusalem', but it creates a logical problem. Some suggest the translation: 'Barnabas and Saul returned, after completing their mission in Jerusalem.'

 Interpretation

Before narrating the story of the missionary journeys by Barnabas and Paul, Luke for the last time moves the spotlight to Jerusalem, telling the last phase of Peter's ministry there. Apart from the brief reappearance in Acts 15, this is practically the last story we hear about him. We get the impression that now Luke wants to wrap up his story about Jerusalem, before he finally moves to the story of Gentile mission which will occupy his attention for the rest of the book.

God's power continues to work in the Church

In this transitional chapter Luke illustrates both the hardship entailed in the service of Jesus (12.1–19) and God's judgement on those who inflict it (12.20–25). Serving Jesus entails sufferings but the word triumphs in the end. Those who persecute the Church will be punished by God who alone holds the power to control history. In this respect we also note that Luke here uses many of the phrases which he had used to describe the passion and resurrection of Jesus. Peter's arrest and rescue is presented as a recapitulation of Jesus' passion and resurrection. The point is: the power at work in Jesus continues to be at work in his Church. 'But the word of God continued to advance and gain adherents' (12.24).

Miracles in the Bible

Stories like Peter's miraculous rescue trouble many modern readers. Luke makes it clear that it was a miracle performed by God. Yet it does not necessarily exclude the use of human agents. That is, God may have intervened 'directly' without using any human help or he may have done so 'indirectly', namely, through human beings. So we need to remember both:

1 that God has the power to do what he wants, and things can and do happen which do not allow any 'rational' explanation; and

2 that God's miracle does not have to be 'inexplicable' to be a miracle.

Perhaps we may ask if our speaking of a 'miracle' does not have an undesirable effect of limiting the scope of 'God's work' in one way or another.

Peter after Jerusalem

After his release Peter went underground 'so successfully that no one to this day has discovered for certain where he went' (F. F. Bruce). He was back briefly for the council in Jerusalem (Acts 15), but disappeared completely thereafter. He was once in Antioch (Galatians 2.11–21), and possibly visited Corinth (1 Corinthians 1.10; 9.5). Later traditions also put him in Rome (1 Peter 5.13; *1 Clement* 5.4; *Acts of Peter* 7), but distinguishing facts from legends is not easy.

Apart from his contribution in the council in chapter 15, Peter seems to have exhausted his role in Acts. His leadership in Jerusalem went to the more conservative James the Just, brother of the Lord, and his role in Gentile territory was also overshadowed by the successful ministry of Paul. In a way Luke's silence about Peter's later activities is as instructive as it is heart-wrenching. The drama is written and directed by God, and we humans are actors and actresses performing the roles assigned by God's gracious wisdom. So we get on the stage and do our part, even at the cost of life. Then when the time comes, we disappear as Peter did, all in the same note of gratitude and loyalty. So Peter was a man of faith, the kind of faith every Christian needs to emulate.

 STUDY SUGGESTIONS

Review of content

1 Who was the King Herod who killed James the brother of John?

2 What was the power that enabled Peter's rescue?

3 Luke describes Peter's rescue as the recapitulation of the death and resurrection of Jesus. In so doing, what does Luke try to say?

4 What were the roles James the Lord's brother played in Acts?

5 Both Luke and Josephus report Herod's death. According to both writers, what was the cause of his death?

Bible study

6 Read the following passages and discuss Peter's role as a disciple of Jesus.

(a) Mark 1.29–31; (b) Luke 8.51; (c) Luke 9.28; (d) Mark 13.3–4; (e) Mark 13.32–33.

7 Read the following passages and observe the role of Mark.

(a) Acts 12.25; 13.13; 15.36–41;

(b) Colossians 4.10; 2 Timothy 4.11; Philemon 24; 1 Peter 5.13.

Discussion and application

8 The Bible often speaks of a (guardian) angel. How are we to understand the idea?

9 In Acts, Peter's role diminishes as the story develops. What can we learn from this about the way God uses us?

10 Peter was rescued but the soldiers died as a result. Jesus escaped to Egypt but numerous children around Bethlehem were killed by Herod the Great. How are we to understand things like these?

Acts 13.1–12

Mission to Cyprus

 Summary

At the Spirit's bidding the Antioch church sends Barnabas and Saul as missionaries and the two display the power of the gospel in the confrontation with the demonic magician Bar-Jesus.

 Notes

13.1. Prophets and teachers: Prophets occupied an important place in the Early Church (11.27; Romans 12.6–7; 1 Corinthians 12.28; Ephesians 2.20; 4.11; Matthew 7.15), and so did teachers (Romans 12.7; 1 Corinthians 12.28–29; Ephesians 4.11; James 3.1). Luke puts these two groups together, suggesting that their roles were not clearly distinguished from each other. Simeon has a Latin surname, Niger ('black'). 'A member of the court of Herod' means 'a childhood companion of Herod', somebody adopted into the family as a childhood playmate. The list is bracketed by Barnabas at the beginning and Saul at the end.

13.2a. Worshipping the Lord and fasting: In the next verse we have 'fasting and praying' (14.23; Luke 2.37; 5.34). These seem to be part of the appointed duties of the prophets and teachers.

13.2b. The Holy Spirit said: Fasting made the church more sensitive to the direction of the Holy Spirit. The Spirit appointed the two most prominent leaders of the church for the missionary work overseas. The appointment of Saul, of course, takes up the story of his conversion in Acts 9.

13.3. They laid their hands on them: As in the appointment of the 'seven' (6.6), they prayed and laid their hands on the two. Some take this as a sign of transmitting power or authority, but that isn't the case here.

13.4. Being sent out by the Holy Spirit: The church sent them off (13.3), but it was the Holy Spirit who took the initiative (13.2). Seleucia is the seaport of Antioch, some 16 miles from the city.

13.5a. Salamis: Cyprus was a Roman senatorial colony administered by a proconsul (13.7). Salamis, located on the east coast of the island, was the chief city of Cyprus.

13.5b. They proclaimed . . . in the synagogues of the Jews: Barnabas and Saul made it their habit to preach first in the Jewish synagogues of the city they visited (13.14; 14.1; 16.13, 16; 17.1, 10, 17; 18.4, 19, 26; 19.8). The purpose is twofold:

1 the gospel has to be preached to the Jews first (13.46–47; cf. Romans 1.16);

2 the synagogue provided a bridgehead for reaching Gentiles.

John was an 'assistant' and his role seems marginal. This prepares us for his upcoming departure in 13.13.

13.6a. Paphos: This city on the southwest coast was the seat of the provincial government.

13.6b. A certain magician, a Jewish false prophet: He was an apostate Jew. Being a magician serving Satan, he was a 'false' prophet. He was attached to the proconsul's entourage.

13.7. Sergius Paulus, an intelligent man . . . wanted to hear the word of God: For the first time the gospel encounters a Roman authority directly. Luke favourably portrays the proconsul as intelligent and open to the gospel.

13.8. The magician Elymas . . . tried to turn the proconsul away from the faith: Elymas does not translate Bar-Jesus, but its meaning is obscure. The 'faith' here refers to the Christian gospel as in 6.7. Probably Bar-Jesus worried about the possible decrease of his influence on the proconsul.

13.9. But Saul, also known as Paul: Paul (Paulus) is Saul's Roman cognomen. From this point Luke regularly calls Saul by his Roman name. However, it is probably a mere coincidence that he begins to do so in the context where another Paul (Sergius Paulus) figures.

13.10. You son of the devil: The 'son of the devil' forms a nice contrast to his name, 'son of Jesus'. This is yet another conflict between the kingdom of God and that of Satan (5.1–11; 8.20–24). By 'making crooked the straight paths of the Lord', he sets himself up as a false prophet (13.6) in contrast to the true one (Luke 3.4).

13.11. You will be blind: Paul's darkening of Bar-Jesus demonstrates that God's power is far stronger than that of Satan. The punishment of blindness recalls Paul's own experience on the Damascus road (9.8). In the OT it was a punishment for wilful disobedience (Deuteronomy 28.28–29).

13.12. He believed, for he was astonished at the teaching about the Lord: Scholars are not sure what Luke means by the proconsul's belief.

But, since he had already been interested in the message of Barnabas and Paul, there is no reason why we should not take the word in its normal sense. Once again, surprise precedes belief, as Luke reminds us over and over again.

 ## Interpretation

Sending of Barnabas and Saul

Acts 13 marks a crucial point in the history of the Church. Luke now leaves Jerusalem and Judea behind to move his attention to a new centre, Antioch in Syria. In line with this, the spotlight also moves from Peter, the apostle par excellence in Jerusalem and Judea, to Saul (later Paul), the hero of the Gentile mission.

The sending of Barnabas and Paul marks the first case of planned mission in Christian history. But it was initiated by the Holy Spirit rather than the Church itself. God through the Holy Spirit told the Church to 'set apart' Barnabas and Paul for the work, and this is the way Paul himself describes his apostleship (Romans 1.1; Galatians 1.15).

In context, the sending of the two means the official confirmation of Paul's calling recorded in Acts 9. Of course, Paul has been busy working in his own way in Syria and Cilicia (Galatians 1.21), but the call to bring Jesus' name 'before Gentiles and kings and before the people of Israel' means more than that (9.15). So the Holy Spirit directed the Church to send the two away, and that marks the beginning of another exciting chapter in the history of the Church.

For that reason it provides a nice illustration of the communal nature of the Church and its ministry. Paul has known his calling for so long, but refrains from acting on his own until the Church receives the instruction from the Holy Spirit. Even then, the Holy Spirit does not talk to him or to Barnabas individually but to the Church as a whole. And he waits until he is commissioned by the Church instead of asserting his own calling.

The confrontation

Paul's confrontation with Bar-Jesus the magician recalls Peter's confrontation with Simon the magician in Acts 8. As in Samaria, the gospel faced the force of Satan trying to thwart its advance at the threshold of a new territory, and overcame it with the power of the Holy Spirit ('filled with the Holy Spirit', Acts 13.9).

Interestingly, Luke says that the proconsul was surprised at 'the teaching about the Lord' (v. 12), when it is clear that he was astounded at the power that blinded the magician. This recalls the people's response to the wonder performed by Jesus in the synagogue: 'What is this? A new teaching with authority. He commands even the unclean spirits, and they obey him' (Mark 1.27). From the first, Luke's concern is to demonstrate the 'certainty' or 'reality' of the gospel. The 'teaching' of Barnabas and Paul did not come as mere words but was accompanied by 'power . . . the Holy Spirit and with full conviction', as Paul puts it (1 Thessalonians 1.5). The gospel is true, not simply because it makes sense but also because it makes things happen, and that is what makes the Christian gospel different from other teachings.

 ## STUDY SUGGESTIONS

Word study

1 What was the role of teachers in the New Testament (Acts 11.27; Romans 12.7; 1 Corinthians 12.28–29; Ephesians 4.11; James 3.1)?

2 What does 'faith' mean in 6.7 and 13.8?

Review of content

3 Who named Barnabas and Paul to go on the missionary journey?

4 What were the two purposes of the missionaries' preaching first in the synagogues?

5 What is the significance of Paul's clash with Bar-Jesus?

Bible study

6 In Luke–Acts when does the Church fast and pray (Acts 14.23; Luke 2.37; 5.34)?

Discussion and application

7 Barnabas and Paul were sent as missionaries but the whole Church was behind them. Discuss the various ways in which the whole Church participates in the mission work.

8 Proclaiming the reign (kingdom) of God involves a confrontation with the Satanic force that tries to thwart it. Can you discern such points of conflict in the Church's evangelistic effort today?

Acts 13.13–52

Mission in Antioch of Pisidia

 Summary

Paul preaches at the synagogue of Antioch in Pisidia. Most Jews reject the gospel, while many Gentiles receive it eagerly.

 Notes

13.13a. Paul and his companions: From now on Luke mostly puts Paul's name first (13.43, 46, 50) with a few exceptions (14.12, 14; 15.12). This indicates that Paul had become the central figure of the mission; Barnabas obviously did not complain about it. Perga in Pamphylia was a river port some 12 miles up the river from the coast. We do not know why they did not stay there. They crossed the Taurus Mountains towards the north.

13.13b. John . . . left them and returned to Jerusalem: Luke does not tell us why, but this would become the bone of contention between Paul and Barnabas which led to a split of the two (15.37–39). See notes on 15.37–39.

13.14. Antioch in Pisidia: This is not to be confused with the Antioch on the Orontes in Syria. The city was actually located in Phrygia near Pisidia. This is the Antioch mentioned in 2 Timothy 3.11.

13.15. After the reading of the law and the prophets: Luke gives us accounts of two synagogue services (Luke 4.16–27 and here). In both cases, Scripture reading was followed by an address. In our passage both the law and the prophets were read. Later Jewish traditions mention the following elements as included in the services: **(a)** recitation of Shema (Deuteronomy 6.4–5); **(b)** benedictions, especially the so-called *Shemone Esre* ('Eighteen Benedictions'); **(c)** prayers; **(d)** the reading of the law.

The synagogue ruler or rulers were responsible for inviting appropriate people to address the congregation. The phrase 'word of exhortation' also occurs in Hebrews 13.22 as the summary of the Letter.

13.16. You Israelites, and others who fear God: Here Paul differentiates the Jews from God-fearers. Paul also uses the designations 'descendants of Abraham's family, and others who fear God' (v. 26) and the 'Jews and devout converts to Judaism' (v. 43). Here Luke seems to use the term 'God-fearers' somewhat loosely to include both proselytes and uncircumcised sympathizers.

13.17. God of this people Israel: The name 'Israelites' is repeated three times (13.17, 23, 24), bearing out the importance of Israel as God's people. On God's choosing Israel, see Deuteronomy 4.37 and 10.15. For the phrase 'with uplifted arm', see Exodus 6.1; Deuteronomy 4.34; 5.15.

13.18. He put up with them: An equally well-attested textual variant reads 'he took care of them'. This is a quotation from Deuteronomy 1.31 (LXX), but there too the same textual problem exists.

13.19. Seven nations: These are listed in Genesis 10.15–20 and Deuteronomy 7.1.

13.20. Four hundred and fifty years: This period includes four hundred years in Egypt, forty years in the wilderness, and ten years of conquering Canaan.

13.22. I have found David: This is a composite citation of Psalm 89.20 ('I have found David'), 1 Samuel 13.14 ('a man after my heart'), and possibly Isaiah 44.28 ('who will carry out all my wishes'). The last phrase from Isaiah is originally about Cyrus who is called 'messiah' there. This citation presents David as prefiguring the Messiah.

13.23. Of this man's posterity . . . a Saviour, Jesus, as he promised: This promise refers to 2 Samuel 7.12. The messianic saviour had been raised up by God in the house of David, and Jesus is that promised Messiah. The Davidic descent of Jesus is also underscored in Peter's first sermon (2.25–36).

13.24–25. John had already proclaimed: Like Peter's sermon in the house of Cornelius, Paul too began with John the Baptist's ministry (10.37). John preached repentance, but he connected it with the coming Jesus, since Jesus was the real One who would bring about forgiveness of sin (13.39–40). This summary of John's ministry reflects traditions both from the Synoptic Gospels (Luke 3.15–17) and from the Fourth Gospel (John 1.20).

13.26. My brothers: Another direct address ('my brothers') begins the second half of the sermon about Jesus. Paul's testimony to Jesus is similar to that of Peter in 2.22–36.

13.27–29. Because the residents of Jerusalem and their leaders did not recognize: As in 3.17–18, the people's ignorance of the scriptural prophecy was seen as a paradoxical means of bringing about its fulfilment. Paul's audience was Diaspora Jews, so he did not put the blame on 'you' but on 'the residents of Jerusalem and their leaders'.

13.30. But God raised him from the dead: Once again, we notice the contrast between human rejection and divine vindication (2.24, 32; 3.15; 4.10; 5.30; 10.40).

13.31. Those who came up with him from Galilee . . . his witnesses: See 1.3, 13–22 and 10.41. It is noteworthy that Paul did not mention the risen Jesus' appearance to himself (cf. 1 Corinthians 9.1; 15.8).

13.32. We bring you the good news: Here Paul presented himself as an evangelist, not one of the original 'witnesses'. God had made the promise bring to Israel a Saviour (v. 23), and has fulfilled it 'for us, their children' by raising Jesus. Some connect this 'raising' with his first coming, but most others relate vv. 33–34 (Psalm 2) to the resurrection of Jesus (cf. 2.36; Romans 1.4).

13.34–35. The holy promises . . . your Holy One: God's promise to David about his protection from decay (v. 35) will be given to 'you', namely, to the present generation (v. 34). These two quotations seem to be connected by the common word 'holy'. This rabbinic method of interpretation is called *gezerah shawah*.

13.36–37. For David . . . but he whom God raised up: Peter also compared David with Jesus to prove the resurrection of Jesus, quoting the same Psalm 16.10 (2.29–36).

13.38. My brothers: The call for repentance begins with another direct address, 'my brothers'. The risen Jesus had told that the message of forgiveness of sin should be proclaimed by his disciples (Luke 24.47; Acts 2.38; 5.31; 10.43). The forgiveness of sin is connected with the resurrection of Jesus (Romans 4.25; 1 Corinthians 15.17).

13.39. Everyone who believes is set free: The 'set free' is normally translated 'justified' (Gk, *dikaioun*). This is the only place in which the doctrine of justification is explicitly mentioned in Acts. Some think that Luke here presents faith–righteousness as supplementing partial justification by the law, but the whole thrust of Acts falsifies such a view. See Interpretation.

13.40–41. A work that you will never believe: Verse 41 quotes Habakkuk 1.5 (cf. Isaiah 28.21–22; 29.14). This warning turns out to be self-fulfilling in vv. 44–47. Also see 28.23–28.

13.42–43. To speak . . . again the next sabbath: The initial reception was favourable, though the actual sender of the invitation is not clear. The exhortation suggests that these have come to believe the message of God's grace revealed through Jesus.

13.44–45. They were filled with jealousy: The popular response to Barnabas and Paul incited the jealousy of the Jews, as in 5.17. By slandering the messengers of God, the Jews virtually blasphemed God himself.

13.46–47. It was necessary that the word . . . be spoken first to you: God had made a promise to Israel, and thus the gospel should first go to them, so that they might 'be a light for the Gentiles', so that they might 'bring salvation to the ends of the earth'. However, Israel has rejected this covenant mission attributed to them in the Servant Songs (Isaiah 49.6), and it has now been transferred to the Church represented by Paul and Barnabas (cf. 1 Peter 2.9–10). This provided a further impetus to the more strenuous Gentile mission: 'we are now turning to the Gentiles'. For Paul, however, this did not mean God's final rejection of his people but a temporary hardening of their hearts in order to allow the full number of Gentiles to come in. After that the Jews would once again return to the Lord (Romans 11).

13.48. As many as had been destined for eternal life: This forms a clear contrast to the response of the Jews: 'you . . . judge yourselves to be unworthy of eternal life' in v. 46. The Jews' rejection of the gospel coupled with the warm welcome of it by the Gentiles raised a serious theological question for the Christians, as Paul's struggle in Romans 9—11 illustrates.

13.49. The word of the Lord spread: This is yet another notice of the successful advance of the gospel (2.41, 47; 6.7; 9.31; 11.24; 12.24).

13.50. The Jews . . . stirred up persecution: In Phrygia, women enjoyed considerable prestige, and there were many such women among the active participants in the Jewish synagogue. The Jews used these to launch a more general opposition. So their jealousy (v. 45) now leads to active persecution.

Here scholars note the similarity between Jesus and Paul: **(a)** the Spirit (Luke 3.21–22; Acts 13.1–3); **(b)** the confrontation with the devil (Luke 4.1–13; Acts 13.4–12); **(c)** proclamation of the fulfilment of the Scripture by himself at the synagogue on a sabbath (Luke 4.4–21; Acts 13.13–41); **(d)** rejection by the Jews (Luke 4.23–30; Acts 13.42–52).

13.51. They shook the dust off: This symbolic act of rejection signifies that these Jews were like pagans and no longer belonged to the people of God (v. 46; cf. Luke 9.5; 10.11).

13.52. The disciples were filled with joy: Luke underscores the fact that returning to God generates joy both in heaven and on earth (Luke 15.7, 10, 22–24; Acts 5.41; 8.8, 39; 11.23).

 Interpretation

This passage divides into three sections:

(a) Paul and Barnabas' entry into Antioch (13.13–14);

(b) Paul's sermon (13.15–41);

(c) people's response (13.41–52).

Paul's sermon in the middle also contains three subjects:

(a) Israel's history until Jesus (13.15–25);

(b) proclamation of Jesus (13.26–37);

(c) call for repentance (13.38–41).

Paul's first sermon

Paul's speech here is probably given as an illustration of the typical message he proclaimed during his missionary journeys. Addressed to the Jews and the Gentile God-fearers, Paul's sermon largely follows the patterns found in the sermons of Peter and Stephen.

(a) A historical survey demonstrating that Jesus is the God-ordained Messiah (vv. 17–23).

(b) The Jewish rejection of Jesus out of ignorance as the fulfilment of God's plan predicted in the Scripture (vv. 27–29a).

(c) The scriptural argument to demonstrate the reality of Jesus' resurrection (vv. 29b–37).

However, the differences are also noticeable. While Stephen spends most of his historical survey on the period from Abraham to Moses, Paul simply ignores the patriarchs and devotes a long section to the kingly rule of Saul and David (vv. 21–41). This is quite natural, since Paul's purpose is to present Jesus as the fulfilment of God's promise given to David.

A different situation also requires a different way of presenting the gospel. Those responsible for the death of Jesus are no longer 'you' but 'the residents of Jerusalem and their leaders' (v. 27). The original witnesses of Jesus' resurrection are not 'we' but 'they', namely, 'those who came up with him from Galilee to Jerusalem' (v. 31). But God has also sent the message of salvation 'to us' (v. 26), 'and we' bring 'you' this 'good news' (v. 32). Therefore, 'you' should also know that through this man Jesus forgiveness of sin is proclaimed 'to you' (v. 38). Likewise, the same warning given to those in Jerusalem (7.51–52) also applies to those in Antioch (13.40–41).

Paul's doctrine of justification

As noted above, this is the only passage in Acts in which the doctrine of justification occurs. The message of forgiveness of sin is a staple ingredient of the apostolic preaching in Acts (2.38; 5.31; 10.43). But in the present speech by Paul that message is connected with the characteristically Pauline doctrine of justification by faith. We also find the same Pauline contrast between justification by the law and justification by faith.

Currently, there exist different views on the precise import of Paul's doctrine of justification, especially about his criticism of the law. Whatever stand we take on this issue, we should not forget the fact that Paul never criticizes those who obey or try to obey the law but only those who

119

disobey it (Galatians 6.12–13; Romans 2). Paul does not say that obeying the law is itself problematic, or that we cannot obey the law perfectly. According to Paul we all are under the reign of sin and death as Adam's descendants, and Christ transfers us from this reign of death to the reign of grace and life. What Paul says is that mere possession of the written code or the outward mark of circumcision is unable to bring about this transition from death to life. That is what only God can do, since he is the One who can give life to the dead through his Spirit (Romans 4.17), and the resurrection of Jesus is the final revelation of this life-creating God (Acts 4.24; Galatians 1.1). Faith justifies us, since it is faith in the One who raised Jesus from the dead (Romans 10.9–10). We need faith, since we receive the gift of the life-giving Spirit through faith and not by works of the law (Galatians 3.2–5, 14; 5.5). And through this life in the Spirit we now enjoy the hope of righteousness and eternal life (Galatians 5.5; 6.7–9; Romans 5.21; 6.19–23; 8.13). So for Paul the key to salvation lies in the Holy Spirit, and the only key to receiving God's Spirit is believing in the death and resurrection of Jesus. And this is also the message we keep hearing throughout the book of Acts. This is what people still need, and this is what the Christian gospel continues to offer (Acts 3.6).

 ## STUDY SUGGESTIONS

Word study

1 What is a 'synagogue ruler'?

2 What does the phrase 'with uplifted arm' mean (Exodus 6.1; Deuteronomy 4.34; 5.15)?

Review of content

3 What were the four elements of a worship service in the ancient Jewish synagogue?

4 What were the two major groups of Paul's audience in the synagogue?

5 What are the three elements that are commonly found in the speeches of Peter, Stephen and Paul?

6 How did Paul interpret Israel's ignorance of the scriptural prophecy?

7 What similarities can we find between Luke's account of Jesus and that of Paul?

Bible study

8 The Greek word behind 'set free' is usually translated 'justified'. In the following passages what does Paul say about 'justification'?

(a) Romans 3.24; (b) Romans 6.7; (c) Galatians 2.15–16.

9 Read Romans 11. What does Paul think of the Jewish rejection of the gospel?

Discussion and application

10 'So for Paul the key to salvation lies in the Holy Spirit, and the only key to receiving God's Spirit is believing in the death and resurrection of Jesus' (p. 120). Do you agree with this statement?

Acts 14.1–28

The mission to Iconium and Lystra and back

 Summary

Paul and Barnabas continue their mission in Iconium and Lystra in the face of severe persecution from the unbelieving Jews.

 Notes

14.1. The same thing . . . in Iconium: Iconium was the easternmost city of Phrygia. Paul and Barnabas went through the same pattern of initial welcome followed by final rejection and persecution. Their speaking at the synagogue shows that the decisive turning to the Gentiles does not necessarily mean ignoring the Jews. The redemptive-historical priority of the Jews remains intact. At the same time, the (circumcised) proselytes and the (uncircumcised) God-fearers in the synagogue provided an ideal bridgehead for reaching the Gentiles. So they won many converts from both Jews and Gentiles.

14.2. The unbelieving Jews stirred up the Gentiles and poisoned their minds: The Jews who would not accept the message tried to prejudice the minds of the Gentiles. The Greek word behind 'to poison' is also used for Herod's antipathy against the church (12.1) and for attacks against Paul in Corinth (18.10).

14.3. Speaking boldly for the Lord, who . . . granting signs and wonders: The apostles' testimony was powerful, and it was only after a long while that the threat became serious. What they proclaimed was 'the word of his grace', namely, the grace of forgiveness and salvation (20.32; cf. 13.43). They spoke boldly, because God was counteracting the Jewish opposition by allowing his workers to perform 'signs and wonders' (2.19, 22, 43; 4.30; 5.12; 6.8; 15.12; cf. 2 Corinthians 12.12).

14.4. The residents of the city were divided: On the one hand, the Jews were poisoning the minds of the Gentiles; on the other hand, God testified to the truth of the proclamation with signs and wonders. The upshot was: the city was divided – some for the unbelieving Jews and others for the 'apostles'. This is the only passage in which Paul and Barnabas are called 'apostles' (v. 14).

14.5–7. When an attempt was made . . . to . . . stone them, the apostles . . . fled: As the opposition became violent and life-threatening, the apostles escaped from the city to other places (Matthew 10.23). 'Their rulers' can either mean 'the Gentiles' rulers' (local magistrates) or 'the Jews' rulers' (synagogue rulers). The apostles fled south to the nearby cities of Lystra and Derbe, but their flight was just another way of spreading the gospel to these cities and to the surrounding country. Wherever they went, 'there they continued proclaiming the good news', just as 'those scattered' did after Stephen's death (8.1–4; 11.19–21).

14.8. A man . . . crippled from birth: The whole verse repeatedly underscores his inability to walk. Readers are made to expect Paul will perform the same miracle as Jesus and Peter (Luke 5.17–26; Acts 3.1–10).

14.9. Looking at him intently and seeing that he had faith to be healed: An intense look heightens tension and expectation (3.4; 13.9). Here salvation is connected with faith (3.16; Luke 5.20. 'To be healed' literally means 'to be saved').

14.10. The man sprang up and began to walk: Both Paul's words and the man's reaction closely resemble the healing story in 3.1–6.

14.11–12. The gods have come down to us in human form: They thought the miraculous healing to be a divine visitation. Ovid tells the story of an old Phrygian couple, Philemon and Baucis, who became the priests of a temple for entertaining Jupiter (Zeus, the supreme God) and Mercury (Hermes, Zeus' messenger) who visited them in the guise of two human beings, while the rest of the villagers were killed by flood (*Metamorphoses* 8.611–725). The Lycaonians would not have wanted to repeat their mistake. Archaeological evidence shows that the cults of these two gods did flourish throughout this region. That they shouted in their local language explains why the response of Paul and Barnabas was not swift enough.

14.13–14. He and the crowds wanted to offer sacrifice: This might have been a most appropriate response from the mortals who had the honour of a divine visitation. But Paul and Barnabas rejected it vehemently, tearing their clothes as an expression of their distress (cf. Genesis 37.29, 34; Joshua 7.6; Matthew 26.65). The attitude of the two resembles that of Peter at the house of Cornelius (Acts 10.26) and forms a sharp contrast to Herod who was punished for usurping divine glory for himself (12.23).

14.15a. We are mortals, just like you: The last part literally means 'of the same nature as you'. With these words the apostles deflect divine glory attributed to them and introduce the true God.

14.15b. Good news, that you should turn from these worthless things to the living God: For Gentiles, conversion means turning from idols to the living God. Without knowing God the Creator, they have been worshipping the created idols rather than the creator himself (Romans

1.18–32). Their attempt to offer sacrifice to human beings like Barnabas and Paul well illustrates such ignorance. But now, here are the apostles bringing the good news that they should turn to the living God who is the Creator of everything (1 Thessalonians 1.9; Hebrews 6.1).

14.16. He allowed all the nations to follow their own ways: Paul makes a similar statement in Athens too (Acts 17.30). Their ignorance of God and their habit of idolatry was not culpable before God's summons, but it would not be so any longer, since now God is calling them to repentance.

14.17. He has not left himself without a witness: People were ignorant, but it does not mean that God had left them in the dark without any clue. All along God has been doing good to all nations, and his ordering of the seasons and giving them food and joy should have made them mindful of him. Paul's speech is typically Jewish with nothing specifically Christian in it. Unlike his speech in Athens, Paul does not appeal to human conscience here (17.27).

14.19. Jews . . . from Antioch and Iconium: The Jews in Antioch and Iconium travelled more than 100 miles to pursue the apostles, and finally had their wish (14.4). Luke's depiction of these Jews recalls the violent 'hooligans' of football games in Europe. The people in Lystra were probably offended by the apostles' refusal to accept divine honours from them. This may explain the success of the Jews in winning them over. Paul himself recalls this incident in his Letter: 'once I was stoned' (2 Corinthians 11.25). Luke does not say why the Jews left Barnabas alone.

14.20. He got up and went into the city: This seems very abrupt, but we need to remember that the report is a very compressed one. Still, Paul shows great courage in entering the city again.

14.21. After they had proclaimed the good news to that city: Derbe, 60 miles south-east of Lystra, was the apostles' last stop, and there the apostles evangelized and 'made many disciples'. This is the only occurrence of the word 'make disciple' (see NASB) in Acts (cf. Matthew 13.52; 27.57; 28.19). No opposition or persecution is reported here.

After Derbe, the apostles could have continued on eastward and arrived at Syrian Antioch through the Cilician Gates. Instead they went back the way they had come to strengthen their new converts.

14.22. They strengthened the souls of the disciples: The purpose of the second visit was to stabilize the new communities. 'To continue in the faith' means to maintain the new life of 'worshipping the living and true God' in the face of opposition and false teaching (1 Thessalonians 1.6; 2.11–12; 3.1–8). The kingdom of God is something believers have to enter in the future by enduring many sufferings in the present (2 Corinthians 4.17–18; Romans 8.17–18; 2 Thessalonians 1.5; Matthew 5.2–12), and thus Paul keeps urging believers to live their lives in a manner worthy of the God who calls them into his eschatological kingdom (1 Thessalonians 2.11–12; 2 Thessalonians 1.11; Ephesians 4.1–4).

14.23. They had appointed elders . . . in each church: Proper organization and leadership structure was an indispensable part of nurturing the Church. There were 'elders' in the Jerusalem church (11.30; 15.2, 4; 16.4), and Paul would make his farewell speech to 'the elders of the church' (20.17). Also see 1 Timothy 5.17 and Titus 1.5. The apostle entrusted these new leaders to God in whom they had come to put their trust. See theological essay 3, below.

14.25. When they had spoken the word in Perga: At first the apostles had not stopped in Perga to preach the word, but they did so on their way back to Syria. We do not know how long they stayed there or how successful their work was.

14.27. All that God had done with them: God was the One who sent Paul and Barnabas on a mission in the first place (13.2, 4), and it was God who had done all the work through them. The significance of their work is that God has now opened a door of faith for the Gentiles, and now there are both Jews and Gentiles in the people of God. Interestingly, 'opening a door' as an evangelistic metaphor is distinctively Pauline (1 Corinthians 16.9; 2 Corinthians 2.12; Colossians 4.3).

 Interpretation

Iconium

The mission in Iconium repeats many of the themes of the Antioch episode: preaching in the synagogue, converts from both Jews and Gentiles, the Jewish opposition, the persecution by inciting the Gentiles. What is specially mentioned in this context is that the apostles spoke boldly for the Lord, and God made their ministry all the more powerful by granting signs and wonders to be done through them (14.3). So Paul and Barnabas were as powerful as Peter was in Jerusalem.

Paul vis-à-vis the Gentiles

In Lystra the apostles had the first direct contact with a purely Gentile crowd. The apostles had fled to the city, and thus their work there was not a planned mission. Interestingly, the story begins with preaching and healing in the open rather than with a sermon in a synagogue.

The healing is very similar to that by Peter. But this time the crippled person was one of Paul's listeners rather than a mere beggar, and Paul saw in him the 'faith to be healed' (14.9). As he listened to Paul, this person perceived the power of God and opened his mind to it. Paul says that such trust in God's power to give life is the essence of saving faith (Romans 4.19–22).

The Gentile idolatry and Paul's Jewish exhortation

The Gentiles' response to the healing was overwhelmingly positive. They clearly recognized divine power working through the apostles and tried to honour them according to their unsophisticated and polytheistic religiosity. So Paul set out to correct their idolatrous misconceptions by proclaiming the living God who is the Creator of all things (14.15). Their ignorance was understandable but still not completely excusable, since the order of nature and its benefits should have made them mindful of the One who has created it (14.17).

As noted earlier, there is nothing particularly Christian in Paul's speech here. It is not surprising at all, since Paul's purpose here was not to proclaim the gospel but to dissuade people from their idolatrous attempt to worship Paul and Barnabas. In a situation like this, simply proclaiming Jesus would have been pointless. To the Jews the apostles could present Jesus as the God-appointed Messiah (Christ), but these Gentiles did not even have a clear concept about the one true God. So Paul had to begin with a sort of natural theology in order to correct their idolatrous misconceptions and direct their attention to the living God. This is incomplete as a gospel, but a necessary preamble to clear the ground for the good news of Jesus Christ.

Paul's natural theology

Paul says that the Gentile ignorance of God the Creator is understandable but not completely excusable, since God has left his mark in nature. In Romans he seems to take a much harder line on this, declaring that God has clearly shown his eternal power and divinity and people are therefore without any excuse (Romans 1.20; but also 1.21–23). The difference seems one of emphasis and can be explained by the respective intention of the two accounts. In Acts Paul's purpose is not to incriminate his audience but to make them realize the folly of their idolatrous behaviour, while in Romans Paul wants to show that all people, both Jews and Gentiles, are under God's righteous judgement (1.18; 3.19–20). The overall perspective remains the same, but the specific way of expressing it varies according to the exigencies of the situation.

Entering God's kingdom through suffering

Paul's exhortation to the young churches was that they had to stand steadfast in the face of affliction, since it is through much affliction that believers can enter the kingdom of God. So Paul calls the present the time of suffering and contrasts it with the glory we will enjoy in the future. Believers have been called to this living hope, the hope of salvation which we did not have before we came to know God through Jesus Christ (1 Peter 1.3–5). Of course, there is a sense in which God's kingdom is already present, but it will only be evident among those who seek after God's will in prayerful obedience, even at the cost of their lives. It will be a fatal danger to mistake the time and take the pleasures of this world for granted.

Instead, our mission here on earth is to proclaim the life of Christ and bear it in our lives in the midst of suffering and despair.

 STUDY SUGGESTIONS

Word study

1 What does 'tearing one's clothes' signify (Genesis 37.29, 34; Joshua 7.6; Matthew 26.65)?

2 What does 'to make disciples' mean in the New Testament (Matthew 13.52; 27.57; 28.19)?

Review of content

3 What typical pattern can we find in the way people responded to the proclamation of Barnabas and Paul?

4 What are the Roman names for Zeus and Hermes?

5 How did Paul explain the idolatrous life of the Gentiles before the coming of Christ?

6 Who stirred the people of Lystra to stone Paul?

7 In Derbe, why did Paul and Barnabas go back the way they had come?

Bible study

8 Read the following passages and observe how the New Testament connects the present suffering and future hope.

   (a) Romans 8.17–18; (b) 2 Corinthians 4.17–18;
   (c) 2 Thessalonians 1.5.

9 Read the following passages. What was the role of 'elders' in the Church?

   (a) Acts 11.30; 15.2, 4; 16.4; 20.17; (b) 1 Timothy 5.17; Titus 1.5.

10 Compare Paul's sermon in Lystra and Romans 1.18–32. What are the similarities and differences?

Discussion and application

11 Paul's address to the crowd in Lystra shows that he was very much concerned about making points of contact and discerning points

of contention between himself and his audience. Discuss the possible ways of making the Christian message intelligible to the people around us who know nothing about our faith.

12 The missionaries had to flee Iconium to avoid persecution but Paul did not leave Lystra at once even after he was stoned. Can you find a principle behind Paul's behaviour? How can Christians decide which is right?

13 How effective is it to use the created natural world to introduce 'the God of Israel' to those who have never heard of Judaism or Christianity?

Acts 15.1–35

The Jerusalem Council

 Summary

The Church debates the value of circumcision and the law of Moses for the believing Gentiles and reaffirms the truth that both Jews and Gentiles are saved by God's grace.

 Notes

15.1–2. Unless you are circumcised . . . you cannot be saved: With a rapid influx of Gentiles into the Church, the question of circumcision was bound to arise. As is well known, the circumcision of the Gentiles emerged as the hardest question which the Church had to deal with in its early stages. This was only natural, since it concerned the very identity of the Jews: who belonged to the 'people of God'? And for the Gentiles the question of identity was closely tied to the ultimate question of salvation: must a Gentile person be circumcised to be saved? The same issue dominates Paul's discussion in Galatians and Romans, as well as part of Philippians (e.g. Romans 2.25–29; 4.1–11; Galatians 3.1–5; 5.1–5; 6.11–15).

Inevitably, the hard-line Jewish Christians clashed headlong with Paul and Barnabas, the champions of Gentile mission. As a result the church in Antioch decided to send the two to Jerusalem 'to discuss this question with the apostles and the elders' and settle it once and for all.

15.3–4. They reported the conversion of the Gentiles . . . they reported all that God had done with them: Paul and Barnabas made visits to various communities on their way to Jerusalem and used the occasions to tell the success of the Gentile mission they had carried out. They did the same to 'the church and the apostles and the elders' in Jerusalem. This is crucial, since this experiential proof of God's acceptance of the uncircumcised Gentiles was an important factor in the Church's decision. The same perspective dominates the speeches of both Peter and James.

15.5. It is necessary for them to be circumcised and ordered to keep the law of Moses: It is not clear whether 'some believers who belonged to the sect of the Pharisees' were the same as those mentioned in v. 1. In this verse the requirement to 'keep the law of Moses' is also added, but its precise nature is not clear. See Interpretation below.

15.7–11. After there had been much debate, Peter stood up and said to them: Speaking on behalf of the apostles, Peter made his point mainly by recalling his experience as the mediator of the paradigmatic case in point: the conversion of Cornelius (10.1—11.18). Through Peter's preaching, the Gentiles had heard the message of the good news and become believers (v. 7). And God had 'testified to them by giving them the Holy Spirit, just as he did' to the Jewish believers (v. 8; 10.47; 11.15, 17). Thus it was clear that God had made no distinction between Jews and Gentiles in his work of 'cleansing their hearts by faith' (v. 9; 10.34–35). Therefore, it amounted to 'putting God to test' to place on the neck of the Gentile disciples 'a yoke that neither our ancestors nor we had been able to bear' (v. 10; 11.17; cf. Matthew 11.29-30; Galatians 5.1). Such an attempt also contradicted the fundamental Christian conviction: 'we will be saved through the grace of the Lord Jesus, just as they will' (v. 11; cf. Romans 3.24; 4.16; 5.21). Circumcision did not matter for the salvation of the Jews, since they still needed to have 'the grace of the Lord Jesus'. If this is the case, how absurd, indeed dangerous, was it to block the way which God himself had opened? A comparison of such passages as Acts 10.47; 11.15, 17-18 on the one hand and 11.8 and 11.12 on the other strongly suggests that Peter had the Holy Spirit in mind, when he spoke of 'the grace of the Lord Jesus' (cf. 2.33). This is Peter's last speech in Acts. Interestingly, as a scholar put it, his last work in Acts was 'the legitimization of the mission to the Gentiles'.

15.12. Barnabas and Paul . . . told of all the signs and wonders that God had done through them among the Gentiles: Once again, they presented the experiential evidence of God's powerful work displayed in their recent ministry. They were present as witnesses, not as participants in the debate. That God worked through them must mean that God approved what they had been doing. This is the third time that Luke draws our attention to this point (vv. 3, 4, 12).

15.13. James replied, 'My brothers, listen to me': James, the Lord's brother, comes into the picture as the leading figure of the Jerusalem church (12.17; 21.18). He seems to represent the 'elders' section of the council.

15.14. Simeon has related . . . a people for his name: James began his speech by summarizing the gist of Peter's address. Simeon is a different spelling for Simon (2 Peter 1.1). 'A people for his name' had been an epithet reserved for the Jews (3.9; 4.10; 5.34; 10.41; Luke 2.10, 32; 7.29) but now James expanded it to include the Gentiles also. The wall of hostility between 'Gentiles' (Gk, *ethnē*) and the 'people' (Gk, *laos*) was now broken.

15.15-18. This agrees with the words of the prophets: James corroborated Peter's argument by adducing a scriptural proof for it. Quoting Amos 9.11-12, he argued that what God began to do with Cornelius and his household had already been foretold in the Scripture.

The primary thrust of the Amos passage is the restoration of the fallen household of David and regaining the rule over its former territory (Acts 15.16), even 'over all the Gentiles over whom my name has been called'. Yet the Septuagint text which James was quoting somewhat spiritualizes its meaning to highlight Israel's role to bring the knowledge of the true God to the Gentiles (v. 17). Thus, by applying this text to the Gentile mission of the Church, James in effect declared that the promised expansion of the Davidic rule over the Gentiles was now taking place through the mission of the Church. In other words, the Gentile mission was God's work, who 'has been making these things known from long ago' (vv. 17b–18).

15.19. We should not trouble those Gentiles who are turning to God: Although the Amos passage says nothing about circumcision, James came to the conclusion that what was now happening in the mission field was indeed the realization of that promise. If so, there was no point troubling the Gentiles by requiring them to be circumcised.

15.20. To abstain only from things polluted by idols and from fornication and from whatever has been strangled and from blood: According to the OT, these regulations apply to both Israel and foreigners who live within Israel (Genesis 9.4; Leviticus 17.8—18.30). 'Things polluted by idols' means food sacrificed to the idols (Acts 15.29; 21.25; Exodus 34.15-16). 'Fornication' includes any form of sexual immorality (Leviticus 18.6-30). 'Whatever has been strangled' refers to animals which are not slaughtered in accordance with the given regulations (Leviticus 17.3; 19.26; Deuteronomy 12.16, 23-27). So it was closely related to the prohibition on consuming 'blood' (Leviticus 3.17; 17.10-14).

15.21. For in every city . . . Moses . . . has been read: The intention of v. 21 is unclear. James wanted to say either **(a)** that the norms from the law should be familiar to the Gentiles, since the law was read in the synagogues of every city; or **(b)** that the Gentiles should respect such norms, which have been an integral part of Jewish life.

15.22. With the consent of the whole church: Luke underscores that the decision was made by the whole church, although the discussion was done by the apostle and the elders. The decision was unanimous (v. 25), and it was made under the guidance of the Holy Spirit (v. 28).

Judas Barsabbas is otherwise unknown, and Silas later accompanied Paul in his missionary journeys (15.40—18.5). He is obviously identical with the Silvanus in Paul's Letters (2 Corinthians 1.19; 1 Thessalonians 1.1; 2 Thessalonians 1.1). These two would act as witnesses to confirm 'by word of mouth' what the letter said (Acts 15.27).

15.24. Though with no instructions from us: This informed the Gentile believers in Antioch that the earlier visitors had not been authorized by the Jerusalem church; Paul and Barnabas, together with the authorized messengers from Jerusalem, would amend the situation according to the decision of the church. The verb 'to disturb' (Gk, *tarassō*) is also used by

Paul to describe those who 'disturb' the believers in Galatia (Galatians 1.7).

15.25–26. Our beloved Barnabas and Paul, who have risked their lives for the sake of our Lord Jesus Christ: 'To risk' is better translated 'to give' or 'to dedicate', the same word used in Acts 14.26. This statement was intended to lend support and authority to the stance of the two.

15.28–29. These essentials: The list is basically the same but in a different order. They were essential not for salvation but for the peaceful fellowship of Jews and Gentiles.

15.31. They rejoiced at the exhortation: The Antioch church received the decision with great relief. And there was no reason why they should not accept those practical guidelines to promote the harmonious fellowship between the two groups within the church.

15.32–33. Judas and Silas . . . prophets: These two stayed in Antioch for some time 'encouraging and strengthening' the believers there, the very thing Paul and Barnabas would do to new converts (14.22).

15.35. Paul and Barnabas remained in Antioch . . . taught and proclaimed the word of the Lord: With many anonymous co-workers Paul and Barnabas continued their ministry of teaching and proclaiming the word of the Lord. This reminds us of their earlier ministry there (11.26), but now with a strong sense of ending. With the resolution of all the theological problems that had troubled the Church, now the first phase of the Church's mission comes to a close. This sense of ending can be felt more strongly, if we compare verse 35 with the almost identical description of Paul in Rome at the end of the book: 'He lived there two whole years . . . proclaiming the kingdom of God and teaching about the Lord Jesus Christ with all boldness and without hindrance' (28.30–31).

 ## Interpretation

The Holy Spirit as the heart of the gospel

Circumcision posed a serious problem for the Early Church, but it also provided a chance to think through the true meaning of faith. Some believers insisted on the necessity of circumcision and observance of the law for salvation, but the Church has concluded that the Holy Spirit, given freely both to circumcised Jews and uncircumcised Gentiles, renders such conditions unnecessary for salvation. As we can see in the story of Cornelius, God's giving his Holy Spirit to the Gentiles means that he has welcomed these uncircumcised people into the Church. In the Jerusalem Council too it was God's powerful work displayed by Paul and Barnabas that led the Church to decide not to require circumcision of the Gentile believers.

Luke does not pursue further the theological logic behind the debate. For that we have to go to the Letters of Paul such as Galatians, Romans and Philippians. Just as the apostles in Acts consider the Holy Spirit as the hallmark of the gospel, so Paul characterizes the gospel as 'power', i.e. the power to bring people to salvation (Romans 1.16; 1 Corinthians 1.18, 24; 2.1–5). Paul objects vehemently to the idea that we can be justified through 'works of law' such as circumcision and dietary regulations. Paul's view is not that 'works of law' are morally bad or doctrinally dangerous but that they are 'weak', in that they cannot mediate the life-creating power of God the Creator. What we need is this life-giving power that can liberate us from the shackles of sin and death and thereby enable us to live a new life under grace. Paul underscores the inability of the law to do this with such phrases as 'flesh' or 'letter'. On the contrary, we receive this power of life through faith, since we believe in God who raises the dead and calls up things that are not as if they were (Romans 4.17). And we come to believe in God by believing in Jesus Christ, since this life-creating God has now revealed himself as 'the One who raised Jesus from the dead' (Romans 4.24; 6.4; 8.11; Galatians 1.1). Christ died on the cross and redeemed us from the curse of the law so that we might receive the promised Spirit through faith (Galatians 3.14). And it is faith, and not works of the law, that justifies us, since we receive the Spirit by faith and not by works of the law (3.2–5, 14). And we wait for the hope of righteousness through this life-giving Spirit (5.5).

Thus, it is not just some doctrinal convictions but God's powerful presence through the Holy Spirit that sets the gospel apart from any other 'human' or 'fleshly' false alternatives. The Christian gospel is good news, because it gives life to those who believe. This truth can manifest itself in various ways in different contexts, but we should never lose sight of this constant of life, without which the gospel can fall into something merely human.

Believing and discerning

This episode well illustrates that believing involves not only passive acceptance of God's gracious gift of life but also active reflection and careful discernment on our part. We are led by the Spirit, but at the same time it means that we walk according to the Spirit. So the question is: how are we to seek the guidance of the Spirit in our Christian walk, especially when dissensions arise among fellow believers? The apostles and elders in Acts 15 appealed to both experience (the undeniable work of the Spirit among the Gentiles) and the scriptural testimony to arrive at the conclusion that circumcision was unnecessary for the Gentile believers. They were both perceptive and open-minded enough to observe and acknowledge the work of the Spirit, at the same time being faithful to God's revelation in the Scripture.

The apostolic decree

Did the Church make a compromise by imposing the apostolic decree on the Gentiles? Some think so, but we have to remember that the point at issue was never observing the law per se but the identity of the people of

God. One does not have to be a Jew in order to be saved, but that does not mean that one can safely ignore God's will expressed in the law (cf. 1 Corinthians 7.19). God requires that we should conduct ourselves in a manner worthy of his calling. So imposing certain regulations by no means contradicts the principle of grace and faith.

Furthermore, the church in Antioch had both Jews and Gentiles. In a situation like this, it was mandatory to respect the cultural sensitivities of each group if they were to maintain a peaceful relationship between the two. The apostolic decree touches on those issues sensitive to the Jews, and it is only right for the Gentiles to respect them in order to avoid unnecessary provocation. Love expresses itself in concrete codes of conduct; the apostolic decree was an expression of such Christian love.

Christians today live in a complex society, which makes it virtually impossible for us to agree with one another all the time. We all believe in the same God but the religious and cultural expressions of such faith often take different forms. Different Christians have different views on many theological issues such as baptism and the Lord's Supper. Some churches welcome the use of contemporary music into worship services, while others consider it to be unfitting for worshipping God. And some Christians are politically conservative, while others lean towards a more liberal position. What we need in situations like this is to learn to tolerate and respect the viewpoints of others. But unity is often easier said than done, since our unity has to be a Christian one and therefore we have to draw the line somewhere. So we struggle to strike the right balance, humbly asking for the guidance of the Holy Spirit.

 ## STUDY SUGGESTIONS

Word study

1   What does 'putting God to the test' mean (Exodus 17.2; Psalm 78.41; Acts 5.9)?

Review of content

2   What was the main point of contention at the meeting in Jerusalem?

3   Why did Barnabas and Paul report the result of their work at the meeting?

4   What did Peter mean by 'the grace of the Lord Jesus'?

5   What was the decision of the Church on the issue of circumcision?

6   What were the requirements imposed on the Gentile believers?

Bible study

7 What does 'the people' refer to in the following passages?

(a) Acts 3.9; 4.10; 5.34; 10.41; Luke 2.10; 7.29; (b) Acts 15.14; 18.10.

8 Read the following passages. What do they say about circumcision? How can we explain their different tones?

(a) Galatians 5.2–4; (b) Romans 3.1; 4.11.

Discussion and application

9 What sets the gospel apart from others is God's powerful presence in the form of the life-giving Spirit. In what ways can we apply this truth in our lives?

10 What are the sort of cultural or religious differences that divide Christians today? What do you think is the best step to take to deal with such divisive situations? What are the cultural or religious differences that affect your community?

Acts 15.36—16.10

The gospel spreads to Macedonia

 Summary

Paul and Barnabas part company due to disagreement over the role of John Mark. Paul begins his second missionary journey, which leads to the unexpected spread of the gospel to Macedonia.

 Notes

15.36. Come, let us return and visit the believers . . . and see how they are doing: This is the beginning of the so-called 'second missionary journey'. The original plan of Paul and Barnabas was to revisit those communities established by their first missionary journey. 'To visit' literally means 'to oversee' (Gk, *episkeptomai*), a word also used for visitation of the sick or taking care of the poor (Matthew 25.36, 43; James 1.27). So their original purpose was of pastoral care rather than establishing new churches. Delivering the message of the Jerusalem church was an important part of such pastoral care (16.4).

15.37–38. Barnabas wanted to take with them John called Mark. But Paul decided not to take with them one who had deserted them: Barnabas wanted to give his nephew John Mark a second chance, but Paul refused to trust one who had previously 'deserted' (Gk, *apostanta*) them (13.13).

15.39. The disagreement became so sharp that they parted company: The two could not reach an agreement at the time, so they eventually parted company. Barnabas returned with John Mark to Cyprus, his hometown, probably to continue the mission there. We hear no more about Barnabas in Acts, but we should not try to read too much into Luke's silence. Paul's positive comments about Barnabas and John Mark in his Letters show that his relationship with them did improve. For Barnabas see 1 Corinthians 9.6 and Colossians 4.10, and for John Mark see Colossians 4.10; Philemon 24; 2 Timothy 4.11.

15.40. But Paul chose Silas: Silas was one of the two representatives of the Jerusalem church who had accompanied Paul and Barnabas to Antioch (15.27, 32). He seems to have been back in Antioch by that time (cf. 15.33).

15.41. He went through Syria and Cilicia, strengthening the churches: Syria and Cilicia were the places where Paul had worked before his move to Antioch (9.31; 11.25; Galatians 1.21, 23). By way of Tarsus and the Cilician Gates, Paul and Silas then retraced the route of the first missionary journey, this time in reverse order. Strengthening believers was an important part of the Church's ministry (14.22; 15.32).

16.1-2. A disciple named Timothy . . . but his father was a Greek: Literally, 'Look! There was a disciple there whose name was Timothy', implying the importance of the encounter. Timothy was raised up in faith by his grandmother and mother (2 Timothy 1.5; 3.15) and eventually became one of the most important associates of Paul. Paul later called him his son (1 Corinthians 4.17; 1 Timothy 1.2), and their relationship would continue until Paul's death. Paul's decision to take Timothy was partly influenced by the latter's good reputation among the believers there (cf. 6.3; 1 Timothy 1.18; 3.7; 4.14; 2 Timothy 1.6).

16.3. Paul wanted Timothy to accompany him; and he took him and had him circumcised because of the Jews: Since Timothy's mother was a Jewess, Paul had Timothy circumcised in order to avoid unnecessary trouble with the Jews. This assumes Timothy's willing obedience to the demand of Paul. (See Interpretation.)

With the earlier addition of Silas, the joining of Timothy to Paul's mission gives us a sense of a new beginning, i.e. the beginning of Paul's independent mission.

16.4. They delivered to them for observance the decisions that had been reached by the apostles and elders: The decisions of the church leaders were not just for Antioch, Syria and Cilicia but for all the Gentile believers. The Gentile Christian communities in Asia Minor acknowledged the authority of the decisions and showed willing obedience to them.

16.5. So the churches were strengthened in the faith and increased in numbers daily: Luke keeps reminding his readers of the effective spread of the gospel (5.14; 6.7; 9.31; 11.21; 12.24; 16.5; 9.20). This time it is linked with the willing adoption of the decrees reached in Jerusalem.

16.6-8. Having been forbidden by the Holy Spirit to speak the word in Asia: Since the missionaries were not permitted to go either south to Asia or north to Bithynia, they inevitably went down to Troas, a harbour city facing the Aegean Sea. However, Luke does not tell us how the Spirit kept them from speaking the word. Interestingly, Luke alternates between 'the Holy Spirit' and 'the Spirit of Jesus', apparently without any change of meaning.

16.9-10. During the night Paul had a vision . . . 'Come over to Macedonia and help us': Throughout Acts, visions or dreams play important roles in guiding the Church to the next stage of its mission (9.10-12; 10.3-6, 10-16; 11.5-10; 18.9-10; 22.17-21; 23.11; 27.23-24). The vision was fairly explicit, so Paul did not have any problem in discerning the message.

This verse begins the so-called 'we' passage where the story is narrated in the first person plural. This first such section extends to 16.17 (20.5–15; 21.1–18; 27.1—28.16). Different explanations have been offered about this: **(a)** it may simply be a stylistic variation; **(b)** the author may be using someone else's travel diaries as his source; **(c)** the author actually accompanied Paul during this part of the journey.

 Interpretation

Evangelism and pastoral care

A hasty reading may give us the impression that Paul is busy establishing new communities without much interest in caring for the existing churches. But such an impression is groundless. We have already seen that Paul on his return journey revisited those cities he had visited earlier to see how they were doing (14.21–26). He did the same at the beginning of his second missionary journey before his move to the European territory (15.41). If possible, he also loved to stay at one place for a long time, preaching the gospel and strengthening believers (11.26; 14.26–28; 15.35). His extensive stays in Corinth and Ephesus provide good cases in point (18.11; 19.10; 20.31). To be sure, he often had to leave the church abruptly; that was mostly because of unavoidable circumstances such as Jewish persecution, as we can see in the case of his Thessalonian and Beroean missions (17.10, 14–15; 1 Thessalonians 1—3). Most of all, his 13 Letters preserved in the NT give eloquent testimony to the fact that he was not just a busy evangelist but also a devoted pastor who dearly loved his converts (2 Corinthians 11.28–29). Behind this lies his strong conviction that his mission as the apostle to the Gentiles was to establish communities of faith which could be offered to God as a holy and blameless sacrifice on the day of Christ (Romans 15.16–19; Ephesians 1.4–5; 5.27; Philippians 2.15–16; Colossians 1.22; 1 Thessalonians 3.13; 5.23). Of course, he was an avid traveller who tried to visit as many places as possible and tell the gospel to as many people as possible. But he never forgot the responsibility of maintaining the communities holy and blameless even in the midst of such busy travels.

Separation of Barnabas and Paul

Many Christians find this incident embarrassing, especially Paul's harsh, even ungrateful, attitude toward Barnabas who had been his mentor and selfless supporter. In all likelihood, Barnabas wanted to give Mark a second chance, just as he had done to Paul, a persecutor turned into a Christian missionary. But Paul could not accept Barnabas' suggestion then; it was only some time later that he was able to take Mark again as a valuable member of his mission. Thus many think that this episode shows the weak side of Paul. On the other hand, there are others who blame Barnabas for plain favouritism for his nephew Mark.

Luke's account is short, and there is no way of telling which is closer to his intention. In any case, we can surely say that human beings are not perfect and thus problems inevitably arise in our works, even when we are guided by the Holy Spirit. Putting it the other way round, it would also be foolish to denounce the work of others altogether in spite of certain problems. God does not use angels but sinful human beings like us and carries out his purpose despite our weaknesses.

Some scholars connect the split of Paul and Barnabas with the so-called Antioch incident where Paul strongly denounced Peter and Barnabas along with other Jewish Christians. We cannot exclude the possibility of different theological positions as the cause of the split, but as far as we can see in Acts we do not find any sign of theological difference between Paul and Barnabas.

Circumcision of Timothy

The Paul of Acts had Timothy circumcised. Such flexibility seems to contradict what he says in Galatians, since there he explicitly forbids circumcision to the Galatians, threatening that such a step would cut them off from Christ (Galatians 5.2–4). This seeming contradiction can be explained by the peculiar situation of the Galatian churches. There the false teachers were promoting the 'works of law' such as circumcision and sabbath regulations as necessary conditions of justification to the detriment of the Galatians' faith and their walk in the Spirit (3.2–5; 5.5–6). Paul forbids circumcision in Galatians, not because it is inherently or doctrinally harmful but because it has become a major cause of the Galatians' defection from their walk in the Spirit. Once the danger is removed, Paul has no problems affirming the positive value of circumcision for the Jews (Romans 3.1; 4.11). As Paul himself affirms it repeatedly (Galatians 5.6; 6.15; 1 Corinthians 7.19), circumcision is in itself irrelevant to the question of salvation; whether one is circumcised or not does not matter, as long as it does not endanger one's faithful walk in Christ.

 STUDY SUGGESTIONS

Word study

1 What are the different ways of describing the Holy Spirit in Acts?

Review of content

2 What was the original purpose of the second missionary journey?

3 Why did Paul not want to take Mark with them?

4 What did Paul do to strengthen the Church?

5   What different explanations are suggested about the 'we' passage?

Bible study

6   Read the passages which refer to Timothy. What kind of a person was he?

(a) 1 Thessalonians 3.1–3; Philippians 2.19–22; **(b)** 1 Timothy 1.2; 2 Timothy 1.5.

7   Read the following verses and try to find out what Luke says about the strengthening of the Church (Luke uses two slightly different words).

(a) 14.22; 15.32, 41; 18.23; **(b)** 3.7, 16; 16.5.

Discussion and application

8   What do you think about the split of Paul and Barnabas? Was it a wrong thing to do? If it is, who is to blame?

9   Do you agree with Paul's decision to circumcise Timothy? What are your reasons?

10   Luke often mentions dreams and visions as ways of God's guidance. Can we still use them in order to receive God's guidance? If we can, to what extent?

Acts 16.11—17.15

Paul in Macedonia

 Summary

Paul's mission in Philippi begins with the conversion of Lydia, the imprisonment of Paul and Silas, and the subsequent conversion of the jailer.

 Notes

16.12. A leading city of the district of Macedonia and a Roman colony: Or 'a city of the first district of Macedonia', since Philippi was not as prominent as Amphipolis or Thessalonica, the capital of the whole district. The city was a Roman colony, and so was exempt from paying land and poll taxes. Naturally, the city was very proud of its Roman citizenship (vv. 21, 37; cf. Philippians 1.27; 3.20).

16.13. On the sabbath day we went outside the gate by the river, where we supposed there was a place of prayer; and we sat down and spoke to the women who had gathered there: It appears that there was no synagogue in the city (ten men were needed to establish a synagogue). As here, women often played a crucial role in the spread of the gospel (16.40; 17.4, 12), while the Jews of the time typically had small regard for women.

16.14. Lydia, a worshipper of God . . . from the city of Thyatira and a dealer in purple cloth. The Lord opened her heart to listen eagerly to what was said by Paul: Paul's mission in Philippi began and ended with Lydia (v. 40). Thyatira was famous for its cloth-dyeing industry, and Lydia probably sold products from there. 'A worshipper of God' means a Gentile who worshipped the God of Israel (without being circumcised in the case of men). The Lord had opened the way to Macedonia for Paul; now God opened the heart of Paul's listeners. Once again, the divine initiative is expressed.

16.15. When she and her household were baptized, she urged us, 'Come and stay at my home': Lydia must have been relatively wealthy, since purple cloth was a luxury trade. Her being a businesswoman and mistress of a household suggests high social status. From the first, the Philippian church was generous to Paul with its financial support (Philippians 4.10–12; 2 Corinthians 11.18). For baptism of a household, see 16.31–34 as well as 10.24, 44–48; 11.14; 18.8.

16.16–18. We met a slave-girl who had a spirit of divination: Literally, 'she had a spirit of the Python', a snake-god in charge of the Delphic oracle. The phrase seems to have become an idiom for divination or fortune-telling.

With demonic insight she kept shouting that the missionaries were 'slaves of the Most High God' and that they were announcing 'the way of salvation'. This reminds us of the stories of the demoniacs met by Jesus in the Gospel of Luke (4.34, 41; 8.28). The salvation proclaimed by the missionaries was what she and later the jailer would get.

Paul cast out the evil spirit 'in the name of Jesus Christ' (Acts 2.38; 3.6, 16; 4.10) and the result was immediate ('that very hour') as was the case with Jesus himself. Luke is silent, but we can naturally surmise that she became a Christian.

16.19. When her owners saw that their hope of making money was gone, they seized Paul and Silas: As the spirit 'went' (Gk, *exelthen*) out of her, the hope of making money also 'went' (Gk, *exelthen*). Here too, the healing led to persecution, this time for economic reasons (3.1–26; 14.8–18). They dragged Paul and Silas to the place where the city's political and economic business was carried out (Gk, *agora*). The owners' disregard for the welfare of the girl is heart-breaking.

16.20–21. These men are disturbing our city; they are Jews and are advocating customs that are not lawful for us as Romans to adopt or observe: The 'magistrates' refers to the chief officials of the Roman colony (*duumvirs*). The charges of riot and promotion of illegal religion were serious ones. The accusation also appealed to the pride of the people as citizens of a Roman colony as well as popular antipathy against the Jews: 'These men . . . are Jews' and 'us as Romans'. The accusers were cunningly silent about the real motive for their action.

16.22–24. The magistrates had them stripped of their clothing and ordered them to be beaten with rods: Even the magistrates disregarded proper legal procedure of formal arrest and trial. Here the beating refers to the Roman method of punishment administered by the lictors (literally, 'rod-bearers'; the word occurs in v. 35, translated 'police' there). For Paul's beating experience, see 2 Corinthians 11.23–25.

16.25–27. Paul and Silas were praying and singing hymns to God . . . Suddenly there was an earthquake: With many beatings, the missionaries must have been seriously wounded (16.23), but their undaunted faith was met by God's powerful intervention (cf. 4.31). They were the object of the prisoners' interested gaze. In 12.19 the guards were executed for losing their prisoner. The jailer wanted to avoid such a disgraceful end by taking his own life (cf. 27.42).

16.28–29. The jailer . . . fell down trembling before Paul and Silas: Under the circumstances the jailer must have judged that Paul and Silas were no ordinary people.

16.30–31. 'Sirs, what must I do to be saved?' They answered, 'Believe on the Lord Jesus, and you will be saved, you and your household': The jailer might have recalled what the slave-girl cried about the missionaries: 'they were announcing the way of salvation'. This question and answer capture the essence of evangelism (cf. 2.37). The phrase 'the Lord Jesus' reflects the early Christian confession that 'Jesus is Lord'.

16.32–34. They spoke the word of the Lord to him and to all who were in his house . . . then he and his entire family were baptized: As in the case of Lydia (16.15) and Cornelius (10.24, 44; 11.14), the conversion involved the entire household, because they all heard the word and believed.

16.35–40. They have beaten us in public, uncondemned, men who are Roman citizens, and have thrown us into prison: Such treatment was against the Roman law. Even Paul's 'sit-in' protest seems to be for the sake of the mission, lest the newly formed church suffer from public prejudice and the advance of the gospel be impeded. The 'we' passage ends here and resumes when Paul comes this way at 20.5; Luke apparently stayed behind, while Paul and Silas and Timothy took their leave.

17.1. They came to Thessalonica, where there was a synagogue of the Jews: Paul and Silas took the Via Egnatia, the Roman road that ran across Macedonia, to the west and then to the south to arrive at Thessalonica, the capital of Macedonia where there was a Jewish synagogue. So Paul's mission was greatly helped by the mobility of the Roman Empire, especially the well-built highways such as the Via Egnatia and the Via Appia in Italy.

17.2–3. On three sabbath days [Paul] argued with them from the scriptures, explaining and proving that it was necessary for the Messiah to suffer and to rise from the dead, and saying, 'This is the Messiah, Jesus whom I am proclaiming to you': Paul's mission here followed his regular custom of proclaiming the word in the synagogue before the rise of Jewish opposition. His first converts usually came from the synagogue, especially from the God-fearing Gentiles. Luke says 'on three sabbath days' but Paul's own words tell us that his stay there was much longer than that (2 Thessalonians 3.8; Philippians 4.16).

Paul made three crucial points about Jesus in his proclamation to the Jews:

1 Jesus was Christ, i.e. the Messiah the Jews had been awaiting;

2 the Christ had to suffer;

3 he had to rise from the dead.

This threefold message resembles the outline in 1 Corinthians 15.3–4, and nicely captures the gist of the early Christian proclamation (*kerygma*).

The early Christians proclaimed this message 'from the Scriptures' (cf. Luke 4.16–21; 24.27, 32, 45; 1 Corinthians 15.3), accentuating the divine necessity in the Christ event: Christ *had to* suffer and rise from the dead (Acts 1.16; 9.16; Luke 2.49; 24.7, 26, 46).

17.4–5. Some of them were persuaded and joined Paul and Silas, as did a great many of the devout Greeks and not a few of the leading women. But the Jews became jealous: Paul's reasoning from the Scripture persuaded some of his Jewish audience (e.g. Aristarchus, 20.4), but most of his converts came from the God-fearing Gentiles, including some women of high social status (e.g. Secundus, 20.4).

Luke specifies the motive behind the Jewish opposition as jealousy. Their plan was to stage a riot with the help of the ruffians and bring the missionaries before the assembly on a charge of sedition.

17.6–7. These people who have been turning the world upside down have come here also . . . They are all acting contrary to the decrees of the emperor, saying that there is another king named Jesus: They could not bring Paul and Silas before the assembly, since the two could not be found, so they dragged Jason and some other brothers to the city officials (Gk, *politarchēs*) for offering hospitality to them.

The charge of sedition was the same as in 16.20. It was certainly a malicious accusation, but since Paul proclaimed the kingdom of God, and the title Messiah practically meant king for Jews, this accusation had a grain of truth in it. In the Gospels the same charge was brought against Jesus himself (Luke 23.2; John 19.12, 15). The gospel is not political in itself, but when it is proclaimed in the real world, it certainly cannot avoid political implications.

17.8–9. The people and the city officials were disturbed when they heard this: The charge was serious, but the city officials apparently did not find any substantial grounds for the accusation. So they had to let the accused go, but with bail, possibly to prevent Paul and Silas from spreading such a dangerous idea. Paul's own words in 1 Thessalonians reflect how he felt about the incident (2.14–16, 18).

17.10. That very night the believers sent Paul and Silas off to Beroea: Paul's departure was abrupt (1 Thessalonians 2.17–18). Beroea was about 45 miles south-west of Thessalonica. The brothers seem to have tried to avoid pursuit, since Beroea was not on the Via Egnatia and was difficult of access. Here too Paul followed his usual custom of beginning his ministry from the synagogue.

17.11–12. These Jews were more receptive than those in Thessalonica, for they welcomed the message very eagerly and examined the scriptures every day to see whether these things were so: The Beroeans were receptive, namely, more open-minded to Paul's message, willing to test it against the testimony of the Scriptures. They did it so eagerly that they searched the Scriptures every day. Sopater, son of Pyrrhus, was among the first converts (20.4). Unlike in Corinth, many of the first converts in Macedonia came from those of high social standing (17.4, 12).

17.13–14. The Jews of Thessalonica . . . came there too, to stir up and incite the crowds: The Jews of Thessalonica pursued Paul to Beroea and caused trouble there. Once again, the believers sent him away 'to the coast' and accompanied him to Athens, leaving Silas and Timothy behind. They were back with Paul's instructions that these two should join him there as soon as possible. Paul's personal circumstances surrounding this escape are recounted in 1 Thessalonians 3.

 Interpretation

This section describes the beginning of Paul's mission in Macedonia: Philippi (16.11–40), Thessalonica (17.1–9) and Beroea (17.10–14). There was opposition from the Jews but Paul had considerable success, especially with the Gentiles.

Practical consequences of proclaiming the gospel

Preaching the gospel in Philippi took Paul and Silas to prison. The Christian gospel is not a political or economic programme in itself. Yet we live in a world where political and economic considerations cannot be avoided. Thus proclaiming the gospel and living it out in our daily lives does carry its own political and economic implications. Loyalty to the gospel often requires us to decide where to stand on various political, social or economic issues such as social welfare, abortion, homosexuality, rich and poor, to name a few. Ever since the birth of the Church, Christians have often been accused of causing political unrest or even of treason. Many believers also suffer physical or economic hardships because of their faith. For this reason, discerning the practical implications of our faith constitutes an important dimension of our spiritual life.

Paul and the Philippians

Paul usually earned his living as a leatherworker and supported his own ministry, since he did not want to put any burden on the shoulders of his Gentile converts (1 Corinthians 9.1–18; 2 Corinthians 11.9; 12.13; 1 Thessalonians 2.9. See p. 158 for this). In Philippi, however, Paul accepted the hospitality of the wealthy businesswoman Lydia; she seems to have supported Paul's ministry throughout his stay in Philippi. It was also at her house that the church was first established. The believers in Philippi continued to support Paul's ministry even after his move to another place, and Paul was very grateful for their generous gifts, as his Letter to the Philippians shows (4.15–16). Paul's primary concern was making his ministry effective, not blindly sticking to his own principle of tentmaking.

The wealthy in the Church

Luke is very much aware of the danger of possessions in Christian life (Luke 1.51–53; 18.25), but this does not mean that God dislikes wealthy people. God also welcomes wealthy people, as long as they show a proper attitude toward material possessions. Jesus bestowed salvation on Zacchaeus on his deciding to give away half of his possessions (Luke 19.1–10). Rather than denouncing the rich indiscriminately, Luke keeps affirming the generous acts of charity by the wealthy for the poorer members of the Church (Acts 2.44–45; 4.32–35). Paul also did not have any qualms about enjoying Lydia's hospitality. But the gospel has no place for those who are 'possessed' by their possessions like the owners of the slave woman in Philippi. The church should be a place for both the rich and the poor, but at the same time it should never allow greed for material possessions to ruin the *koinōnia* of the Spirit.

In this respect, the recent rise of the 'prosperity gospel' in certain areas of Christianity (including South Korea) is rather alarming, since it may mislead people into considering material prosperity itself as an expression of God's favour, a view which cannot be supported by the NT. There are numerous Christians who are poor yet faithful, and many of them are poor because they are faithful. We can demonstrate that God's favour has been given us by using our possessions wisely, but the possessions themselves should never be taken to be the mark of God's favour.

'We are Roman citizens'

People in Philippi were proud of their Roman citizenship. Such pride is also reflected in Paul's Letter to the Philippians. Paul exhorts believers there: 'Live your life in a manner worthy of the gospel of Christ' (1.27). The verb 'live your life' literally means 'live as a citizen' (Gk, *politeuomai*). The Philippians were proud of their Roman citizenship and loved to conduct their lives as such. But the believers no longer have their real citizenship here on earth, either in Rome or anywhere else, but 'in heaven' (3.20). So Christians are to make every effort to live their lives as citizens of this heavenly kingdom. In other words, we should live our lives here on earth 'in a manner worthy of the gospel of Christ' (Ephesians 4.1; 1 Thessalonians 2.12).

Of course, Christians are also citizens of a particular nation, and live their lives accordingly. Paul often declared before the Romans that he was a responsible citizen of the Roman Empire. He also used his Roman citizenship whenever it was appropriate. In Romans he teaches that Christians should respect the God-given authority of the government, unless the policy of the government is explicitly against the will of God. We too know that there are times when we have to disobey the authority of our earthly government, since our ultimate devotion goes to God, not to the earthly government. Striking the right balance is not always easy, so Christians keep asking for the guidance of the Holy

Spirit in order to discern the best way of conducting their lives here on earth.

Reasoning from the Scripture

God's word should be proclaimed so that people may listen. But proclamation does not mean announcing the message on a take-it-or-leave-it basis. The gospel should be communicated, and so we also need to 'discuss' (Gk, *dialegomai*) it and 'reason' with our listeners. That is what Paul regularly did with his audiences (17.2, 17; 18.4; 19.8, 9; 20.7, 9). Sometimes we boldly proclaim, but sometimes we also explain or even argue, defending the truth of the gospel. Bold proclamation does not exempt us from the responsibility of proper reasoning and careful argument. We should be ready to do everything in order to get across the message to our listeners.

On the part of the listeners, welcoming the proclaimed message eagerly does not mean swallowing it indiscriminately. God's word is trustworthy, but human interpretation and proclamation of it is not necessarily so. Ignoring this obvious fact runs the risk of turning human ideas into God's word, what we may call 'hermeneutical idolatry'. The people in Beroea received Paul's message 'with great eagerness' but that made them 'examine' the Scripture all the more astutely to see if what Paul said was true to the testimony of the Scripture. (The verb 'to examine' often meant 'legal examination', Luke 23.14; Acts 4.9; 12.19; 24.8; 28.18.) We should receive eagerly the message proclaimed by our ministers, but it does not exempt us from the responsibility of careful examination against the testimony of the Scripture, which is the final authority of truth.

 STUDY SUGGESTIONS

Word study

1 What is the background of the phrase, 'a spirit of divination'?

2 What is the meaning of 'fearing God' in Acts (13.43, 50; 16.14; 17.4, 17; 18.7, 13; 19.27)?

Review of content

3 Why did the owners of the slave-girl persecute Paul?

4 What charges were brought against Paul and Silas in Philippi?

5 What three points did Paul make in the synagogue of Thessalonica?

6 What charges were brought against Paul in Thessalonica?

Bible study

7   Compare the charges brought against Paul in Philippi and Thessalonica and see similarities and differences between the two (16.20–21; 17.6–7).

Discussion and application

8   Paul's evangelism included active discussion and careful argument with his listeners. How does it help us to speak the word to others more effectively?

9   Preaching and believing the gospel carries economic and political implications. Can you give concrete examples of such practical implications?

Acts 17.16–34

Paul in Athens

 Summary

Waiting for the other missionaries, Paul proclaims the word to the Jews and to the Gentiles, and delivers the 'Areopagus speech' before the purely Gentile audience.

 Notes

17.16. The city was full of idols: He had not intended it, but now Paul was in Athens, the intellectual capital of the whole empire. Paul saw numerous representations of gods and demigods there; they might be beautiful, but Paul was enraged by the senseless and idolatrous notions behind them. Other ancient authors also expressed similar views.

17.17. He argued in the synagogue . . . and also in the market-place: Without abandoning his habit of preaching in the synagogue, Paul was also active in discussing the gospel with the Gentiles in the market-place. The market-place was practically the centre of the city, where people could meet one another and listen to public speakers.

17.18. Some Epicurean and Stoic philosophers debated with him . . . 'What does this babbler want to say?' . . . 'He seems to be a proclaimer of foreign divinities': The Epicureans were materialists. According to them, the world was formed by chance, and gods were not interested in human affairs. So they denied divine judgement. Their object of life was happiness, i.e. freedom from pain and disturbance. The Stoics believed that the world was governed by universal reason ('nature, logos'), and that happiness lay in living according to the law of nature. Their ideal was self-sufficiency.

Some philosophers dismissed Paul as a 'babbler' (lit. 'one who picks up seeds'), which means 'retailer of second-hand ideas' or 'one who picks up new ideas indiscriminately'. Others probably mistook Paul's proclamation of Jesus and resurrection from the dead to be a message about two foreign deities, namely, Jesus and Anastasis (the Greek word for resurrection).

17.19-21. They brought him to the Areopagus: Areopagus may refer to the place itself, namely, the 'Hill of Ares' to the south of the city, or to the administrative council of that name (NIV). Athenian curiosity about new teachings is also attested by other ancient authors. But their interest in Paul seems purely academic and Luke's description reflects a degree of sarcasm. No wonder the outcome of Paul's preaching was not impressive.

17.22. I see how extremely religious you are in every way: This can either be pejorative ('superstitious') or neutral ('religious'). It is possible that Paul deliberately chose an ambiguous word: 'your idolatry is understandable yet mistaken'.

17.23. What therefore you worship as unknown, this I proclaim to you: No inscription with 'To an unknown God' has been found but there are altars dedicated to unknown gods. Paul did not mean that the Athenians were unconsciously worshipping God; he was using their idolatrous notion of god to introduce the 'living and true God' (1 Thessalonians 1.9).

17.24-25. God . . . does not live in shrines made by human hands, nor is he served by human hands . . . since he himself gives to all mortals life and breath and all things: David's prayer in 1 Chronicles 29.1-16 captures the point of this verse. Here Paul was exposing the foolishness of idolatry: dedicating altars to gods and offering sacrifices to them (cf. Acts 7.48). Many of Paul's hearers would have heartily agreed with him.

17.26. From one ancestor he made all nations . . . he allotted the times: The Greek text says simply 'one', meaning 'one man' (NIV) or 'one ancestor' (NRSV). 'Every nation' can also mean 'the whole human race'. If so, the 'times' refers to the cycle of seasons (14.17) or the lifespan of each person, and 'the boundaries of places where they would live' means the natural boundaries between sky and land, land and sea (Psalm 74.17). Paul was perhaps mildly criticizing the fatalism of his Stoic hearers.

17.27. So that they would search for God and perhaps grope for him and find him – though indeed he is not far from each one of us: On Gentiles' search for God, see Wisdom 13.6. For the biblical notion of seeking God, see Psalm 14.2; Proverbs 8.17; Isaiah 55.6. On the nearness of God, see Psalm 145.18 and Jeremiah 23.23. But Paul's idea of the personal God is far from the pantheistic immanence of the Stoics.

17.28. For 'In him we live and move and have our being' . . . 'For we too are his offspring': The first line comes from the Cretan philosopher Epimenides, and the second from *Paenomena* 5 by the Cilician poet Aratus. Paul saw a grain of truth in these pagan writers, but turned their words to the service of his own, distinctively biblical, idea of God.

17.29. We ought not to think that the deity is like gold, or silver, or stone, an image formed by the art and imagination of mortals: This is a familiar Jewish polemic against pagan idolatry (Psalm 115.4; Isaiah 37.19;

44.9–20; Wisdom 13.10; Romans 1.23). As we saw earlier, Stephen used the same polemic against the Jews (7.41–43).

17.30. While God has overlooked the times of human ignorance, now he commands all people everywhere to repent: Ignorance had been overlooked for both Jews and Gentiles (3.17; 13.27; 14.16; Romans 3.25), but now, with the announcement of the new revelation in Christ, people had to repent from their idolatry (Acts 2.38; 3.19; 8.22; 11.18; 26.20).

17.31. He will have the world judged in righteousness by a man whom he has appointed, and of this he has given assurance to all by raising him from the dead: This verse tells us why repentance is called for. People have to repent, since God will judge the world with justice. For this he has appointed 'a man', no doubt, Jesus of Nazareth (10.42; Romans 2.16). Paul presented resurrection as the proof of Jesus being the God-appointed Judge (cf. Acts 2.36). Curiously, the name 'Jesus' is never mentioned in the speech. In all likelihood Paul meant to bring his speech to that core of the gospel but was probably cut short at the mention of resurrection.

17.32–34. When they heard of the resurrection of the dead, some scoffed . . . But some of them joined him and became believers: Paul's speech was interrupted at the mention of resurrection, which was, and still is, the greatest stumbling block of the gospel. Notions such as judgement and resurrection ran counter to the views of the Greek philosophers. So most of them rejected Paul and some deferred judgement, which was in fact a polite way of ending the conversation (cf. 24.25).

But his effort was not completely in vain, since there were a few who believed and became Christians. Such a positive response assumes that Paul said a lot more than what is recorded here. Tradition has it that Dionysius, a member of the Areopagus, became the first bishop of Athens (Eusebius, *Ecclesiastical History* 3.4.10; 4.23.3).

 Interpretation

Paul's Areopagus speech is very different from his sermons preached in Jewish synagogues. There are some who tend to consider it a failure in that Paul failed to present the gospel pure and simple, but that would be too hasty a conclusion. Rather what we have here is an excellent example of reaching out to people whose cultural background is different from ours.

Preaching the word to the Gentiles

Like Paul in Athens, missionaries from Western countries are often enraged by the idolatrous culture of the country in which they serve. Some are quick to denounce it as 'demonic' but such hasty condemnation usually does not help. Here we can learn from Paul who was rightly enraged by the idolatry of the Athenians but patient enough to understand what they were doing, and who tried to find possible points of contact between their culture and the gospel. Paul could not approve what they were doing, but he tried to establish possible contact points by acknowledging the religiosity behind it. Hence such a 'natural theological' approach as we see in the present episode, which provided a critique of the folly of idolatry in a sympathetic manner. This, of course, will have to lead to a clear presentation of the gospel and a solemn call for repentance, and that will require 'revelation', which goes beyond the simple observation of nature.

One common mistake Christians often commit is to consider a particular culture to be Christian and denounce others as unchristian or even demonic. For example, about a century ago some Western missionaries denounced Korean traditional folk music as demonic and banned it from the church. But Korean Christians were very much offended when they found out that many of the 'holy' hymns they had learned from their missionaries also used the traditional folk music of some Western countries.

Worshipping idols and worshipping the life-giving God

The Bible is full of polemics against idolatry, since even Israelites, the chosen people of God, were not free from the temptation. Human beings are worshipping animals. They either worship the true God or end up worshipping some other things that do not deserve devotion. Some say that they believe in themselves and therefore do not need a god, but to say that does not mean that they are masters of their own lives. We can worship things or creatures of nature or make idols out of inanimate materials such as gold, silver or wood. Or we can follow certain philosophical ideas. We can also indulge in gratifying our fleshly desires. What are the typical idols that people follow in your culture? What distracts you from worshipping God in your life?

Whatever we worship or seek after, the folly of idolatry lies in the fact that we devote our lives to the things that cannot give life (Jeremiah 2.13). This is the ultimate message that God proclaims to human beings. Even Paul's doctrine of justification is the call to return to God who is the only one who can justify us. It is foolish to rely on any human values such as national identity, money or social status, since they are inherently 'weak' and cannot give life to us. God is the only one who can justify us, since he is the God who can give life to the dead (Romans 4.17), the truth finally confirmed by his raising Jesus Christ from the dead (Romans 4.24–25).

 STUDY SUGGESTIONS

Word study

1 What are the two ways of interpreting the word 'religious' in Acts 17.22?

2 What Greek myth lies behind the name 'Areopagus'?

Review of content

3 What were the major venues of Paul's mission in Athens?

4 What positive point did Paul draw from the idolatrous culture of the city?

5 What was the main point of disagreement between Paul and the philosophers?

6 What role did Paul attribute to Christ ('a man')?

7 What were the three different responses to Paul's speech?

Bible study

8 Read the following passages and discuss what it means that God 'overlooked ignorance'.

(a) 3.17; 13.27; 14.16; (b) Romans 3.25.

9 Read 2 Chronicles 6.18–41. What was the role of the Temple in Israel's relationship with her God?

Discussion and application

10 What are some philosophies of our time which we need to take into account when we speak the gospel to others? In what ways do they differ from the gospel?

11 The folly of idolatry lies in worshipping something that cannot give us life. Can you name some things around us that keep soliciting our attention and devotion?

Acts 18.1–28

Paul in Corinth

 Summary

In Corinth Paul meets Priscilla and Aquila. Paul preaches the word first in the synagogue, and then in the house of Titus. Jews accuse him without success. Apollos is introduced.

 Notes

18.1. Paul ... went to Corinth: The city was the Roman capital of Achaia. It was economically prosperous, culturally diverse and morally decadent. In those days, 'to behave like a Corinthian' meant 'to lead a morally decadent life'. Such an atmosphere posed a serious challenge to Paul as he tried to build a solid Christian community. Luke's description of Paul's mission there deals only with its beginning phase. We learn a lot about the fascinating relationship between Paul and the church there from his two Letters in the NT.

18.2. He found a Jew named Aquila ... with his wife Priscilla: Expelled from Rome by the edict of Claudius, they met Paul in Corinth and worked with him. (The expulsion was due to the friction between the believing and non-believing Jews.) They had been Christians before they met Paul and became his life-long supporters (1 Corinthians 16.19; 2 Timothy 4.19). Interestingly, in many other places Priscilla is named before her husband, which suggests that she played a more important role than her husband (18.18, 26; Romans 16.3; but also 1 Corinthians 16.19). The couple subsequently moved to Ephesus with Paul, where he left them to return to Syria. They were back in Rome by the time Paul wrote Romans (Romans 16.3), which provides a good illustration of mobility in the Roman Empire of the first century.

18.3. They were tentmakers: While maintaining his usual pattern of preaching in the synagogue (18.4; 13.14), Paul also worked during the week to support his own ministry (1 Corinthians 4.12; 9.3–19; 2 Corinthians 11.7–9). Being a leatherworker ('tentmaker'), he stayed with Aquila and Priscilla and worked for them.

18.4. Every sabbath he would argue in the synagogue and would try to convince Jews and Greeks: Here 'Greeks' means the God-fearing Greeks. Paul took pains to persuade those in the synagogue, but the result was mostly negative.

18.5. When Silas and Timothy arrived from Macedonia, Paul was occupied with proclaiming the word: It appears that Timothy had accompanied Paul to Athens but had been sent back by Paul to Thessalonica (17.14; 1 Thessalonians 3.1–2, 6), while Silas stayed behind. They came to Corinth together to meet Paul there (for the second time for Timothy). Their arrival allowed Paul to concentrate exclusively on ministry; they had probably brought gifts from the Macedonian churches (2 Corinthians 11.9; Philippians 4.15–16).

18.6–8. From now on I will go to the Gentiles: On two other occasions Paul made similar announcements (13.46; 28.28). These passages make it clear that Paul's announcement here concerned only the local situation in Corinth, not Paul's mission policy as a whole. Shaking the dust recalls 13.51 and Luke 9.5. For the expression 'Your blood be on your own heads!' see Acts 5.28; 20.26 (Ezekiel 18.13; cf. Matthew 27.25). Opposed by the Jews, Paul was forced to withdraw from the synagogue and found new headquarters at the house of a God-fearer, Titius Justus. Despite opposition, Paul's mission was fruitful, as illustrated by the conversion of Crispus, the synagogue ruler (1 Corinthians 1.14).

18.9–11. 'Do not be afraid . . . speak' . . . [Paul] stayed for a year and six months: Preaching the gospel in a city like Corinth must have been daunting, as reflected in Paul's own words (1 Corinthians 2.3). Probably Paul was giving way to fear or depression, but the Lord encouraged him in a vision (Acts 18. 9–10). 'I am with you' was God's word of encouragement (Joshua 1.9; Isaiah 41.10; 43.5; Jeremiah 1.8). In Luke–Acts the 'people' (Gk, *laos*) usually refers to the Israelites, but in Acts 15.14 and here the word also includes the Gentiles. Paul was busy carrying the gospel throughout the empire, but he also knew the importance of sustained pastoral care, as his extensive stay in Corinth and Ephesus exemplifies.

It was during his stay in Corinth that he wrote his two Letters to the believers in Thessalonica.

18.12–17. When Gallio was proconsul of Achaia, the Jews made a united attack on Paul: Gallio was a brother of the Stoic philosopher Seneca. An inscription from Delphi identifies him as proconsul of Achaia in AD 51, indicating that Paul worked in Corinth around that time.

The accusation sounds ambiguous, since 'the law' can either be the Jewish law (6.13) or the Roman law (16.21; 17.7). The Jews probably intended the latter, but Gallio did not even feel the need to hear Paul's defence. He decided that the dispute was about matters of Jewish religion, nothing for a Roman magistrate to bother about: 'I do not wish to be a judge of these matters.' So he dismissed them all and thereby vindicated

Paul's cause (cf. 24.14–15; 25.19; 26.2–3). The interjectory 'you Jews!' (in Greek) suggests a tone of rebuke.

What happened next is not clear. Luke says that 'all of them' seized Sosthenes, but it is unclear to whom he is referring. It is possible that the Greeks lynched the head of the Jewish synagogue for causing unwanted trouble. Or it may be that the Jews vented their frustrated anger on their synagogue ruler, apparently for handling the matter so inadequately. Or is this Sosthenes identical with his namesake mentioned in 1 Corinthians 1.1? If so, it is also possible that he was lynched by the Jews for his sympathy toward the missionaries. In any case, the Roman magistrate could not care less about the life and limb of Jews, whether Christians or not.

18.18. At Cenchreae he had his hair cut: Cenchreae was a port seven miles east of Corinth. A church was established there, probably during Paul's stay in Corinth. Phoebe was the leader of the church (Romans 16.1). It seems that Paul had taken a Nazirite vow (Numbers 6.1–21), and cutting his hair marked its conclusion. It was usually done in Jerusalem but this case might be an exception. Or it may have been a preparatory cutting before beginning the Nazirite period (21.20–26). Paul remained a devout Jew throughout his life, before and after his conversion to Christ.

18.19. When they reached Ephesus, he left them there: Ephesus, the capital of Asia, was a great port city serving as the commercial and religious centre. Here Paul parted from Priscilla and Aquila (we do not know why), and preached in the synagogue as was his habit.

18.20–21. I will return to you, if God wills: The Jews were quite eager to hear Paul's message, but it is unclear why he had to refuse such a good chance of evangelism (19.1; cf. 20.16).

18.22. He went up . . . and greeted the church: Luke does not mention Jerusalem, though NRSV includes it here. But since 'going up' and 'going down' usually referred to movement toward or from Jerusalem, it is quite probable that Paul paid a visit to the Jerusalem church. Paul was an apostle for the Gentiles but Jerusalem remained a theological centre of his ministry (Romans 15.19).

18.23. After spending some time [in Antioch] he . . . went . . . through the region of Galatia and Phrygia: Antioch still remained a crucial base for Paul's mission (11.26–30; 13.1–3; 14.26–28; 15.30–35). This verse describes the beginning of the so-called 'third missionary journey', though Luke does not seem to make much of it. In this trip Paul paid a pastoral visit to the communities established in his previous mission (cf. 14.21–22; 15.41).

18.24. There came to Ephesus a Jew named Apollos: Being an Alexandrian Jew, Apollos was learned and so was an eloquent communicator. He was also well-versed (lit., 'powerful') in the Scriptures (our OT).

18.25–26. He had been instructed in the Way of the Lord . . . though he knew only the baptism of John: He had already become a Christian of sorts in Egypt, and had a passion for proclaiming Jesus. 'With burning enthusiasm' literally means 'ardent in the spirit' or 'ardent in the (Holy) Spirit'. Yet he had not received Christian baptism in the name of Jesus and so had never acknowledged Jesus as his 'Lord'. He may not have been full of the Holy Spirit, but he was certainly different from those 'disciples' in Acts 19.1–7 who had to be baptized and receive the Holy Spirit. Priscilla and Aquila gave Apollos further instructions on the Christian way, thereby making his already 'accurate' knowledge 'more accurate' (NRSV: 'more adequate').

18.27–28. [Apollos] wished to cross over to Achaia: That Apollos arrived at Corinth after Paul and his ministry there is well reflected in 1 Corinthians 1—4. Although some Corinthians tried to make the two rivals (1 Corinthians 1.12), Paul himself considered Apollos to be his valuable co-worker (3.6, 9; 4.6; 16.12). Writing and carrying letters of recommendation was common in those days (2 Corinthians 3.1; Romans 16; 2 Corinthians 8; Acts 15.22–29).

Apollos put his knowledge of Scripture to good use in his debate with the Jews; using the Scriptures he 'powerfully' refuted the Jews, since he was 'well-versed' in the Scriptures (18.24). For proving the messiahship of Jesus from the Scriptures, see 8.35; 17.2–3; Luke 24.26–27, 45–46.

 Interpretation

This section describes Paul's mission in Corinth. Paul's mission to the Jews there was not successful, but his ministry among the Gentiles proved fruitful, as is indicated by his unusually long stay in the city (Acts 18.11). So here Luke underscores the Jewish rejection of the gospel and Paul's turning to the Gentiles. Paul's two Letters to the believers at Corinth tell us many more details about the initial stage of his ministry there as well as the subsequent deterioration of the relationship between him and the Corinthians.

Paul's ministry in Corinth

In Romans and Galatians Paul had to deal with Jewish problems related to 'works of the law'. But such a threat was not visible in Corinth; the problems there were largely the problems caused by the Gentile culture of Corinth. For Paul the root of all the problems in the church was divisive dissension (1 Corinthians 1.10; 3.3–4; 11.18). Behind the problem lay the competitive and self-seeking pursuit of secular values such as knowledge, eloquence or economic and political influence. But such things were 'fleshly' or 'merely human' values which could not bring about salvation. Paradoxically, the real power of salvation could only come from the message of the crucified Christ, which seemed foolish to those who were perishing but really powerful to those who were being saved. So Paul was determined to proclaim nothing but the cross of Christ, 'so that your faith might rest not on human wisdom but on the power of God' (1 Corinthians 2.5).

Paul's own ministry exemplified this truth. Humanly speaking, his presence in Corinth was ignorable. He came to Corinth 'in weakness and in fear and in much trembling' (2.3) and his speech lacked 'plausible words of wisdom' (2.4). And he proclaimed the crucified Christ (2.2), which seemed mere folly to humans. Yet his ministry was accompanied by a 'demonstration of the Spirit and of power' (2.4), since the crucified Christ is at the same time the risen Christ who comes to us as the 'life-giving spirit' (15.45). Since salvation comes through this Christ, all human values become meaningless and no one is able to boast of themselves. This provided the basis for the unity of the Church. Yet, the Corinthian believers continued to be influenced by the atmosphere of their pagan environment, boasting meaningless human values and creating divisions among themselves. So Paul reminded them of the gospel of the cross once again, which should express itself in the form of self-sacrificing love for the building-up of the community.

Modern Christians are not free from such a danger either. We often experience that even in the Church those who are rich, powerful or learned tend to have a stronger voice than those who are not. There are also those who use what God has given them for their own benefit rather than for the building-up of the local church. Some look at various positions in the church (pastors, elders, deacons) in terms of political power and social honour rather than loving and self-effacing service for others. Celebrating the God-given unity of the whole Church requires us to leave all our human differences behind and to stand hand in hand on the firm and sole foundation of the cross of Christ.

Paul as a tentmaker

Paul had been trained as a rabbi and, as was usual with rabbis, Paul had also learned a trade. Paul put his skill as a leatherworker to good use for his ministry. Many times in his Letters Paul draws his readers' attention to the fact that he worked with his own hands to support his ministry. Not that he was against receiving financial support from the believers; he explicitly affirms the right of support for those who preach the gospel (1 Corinthians 9.4–14). But on many occasions he voluntarily gave up this right. Sometimes he did so in order not to burden his converts (1 Thessalonians 2.9; 2 Thessalonians 3.8; 2 Corinthians 12.13); at other times he did so to avoid unnecessary complications in the relationship with his converts (1 Corinthians 9.15–18; 2 Corinthians 11.7). In Corinth, his tentmaking ministry was intended to distance himself from the 'peddlers of the gospel' (20.33–34; 2 Corinthians 2.17). However he did his ministry, his purpose remained the same: to save as many souls as possible (1 Corinthians 9.22). Even today, there are numerous numbers of voluntary 'tentmakers', especially in those countries where working as a missionary is not legally possible.

Today many Christians ask whether or not an ordained minister should have a trade, as Paul did. Paul does affirm the right to be supported by the believers, and many apostles such as Peter effectively used their right to facilitate their ministry. So it does not seem wise to say that all ministers should have a trade. On the other hand, however, we should also consider Paul's practice and the reasons behind it. Sometimes he supported his own ministry and at other times he gladly received financial assistance from his converts. Whether working or not, Paul's single concern was the benefit of his converts, and that should be the most important criterion for deciding the matter. In Korea most pastors concentrate on their ministry and do not have to take on other work to support themselves financially. But in many small Korean churches in America pastors work during weekdays to support themselves, since the membership is usually too small to expect full financial support. So both ministers and congregations need discretion in deciding what is most beneficial for the building-up of the church.

Priscilla and Aquila instruct Apollos

Apollos was both learned and well-versed in the Scriptures. He was also instructed in 'the Way of the Lord' and taught about Jesus 'accurately'. Yet Priscilla and Aquila soon found out that there was a problem in his message. So they invited him to their house and explained to him 'the Way of God . . . more accurately'. Apollos had been an effective communicator of the word, but he was humble enough to sit at the feet of Priscilla and Aquila and learn from them. On the other hand, the couple were considerate enough to correct him privately at their house, so as to avoid unnecessary embarrassment on his part. This short episode gives us a heart-warming example of how we can exercise our gifts properly and effectively to build up the whole Church.

 STUDY SUGGESTIONS

Review of content

1   Why did Aquila and Priscilla leave Rome?

2   What Letters did Paul write during his stay in Corinth?

3   What was Gallio's verdict on the Jewish accusation of Paul?

4   What was Paul's principle in the matter of financial support?

5   What was the problem of Apollos before he met Priscilla and Aquila?

Bible study

6   Read Acts 18.26–28 and 1 Corinthians 3.4–6. What was Apollos' ministry in Corinth?

7   Read Romans 16.3–5, 2 Timothy 4.19 and 1 Corinthians 16.19. What do we learn about Priscilla and Aquila from these verses?

Discussion and application

8 Some ministers have a trade of their own and some are supported fully by the Church. Which do you think is better? What are your reasons?

9 Even such an effective communicator as Apollos needed further instruction from others. What can we learn from this episode about Christian ministry?

 # Theological essay 3
Women in Acts and in Oceania

MERCY AH SIU-MALIKO

Introduction

This essay is based on case studies in the Pacific Islands (Oceania) which stimulate a contextual theological reflection on the parallels between the stories of Oceanian women and women in the book of Acts. Having worked with women in theological colleges and churches from across the South Pacific, I have observed that the experiences of women reflect very diverse contexts. Women make up around 60 per cent of the membership of many island churches. Still, this reality is not enough to grant women their God-given place in the ministry of the church because some island churches are operating from the dominant biblical ideology of patriarchy. Clear evidence of this is exemplified in the following remarks:

'Excuse me, you are sitting in my place. This is the place set aside for ministers only.'
'What made you think I am not a minister?'
'Because you are a woman, dear.'
'You will never be a minister, you will fall in love and follow your husband.'
'The church structure will not allow it.'
'You are a woman and you are young. You cannot make a final decision for a parish like ours.'
'We want a man to be our minister. A man is stronger. We are comfortable with a man.'
'You are destructive to the church and too radical.'
'There is no need for you to study theology because your husband is the only one who can minister.'
'There is no need for you to be forward about women's leadership in the church. Time will come and then you will be allowed in.' (Johnson and Filemoni-Tofaeono, 2003, p. 133)

These are the patriarchal attitudes that have been internalized by most Oceanian people. They have become norms that control the churches in the region, as in many other parts of the world. Such views hinder the recognition and utilization of women's God-given gifts. We need to learn about the social, political and church structures that restrict women, to understand how they have come about and how to take steps to be in solidarity with others who work for change.

In the book of Acts we learn that the events of Pentecost gave those who were present (women as well as men) the power to witness to the good news of the gospel. It is thus valid to make the claim that women were also empowered by the Spirit to become witnesses of God's salvation in Jesus Christ. This Pentecost experience is also a fulfilment of Joel's prophecy of a new order of equality for all of God's creation (Acts 2.17–18).

This is a prophecy that brings to reality the signs of the times. Even the late Pope John Paul II affirmed that this is the time

> when the vocation of women is being acknowledged in its fullness, the hour in which women acquire in the world an influence, an effect and a power never hitherto achieved. That is why, at this moment when the human race is undergoing so deep a transformation, women imbued with a spirit of the Gospel can do so much to aid humanity in not falling. (Pope John Paul II, 15 August 1998)

In contrast, Oceanian women's experiences of oppression and marginalization in the Church often lead to their passivity and withdrawal from activities that enhance their spiritual development and participation. As the former coordinator of Weavers, a region-wide programme that advocates for women in theological education, part of my responsibilities included visiting theological schools and churches across the region to share with them the Weavers' mandate, as well as listening to women's concerns. It was unfortunate that the majority of island women I encountered suffered from the effects of presumed cultural notions that tended to place them in subordination. This attitude has become a normative practice in most of the religious institutions in the Pacific, hence denying women the opportunity to be recognized and to develop their God-given potential.

A contextual dialogue

What follows is a contextual dialogue based on the story of two Oceanian women from two mainline denominations in Samoa. Ana and Sina are both married. Ana is 38 years old and the wife of a pastor. She holds a degree in arts as well as in theology. She lectures at a university in her country. Sina is 41. She likewise has a degree in arts and theology and is a minister's wife. Sina used to work for a regional women's organization in another island country, but the church called her husband back to work in their local theological college. These two women have much in common. They both have good educational backgrounds that could contribute to the enhancement of their churches' ministries. But because of assumed cultural norms and church policies on women's status, Ana now works outside of the church, while Sina stays at home as a housewife, in compliance with her intended role as *faletua* (translated as 'minister's wife' but literally meaning 'house at the back'); this is her 'shadow identity'.

Ana and Sina are having a conversation about some of the frustrations they experience with regard to their respective churches. They are discussing ways in which they might be able to move forward. They bring into their conversation the stories of women in Acts, especially in the way that 'women believers sought ways to hear their own voices and stories in worship, freed from the dictates of the male-dominated church' (O'Day, 1998, p. 397).

Ana: Sina! How are things in your church?

Sina: I am not quite sure. I think it is best for me to stay home, because I am not allowed to work. As trained women theologians, we are seldom given a chance to share our God-given gifts to help our church. Aren't we part of the Pentecost empowered community? Weren't both men and women present when the Holy Spirit came upon them?

Ana: Actually, I feel the same way. That is why I am enjoying working in the secular sphere, where there are no gender divisions. Everything depends on what a person offers in terms of qualifications, expertise and experience.

Sina: Well . . . ! I love the church because it is supposed to be the 'body of Christ' and the 'community of faith'. But it is far from that in terms of how it is organized. It discourages me from sharing what God has gifted me with. I don't really know where to start. But I thank God for using me in mysterious ways. I am working as a freelance for some women's organizations overseas. They have given me the opportunity to use my gifts through writing. And this has really lifted my spirits!

Ana: Isn't that a blessing! I think we should continue studying and writing about the ministries of women. I am also interested in the stories of women's ministries, especially in the context of the Early Church.

Sina: I think the approach is not to fight against the existing patriarchal system, because we have gone past that stage. We are not going to waste our energies doing that any more! But it is time to bring on board a new and appropriate approach that suits our global context – an approach that can demonstrate our inevitability. This can be done through our being in solidarity with others and especially our continued efforts to express our passion in 'women's theologies'.

Ana: Why don't we prepare a study on women in Acts, perhaps beginning with women who are mentioned only in passing, then going on to look at women who are particularly named in relation to their ministries? This would help a lot in enabling women to understand that we are also called to serve God, no matter what!

Searching the text

In order to gain a clear understanding of women in Acts, it is important to begin from the narratives of their experiences. Luke frames Acts around the ministries of Peter and especially Paul, because they embody for him the movement of the gospel from Jews to Gentiles. Moreover, women were regarded as second-class citizens in the Roman Empire and public leadership roles were all held by men. Luke shapes his treatment of women in Acts to conform to this Roman model.

Brief references to women

In Acts, women are often mentioned only briefly in specific stories; Luke also includes five stories in which women's names are particularly mentioned. Although the stories mentioning women tend to portray them as comparatively trivial characters in the making of the Early Church, still women's ministries and contributions to the life of the Early Church clearly speak of them as destined members of the empowered community. This is evident in the specific ministries implemented by women. Such ministries were successful in many ways, regardless of the barriers placed before women.

Acts 1.14 Women who stayed with the disciples after Jesus' Ascension

The first mention of women in Acts is recorded in Acts 1.14. The 'certain women' may refer to wives of the apostles, or to the women who accompanied Jesus, as named in Luke 8.2–3. They may also include those who witnessed the crucifixion (23.49), the burial (23.55–56) and the announcement of the resurrection (24.1–11).

Women who were present in the beginning of the Church played an important role in the early Christian community in Jerusalem. Luke mentions only Mary, the mother of Jesus. Although readers may question the intention behind Luke's mention of Mary (and not the other women), still the specific mention of Mary does establish a continuity between the birth of Jesus and the birth of the Church. This role is very much part of the Church's ongoing mission even though patriarchal views hinder the fulfilment of women's calling.

The primary characteristic that marked the Early Church's life was prayer. Luke's specific mention of certain women devoting themselves to this vital element of worship indicates a characteristic associated with the psychological nature of women as caring and responsible human beings. This was nurtured by the promised Spirit that empowered women (and men) to become Christ's witnesses. However, because of cultural norms, this witnessing characteristic tends to be associated only with men, even in many cultures today.

Acts 2.17–18 Prophesying daughters and female slaves

The disciples were meeting on the Day of Pentecost, and 'all of them were filled with the Holy Spirit and began to speak in other languages'

(v. 4). Peter explained to the crowd that this happened in fulfilment of the prophet Joel's prophecy. This passage envisions a new order, not only of women and men in the community of those filled by the Spirit, but also of enslaved persons of both genders, and further implies that their inclusion signals the imminence of the 'end'. In this early church meeting, God caused women to speak in tongues and prophesy in a place where men and women had gathered to pray and worship. Nevertheless, women are not portrayed as public speakers in the remainder of Acts. Jewish and Greco-Roman society had few if any precedents of women speaking in public settings. The attitudes of Jewish men towards women can be seen in the fact that they did not permit women to testify in court. It is therefore not likely that men would view female preachers as credible sources for new religious ideas. Because of those attitudes, women supported the gospel in other ways.

Acts 5.14 Women (and men) as new believers

In one place, Luke describes the growth of the Church in terms of 'the number of the men' (Acts 4.4, NASB); in another place he mentions both 'men and women' (5.14). The mention of women is another reminder of their role in the life of the Church. The tense of the Greek verb 'were added' (imperfect) gives the sense that men and women kept on being added, whereas the passive voice carries the implication that it was God who did the adding.

Acts 16.16–18 The slave-girl

The unnamed slave-girl was exploited by her owners, because of her gift of divination, to make money for themselves (v. 16). When Paul passed this woman in the streets of Philippi, she proclaimed him to be a man of God (v. 17). We may wonder why Paul was annoyed with the slave-girl's repeated utterances. The silencing of the woman may reflect Luke's discomfort with the prophetic voice of women in the Church. The scene can be read as emblematic of Luke's silencing of women prophets throughout Acts. It is also noted that this anonymous slave-girl may be the most marginalized person in the New Testament, for she is a demon-possessed, exploited, pagan, female slave. Isn't driving out demons a good thing?

Acts 21.9 Philip's daughters

Paul was visiting Philip (one of the appointed seven in Acts 6.5). Philip had four unmarried daughters who had the gift of prophecy, as in Acts 21.9. This is the only comment Luke makes about these women and their ministry. The mention of Philip's daughters is unusual, since they play no role in the story. The fact that they are mentioned in this particular account reveals their significance in terms of their divinely inspired gift. Although the daughters' gift of prophecy seems trivial in the story, still the truth remains that their gift of prophecy brings to fulfilment Joel's prophecy, 'and your sons and your daughters shall prophesy' (2.17).

Acts 24.24 Drusilla

Drusilla is the daughter of Herod Agrippa I, the Herod who murdered James and would have murdered Peter (12.1–23). She had previously been married to the Syrian Azizus of Emesa but had left him for Felix, who reportedly pursued her for her great beauty. Although her name is mentioned, it is only in relation to her husband Felix. This may reflect her influence on Felix or her own personality. Luke continues to present contrasting images of women in the Early Church. There are those empowered by the Spirit and those whom the apostle Paul yearned to win to Christ.

Stories about particular women

Luke mentions women also in relation to two ministries of the early Christian communities. The first concerns ministry to and by widows, as instigated by Dorcas. The second is prophetic ministry. This ministry is a sign of the Holy Spirit working among both women and men in the Early Church, although Luke almost completely ignores women's prophetic ministry.

Acts 5.1–11 Sapphira

The account of Sapphira and her husband Ananias is the first story in Acts in which an individual woman plays a very influential role, as described by Luke (vv. 1–2). It is a story about two people who conspired to deceive their fellow believers, the Church. They promised to give the money to the Church but did not fulfil their promise. In this story, Luke pictures women as participating not only in the blessings of the new community but also in its problems and failures. In fact, it is not only Ananias who is held responsible and punished for withholding some of his resources, which he claimed to have given to the pooled funds of the community, but his wife Sapphira as well. Their actions failed to comply with the meanings behind their names: the Hebrew form of Ananias means 'Yahweh is gracious', and Sapphira means 'beautiful'. The story also shows Sapphira as having an equal voice in the economic management of her marriage. This supports the egalitarian nature of the early Christian community, where men and women had equal shares in decision-making and the regular distribution of funds (6.1).

Acts 9.36–42 Dorcas

Dorcas or Tabitha was a compassionate woman who was, first of all, a disciple. It is only here in the book of Acts that a woman is explicitly called a disciple. In fact, the feminine noun for 'disciple' appears nowhere else in the New Testament. Her name has been used for many women's charitable societies.

We read in the book of Acts that widows made up a separate group with their own ministry. By the end of the first century, Christian widows had their own order, to which only certain highly qualified widows could belong. Perhaps those who belonged to this order were being recognized for their hard work, as in the case of Dorcas. And since there are so many stories about widows in the Gospel of Luke and the book of Acts, it is possible that these stories were told by some of the women who belonged to the established widows' order.

The story of Dorcas and the widows occurred at a time when the Church was facing persecution. Both men and women had suffered persecutions led by Saul, and the community in Jerusalem had scattered. As a result, the gospel was carried to Samaria, the coastal cities of Gaza, Lydda, Joppa and Caesarea, and even to Antioch in Syria. But with Saul's conversion had come a temporary peace: 'And walking in the fear of the Lord and in the comfort of the Holy Spirit, [the church was] multiplied' (Acts 9.31, KJV).

Acts 12.12–19 Rhoda at the gate

When Peter was miraculously released from prison, he went to the home of the mother of John Mark, where many were gathered together for prayer (vv. 12–17). The account of Rhoda and Peter is a masterful piece of storytelling, full of comedy and suspense. It is comic when Rhoda, overwhelmed with joy at the sight of Peter, runs to announce his arrival without letting him in (vv. 14–15). Her joy in rushing to tell the disciples and their response, accusing her of madness, recalls details of Luke's resurrection narrative (Luke 24.9–11). Yet the story is also suspenseful, because the reader wonders whether Peter will be re-apprehended while he waits to be admitted to his own community.

Acts 16.11–15 Lydia

The story of Lydia, in Acts 16.11–15, took place in the city of Philippi, a district of Macedonia (although Lydia herself was from Thyatira). Lydia was a businesswoman who sold purple cloth, which was a luxury item for the wealthy. Lydia was a Gentile woman who worshipped God but was not, initially, a member of the Christian community. She offered her home as a centre for Paul and the other missionaries. Being already a devout person, when she heard the word of God she took what she heard seriously. Lydia opened her heart to the gospel, which then enabled her to respond by inviting Paul and his team to her house as guests. Her generosity is also to be noted. Since she was a businesswoman, she had the means to use her resources to build up the church, and she gave both hospitality and material gifts without reservation. She was a pillar of the church at Philippi.

Acts 18.1–4, 18–28 Priscilla

The apostle Paul does at times acknowledge the important contributions of women to the life and growth of the Church. Priscilla receives particular mention. She was engaged with her husband, Aquila, in teaching people, including the gifted and learned Apollos. Priscilla means 'old', or 'of ancient blood'. Some suggest that Priscilla herself was of noble birth, a distinguished and well-educated Italian woman who married Aquila, a rich Jew of Pontus. She actively engaged in promoting the cause of Christ in Corinth, Ephesus and Rome, three of the most important cities in the Roman Empire. Even though Priscilla worked in partnership with her husband Aquila, in three out of five times they are mentioned she is named first. This is a clear indication of her outstanding contribution to their ministry as well as being well educated in the teachings of the Christian faith.

Conclusion

Women in Acts became the backbone of the Early Church's ministry. Their domestic and prophetic ministries were divinely inspired by the Spirit. They were present in the upper room praying prior to Pentecost, when the Holy Spirit came upon the disciples. And from that moment women were added to the Christian community, endured persecution and suffering, and brought others to faith in Christ. Women were also involved in the building-up of the body of Christ. The activities in which women participated varied, but they included prophesying, performing charitable services, and serving as missionary workers. This has been repeated through the centuries, from one generation to the next, as the history of the Church demonstrates. These (and other) aspects of women's ministry gifts have penetrated our contemporary world and our respective Oceanian (and other) contexts. They are pivotal forces that strengthen Christian women's calling to ministry.

As an Oceanian woman theologian, I believe that women are a crucial element in all societies. The maintenance, continuation and survival of the community, local church, family and individuals depend on the service and efforts of women. Therefore, the Church must defend the dignity of women and their calling. By so doing the Church is showing honour and gratitude for those women, such as the women in Acts, who were pioneers in the apostolic mission of the whole people of God.

Likewise, Oceanian women must raise prophetic voices within their churches. According to Ana and Sina's conversation, 'This can be done through our being in solidarity with others and especially our continued efforts to express our passion in "women's theologies".' More importantly, this ministry of women is a fulfilment of a divine prophecy (Acts 2.17).

 References

John Paul II, 'Introduction' in *Apostolic Letter* Mulieris Dignitatem: *On the Dignity and Vocation of Women on the Occasion of the Marian Year.* Rome: St Peter's, 15 August 1988. <http://www.vatican.va/holy_father/ john_paul_ii/apost_letters/documents/hf_jp-ii_apl_15081988_mulieris-dignitatem_en.html>; accessed 19 October 2011.

Johnson, Lydia and Joan Alleluia Filemoni-Tofaeono (eds), *Weavings: Women Doing Theology in Oceania*. Suva, Fiji: University of South Pacific, 2003.

O'Day, Gail R., 'Acts', in Carol A. Newsom and Sharon H. Ringe (eds), *The Women's Bible Commentary: Expanded edition with Apocrypha*. Louisville, Ky.: Westminster/John Knox, 1998.

Acts 19.1–44

Paul in Ephesus

 Summary

Paul baptizes a group of disciples of John the Baptist. He carries out his ministry for two years with numerous miracles. Paul's work of exorcism leads to a riot.

 Notes

19.1. While Apollos was in Corinth, Paul passed through the inland regions and came to Ephesus, where he found some disciples: The 'inland regions' literally means 'higher', referring to the mountainous countryside. While Paul was going through these regions including Galatia and Phrygia, strengthening the disciples (18.23), Apollos was in Corinth, 'watering' the church which Paul had 'planted' (1 Corinthians 3.6).

19.2–3. Did you receive the Holy Spirit when you became believers?: In the Early Church, confession of faith and baptism in the name of Jesus typically led to the reception of the Holy Spirit (1.5; 2.4; 8.17; 9.17; 10.44). However, the pattern was by no means uniform. It is not easy to define the exact status of the 'disciples' we meet here. Luke says that they 'believed' and baptized but they believed what John had taught them and they had received only 'John's baptism'. So Paul checked if they had received the Holy Spirit, which was the surest litmus test of the authenticity of faith. But these disciples had not received the Holy Spirit, since they had not yet been baptized in the name of Jesus.

Their response in verse 2 is also problematic, since John had proclaimed Jesus as the one who would baptize people with the Holy Spirit, as Paul reminded them (v. 4). It is possible that they had heard about the Holy Spirit but were unaware of the actual coming of the Spirit (the Pentecost). But Paul's instruction about Jesus suggests that they were merely baptized by John without learning either about Jesus, the one predicted by John himself, or about the Holy Spirit (v. 4).

19.4. Telling the people to believe in the one who is to come after him, that is, in Jesus: John's baptism of repentance (Luke 3.3–15) was a preparation for the coming of Jesus who would baptize people with the Holy Spirit (Acts 1.5; 11.16; 13.25; 18.25).

19.5–7. When Paul had laid his hands on them, the Holy Spirit came upon them: With Paul's accurate instruction about Jesus, they were 'baptized into the name of Lord Jesus' (2.38; 8.16; 10.48). The fact that the coming of the Spirit was directly linked with Paul's laying on of his hands signified the full membership of these disciples within the community of believers, as in the case of the Samaritan mission (8.17). Their speaking in tongues and prophesying also had the same legitimating function (2.4, 11; 10.46).

19.8. [Paul] entered the synagogue and for three months spoke out boldly: Paul's Ephesian mission followed his usual pattern of beginning his preaching in the synagogue. Paul's message is here summed up as about the kingdom of God: preaching about Jesus and about the kingdom of God is one and the same (28.31).

19.9–10. He left them, taking the disciples with him, and argued daily in the lecture hall of Tyrannus: Opposition arose after three months. Paul withdrew from the synagogue and continued his ministry in the public hall called Tyrannus for two years (cf. 20.31). Some manuscripts of Acts (the Western text; see Introduction) add here that Paul held the meeting 'from the fifth hour to the tenth', i.e. from 11 a.m. to 4 p.m. when most people were resting from work to avoid the heat. So Paul, while working to support himself (20.34; 1 Corinthians 4.12), used his resting time to do his ministry. The Tyrannus probably offered him 'off-peak' rates during these hours. Paul's preaching was not confined to Ephesus but covered the whole province of Asia. The churches in Colossae, Laodicea and Hierapolis were probably established during this period (Revelation 2—3; 1 Corinthians 16.19).

19.11–12. God did extraordinary miracles through Paul: The 'miracle' is literally 'power' (Gk, *dunamis*). Paul's preaching was accompanied by powerful manifestation of the Holy Spirit, and Ephesus was no exception (Romans 15.19; 2 Corinthians 12.12). The people's attitude was not free from the culture of magic and superstition, but God acknowledges their purity of heart and often meets them at their level.

19.13–16. Some itinerant Jewish exorcists tried to use the name of the Lord Jesus: 'Exorcists' translates the Greek word *exorkistēs*. The Jews were renowned for their magical practices (13.6–11; cf. Deuteronomy 18.10–14). Exorcism usually involved the incantation of powerful names. The sons of Sceva had seen the power Paul wielded by invoking the name of the Lord Jesus and probably thought to add that name to their repertoire.

God's power cannot be concocted by magical formula. Like the demoniacs of the Gospels (Luke 4.34, 41; 8.28) and the slave woman in Acts (16.17), the evil spirit showed demonic insight into the identity of Jesus. Ironically, the word Luke uses for the 'leaping' of the evil spirit is used in

LXX to describe the 'leaping' of the Spirit of the Lord (1 Samuel 10.6; 11.6; 16.13). The helpless defeat of the Jewish exorcists is sharply contrasted with the effectiveness of Paul's healings and exorcisms.

19.17. Everyone was awestruck; and the name of the Lord was praised: The defeat of the evil power represented by evil spirits and charlatan exorcists prompts serious reactions: (negatively) fear (3.10; 5.1, 11) and (positively) praise of God (4.21).

19.18. Many of those who became believers confessed and disclosed their practices: Literally, 'many of those who had believed began to confess and announce their practices', suggesting that such confession was not just a single act. Growing as 'infants in Christ' (1 Corinthians 3.1) inevitably involves ongoing confession of their sins (James 5.16; 1 John 1.9).

19.19–20. A number of those who practised magic collected their books and burned them publicly: The scrolls contained magical spells and formulae. Public burning was a way of stopping the spread of unhealthy ideas or habits. 'Fifty thousand silver coins' must have been enormous, though it is not easy to tell the modern equivalent value. The great value of the scrolls burned indicates the seriousness of their repentance and the power of the word of God. Luke introduces this episode to illustrate how widely and powerfully the word of the Lord was spreading throughout the region.

19.21–22. Now after all these things had been accomplished, Paul resolved . . . to go on to Jerusalem . . . So he sent two of his helpers: 'Resolved' literally means 'determined in the spirit/Spirit'. Paul's resolve to go to Jerusalem and sending ahead of two messengers parallels Luke 9.51–52 (NIV): 'As the time approached for him to be taken up to heaven, Jesus resolutely set out for Jerusalem. And he sent messengers on ahead.' Clearly, this marks a crucial turning point in Paul's mission, the beginning of Paul's journey toward his final destiny. Like the 'travel narrative' in the Gospel (Luke 9.51—19.44), the motif of Paul's journey to Jerusalem and Rome frequently recurs in the following narratives (Acts 20.22; 21.13; 25.9–12; 28.14).

Paul wanted to go through Macedonia and Achaia on his way to Jerusalem. Here Luke does not give us the reason, but Paul himself links it with the collection that he had been organizing for the saints in Jerusalem (24.17; Romans 15.25–31; 1 Corinthians 16.1–4; 2 Corinthians 8—9). The sending of the two assistants was probably to make sure that the relief fund would be ready by the time of Paul's arrival. Timothy is said to have worked both in Macedonia (Acts 18.5; Philippians 2.19–24) and in Corinth (1 Corinthians 4.17; 16.10). Erastus was a common name, so it is not certain whether this Erastus was the same as the one mentioned in Romans 16.23 (cf. 2 Timothy 4.10).

The reference to 'Asia' suggests that Paul's ministry in Ephesus was not confined to the city itself, a fact also confirmed by verses 10 and 26.

19.23. No little disturbance broke out concerning the Way: 'No little disturbance' is a figure of speech called litotes, which Luke uses frequently in Acts (see 12.18–19; 19.24). Luke often uses 'the Way' to refer to the Christian movement (9.2; 16.17; 18.25–26; 19.9). The gospel is not just a philosophical idea but a 'way' of life to walk.

19.24. Demetrius, a silversmith who made silver shrines of Artemis: The following episode provides a vivid vignette of one of those 'dangers in the city' (2 Corinthians 11.26). Unlike those practitioners of magic who gave up their livelihood for faith, Demetrius and his colleagues incited a great uproar. The 'Artemis of the Ephesians' (19.28, 34) was originally the mother-goddess of the East but was later identified with the Greek huntress-goddess Artemis (Latin: Diana). The temple of Artemis in Ephesus was among the Seven Wonders of the World. The 'silver shrines of Artemis' refer to its miniature replicas. Many examples of such model temples in terracotta and marble have been found (but none in silver).

19.25–27. This Paul has persuaded and drawn away a considerable number of people: We can picture the members of a craftsmen's guild (Latin, *collegium*) called to respond to a threat to their thriving business. As in 16.16–21, the major motive of such a move was economic in nature. Demetrius pinpointed a crucial point of Paul's message: 'Man-made gods are no gods at all'. Addressed to the idol-worshipping Gentile audiences, polemic against idolatry must have been a constant theme of Paul's preaching (14.15–17; 17.29; cf. 7.48–50; 1 Thessalonians 1.9). The charge also indicates how successful Paul's ministry had been: 'almost the whole of Asia'. Demetrius was a demagogue; his appeal to the religious feeling of the people was specious but nevertheless effective.

19.28–29. The city was filled with the confusion: Demetrius provoked the people by saying that the great goddess might be brought down from her greatness (NRSV: 'majesty'). At this, the furious people began to shout, 'Great is Artemis of the Ephesians' (vv. 28, 34). The Macedonian Gaius introduced here should be different from his namesake in 20.4 who was from Galatia (cf. Romans 16.23; 1 Corinthians 1.14; 3 John 1). Aristarchus was from Thessalonica; he would later accompany Paul to Jerusalem (Acts 20.4; 27.2; Colossians 4.10).

19.30–31. Paul wished to go into the crowd, but the disciples would not let him: Paul wanted to face the assembly himself (Gk, *dēmos*; NRSV: 'crowd'), but was dissuaded from doing so, since the gathering was more like a wild mob than a citizens' assembly. Among Paul's friends were some of the 'officials' (Gk, *asiarchēs*). Their exact function is obscure but they certainly belonged to the higher strata of the society. This reflects the success of Paul's mission among the higher classes (17.4, 12, 34).

19.32. The assembly was in confusion: The Greek behind the 'assembly' is *ekklēsia*, the technical term for such a meeting. But the picture Luke draws belies its name, and Luke soon switches back to 'the crowd' (19.33, 35).

19.33–34. But when they recognized that he was a Jew . . . all of them shouted in unison, 'Great is Artemis of the Ephesians!': It is difficult to grasp what is going on in these verses: who was this Alexander? Was he a Christian or not? Why did the Jews push him forward? What instruction did they give him? In any case, the crowd saw that he was a Jew and shouted him down. The Jews, Christian or not, all repudiated the Gentile idolatry; the crowd of Ephesus apparently took the matter from that perspective.

19.35. The city of the Ephesians is the temple-keeper of the great Artemis and of the statue that fell from heaven: The city-clerk (Gk, *grammateus*), the highest official in Ephesus, managed to gain control. The 'guardian of the temple' was the title given to cities that maintained temples honouring the emperor or other gods or goddesses. The idea that the image of Artemis had fallen 'from heaven' (Gk, *diopetēs*, literally 'fallen from Zeus') may have been the clerk's response to Paul's attack on the human-made gods (19.26). His advice was simple: 'There is no need for such a commotion, since nobody can deny our honour as the guardian of the temple of Artemis.'

19.37–39. Neither temple-robbers nor blasphemers of our goddess: The clerk knew that the Christians had neither robbed temples (cf. Romans 2.22) nor blasphemed the goddess, so no specific charges were made against them. Verse 38 is filled with legal terminology. Demetrius and his colleagues should follow a proper legal process ('proconsuls' and the 'courts'). He could also appeal to the civil assembly, but it had to be a 'legal assembly', not a commotion like this.

19.40. We are in danger of being charged with rioting . . . since there is no cause: The clerk considered the present rioting as a far greater threat to the welfare of the city than the activity of the missionaries, since the Roman authorities would not tolerate such disorder.

 ## Interpretation

This section deals with Paul's second, and much longer visit to Ephesus. He had already visited the city on his way back to Jerusalem and Antioch but had not stayed long. He just promised that he would return if God would allow it (18.19–21). Now he returned and ministered there for no less than three years. As far as we can tell from the account in Acts, this was his longest stay in one particular place. Four different episodes are recorded in this section: re-evangelizing a group of John's disciples (vv. 1–7); Paul's powerful ministry (vv. 8–20); sending of emissaries to Macedonia (vv. 21–22); and the public commotion (vv. 23–41).

The litmus test of the Holy Spirit

Paul's mediation of the Holy Spirit for the 12 disciples confirms once again the importance of the Holy Spirit as the key element of Christian faith. In Acts it has to be so, since the Holy Spirit functions as the surest sign of God's acceptance, as is aptly illustrated by the Cornelius episode (10.44–48; 11.15–18). But in Paul's gospel the Spirit means far more than that. The Holy Spirit is not just the evidence of God's acceptance but also the ongoing source and principle of Christian life (Romans 7.6; 8.4–9; Galatians 5.16–18, 25) and, for that reason, the surest guarantee of future hope (Romans 8.11, 14–17; Galatians 5.5; 6.8). So the Christians are exhorted to finish their race under the guidance of the Spirit, just as they began it through the Holy Spirit (Galatians 3.3).

Faith and magic

God performed many extraordinary miracles through Paul. Paul's ministry was so powerful that even garments that had touched his skin had healing power. Naturally, some 'magicians' mistook this manifestation of God's power for magic and attempted to drive out evil spirits by invoking the name of Jesus. But they could not do it, since the power of healing was not something they could possess and use at will. Paul's power was derived from his faith in the risen Jesus who is the 'life-giving Spirit' (1 Corinthians 15.45), a point Peter also made clear earlier in the book (Acts 3.12–16).

Repentance in action

Genuine repentance leads people to confess and renounce old practices to bring their life into line with their faith in Christ. History tells us that many great awakenings, such as the 1907 Great Awakening in Pyongyang, Korea, began with the Spirit-prompted confession of sins both by the preachers and their audiences. For this reason, believing the gospel has direct bearings on our everyday life, as we can see in the Ephesian episode above.

Faithful life often requires us to renounce economic gain or even suffer loss. It also involves a serious cultural reorientation. For example, in Korea important public exams or tests are often held on Sundays, but many Christians who want to observe the 'Lord's day' properly refuse to take the test and accept the consequences. Many shop-keepers also close their shops on Sundays for the same reason. And many Korean Christians are criticized or even harassed by their family members and relatives for refusing to participate in *jesah*, the traditional rite of ancestor veneration, since they consider it a form of idolatry. We may question their viewpoint but their willingness to be faithful in all areas of their lives is surely to be applauded. We can also think of those believers living in Islamic or Communist countries who have to suffer all kinds of hardships simply because they are Christians. Concrete situations may differ, but the cost of discipleship still seems high for many Christians throughout the world.

Proclamation and defence

In his address to the roused crowd, the city-clerk of Ephesus declared that the Christian missionaries were 'neither temple-robbers nor blasphemers of our goddess' (Acts 19.37). In the stories to follow, Paul would have to defend himself in both Jewish and Roman courts (cf. 22.1; 24.10; 25.8, 16; 26.1, 2, 24), and many Roman officials would declare Paul's innocence in the face of the political and religious accusations of the Jewish leaders (18.14–15; 23.29; 25.18–19, 25; 26.32). So Luke reveals a clear apologetic motive in writing his book, and this purpose seems to have to do with the situation of the Christian communities of his day which were under threat both from the Romans and the Jews (cf. 1 Thessalonians 2.14). Christians surely know the word of Jesus, 'Blessed are those who are persecuted for righteousness' sake' (Matthew 5.10–12), but it does not mean that we should not avoid unjust wrongdoings or persecutions when possible. Proclaiming the gospel sometimes involves defending it from unnecessary misunderstandings and malignant accusations, though we should never do so by removing the stumbling block of the cross itself (cf. Galatians 5.11).

 STUDY SUGGESTIONS

Word study

1 What is the meaning of 'power' in the following verses?

(a) 1.8; 4.33; **(b)** 2.22; 3.12; 4.7; 6.8; 8.13; 10.38.

Review of content

2 What was the disciples' condition when they met Paul?

3 What did Paul do when he faced the opposition of the Jews?

4 What were the visible results of the Ephesians' conversion?

5 What charge did Demetrius bring against the Christian missionaries?

6 What was the city-clerk's view of the Christian missionaries?

Bible study

7 Read the following passages. What was the message of John the Baptist about Jesus?

(a) Luke 3.4, 16; **(b)** Matthew 3.11; **(c)** Mark 1.4, 7–8; **(d)** John 1.26–27.

8 The Spirit is God's gift that we receive. What other expressions are used to describe our relationship with the Spirit?

(a) Romans 8.3; **(b)** Romans 8.9–11; **(c)** Romans 8.13; **(d)** Romans 8.14; **(e)** Galatians 5.16; **(f)** Galatians 5.25.

Discussion and application

9 In the New Testament the Holy Spirit manifested itself both charismatically and morally. What do you think are the concrete ways of showing that we have received the Holy Spirit?

10 Magic still seems to have a great influence on people's lives even in more developed countries. What kinds of magical thoughts or practices can we find around us?

11 Believing in Christ sometimes means economic loss. Can you give an example of such cases?

Acts 20.1–38

Paul begins his journey to Jerusalem

 Summary

After visiting Macedonia and Greece, Paul begins his journey to Jerusalem. Paul speaks to the believers in Troas and then makes a farewell speech to the Ephesian elders in Miletus.

 Notes

20.1–3a. After encouraging them: Encouragement or exhortation (the Greek word can mean both) was a crucial part of Paul's apostolic ministry (14.22; 15.36, 41; 16.40). He went through Macedonia for this pastoral purpose (cf. 19.21). It is probable, though not certain, that Paul visited Illyricum about this time (Romans 15.19). Then he went on to Greece, i.e. Achaia. Paul probably stayed in Corinth, and from there he wrote Romans in preparation for his long-awaited visit (Acts 19.21; Romans 15.22–29). He stayed there for three months, probably waiting for the travelling season to come (cf. Acts 27.12; 28.11; Titus 3.12).

20.3b–4. When a plot was made against him by the Jews: Luke mentions many such plots against Paul (9.24; 20.19; 23.30). The plot made Paul change his plan and instead 'return through Macedonia' on foot. (It would have been much easier to stir the crowd and kill Paul on the ship.) Delegates from the churches of diverse regions (Macedonia, Galatia, Asia) accompanied Paul: Sopater son of Pyrrhus (Beroea); Aristarchus and Secundus (Thessalonica); Gaius and Timothy (Derbe); Tychicus and Trophimus (Asia). Luke is silent about their purpose, but it was probably related to the relief fund which Paul had been collecting for the Jerusalem believers. Their existence explains why Paul could greet the Romans on behalf of 'all the churches of Christ' (Romans 16.16).

20.5–6. They went on ahead . . . but we sailed from Philippi: Two scenarios are possible:

1 The delegates set sail from Corinth as planned, disembarked at Troas and waited for Paul there.

2 The whole group travelled together through Macedonia but in Philippi the delegates 'went on ahead' to Troas.

In any case, Paul celebrated the Passover in Philippi, before he set sail for Troas. The crossing from Philippi to Troas took five days (twice as long as the first crossing, 11.11–12). Though he was in a hurry (v. 16), Paul stayed a week in Troas, ministering to the believers there.

Verse 5 resumes the so-called 'we' passages which continue through 21.18. See note on 16.10.

20.7. On the first day of the week, when we met to break bread: This verse provides clear evidence for the weekly Sunday gathering of the Early Church. 'The first day of the week' was a definite day of Christian 'gathering' (1 Corinthians 16.2; 'Lord's day', Revelation 1.10), worshipping God and celebrating the resurrection of Christ by way of breaking the bread (Luke 24.1; 22.19; 24.30; 24.35; Acts 2.42, 46). The believers at Troas met at night, since at that time it was still an ordinary working day. Paul's conversation went on until daylight (v. 11), since the company intended to leave the next day.

20.8–12. A young man named Eutychus . . . fell to the ground: Probably, the warmth of the crowd, the fumes of the oil lamps and the length of Paul's sermon all contributed to the boy's sleepiness. Paul's action resembles the artificial resuscitations by Elijah and Elisha (1 Kings 17.21; 2 Kings 4.34–35). Some explain it differently, but the body had been dead and now was alive, as far as Luke is concerned. This puts Paul on a par with Jesus and Peter (Luke 7.11–15; 8.49–56; Acts 9.36–41). So Paul went on with the journey to the city of his destiny as the victor over death.

20.13–17. He was eager to be in Jerusalem, if possible, on the day of Pentecost: Why Paul walked 30 kilometres to Assos is unclear. From there the ship made its way from one port to another in short one-day journeys to Miletus, stopping at Mitylene, Chios and Samos, all ports of the Aegean islands. Paul had already decided not to visit Ephesus, since he wanted to celebrate Pentecost in Jerusalem. Yet, he stayed in Miletus a few days and he had the elders of the Ephesian church come there for him to make a farewell speech.

There were 'elders' in the churches both in and outside Jerusalem (11.30; 14.23; 15.2, 4, 6, 22, 23; 16.4). For Ephesian elders, see 1 Timothy 5.1, 2, 12, 19 (cf. Titus 1.5; James 5.14; 1 Peter 5.2; 2 John 1; 3 John 1). The verb 'sent for' means 'summoned', suggesting a sense of earnestness and authority.

20.18. You yourselves know how I lived among you the entire time: This is the only speech by Paul in Acts addressed to Christians. Paul began his speech by reminding the elders of his Ephesian ministry in the past. In Greek a special emphasis falls on 'you' (so NRSV). In his Letters too Paul often appeals to the memory of his readers (1 Thessalonians 2.1; Philippians 1.5; 4.15; Colossians 1.6).

20.19. Serving the Lord with all humility and with tears: Humility was a fault, not a virtue in those days. It befitted only a slave, but Paul considered himself as a slave (NRSV: 'serving') of the Lord (Ephesians 4.2; Philippians 2.3; Colossians 2.18; 3.12; cf. Galatians 5.13; 6.2). The reference to 'the plots of the Jews' recalls earlier incidents (Acts 9.23; 20.3) and anticipates later episodes (23.12; 25.3).

20.20–21. Proclaiming the message to you and teaching you publicly and from house to house, as I testified to both Jews and Greeks: These verses provide an excellent summary of Paul's ministry. It was comprehensive, involving preaching (19.8–9; cf. 14.27; 15.4) and teaching (11.26; 15.35; 18.11; cf. 1 Corinthians 16.19) in both public and private settings. It was for both Jews and Greeks (Romans 1.16; 2.9, 10; 3.9; 1 Corinthians 1.24). He preached the need to turn to God in repentance and have faith in the Lord Jesus (cf. Acts 2.38; 1 Thessalonians 1.9). Paul held nothing back that would help his hearers to their salvation; bold speech was a crucial mark of a Spirit-filled witness (Acts 4.13; 9.27–28; 13.46; 19.8).

20.22–24. As a captive to the Spirit, I am on my way to Jerusalem: The Greek can mean either (psychologically) 'I am determined' or (theologically) 'I am compelled by the Spirit' (NIV). Paul himself did not know what would happen, but 'in every city' he would be warned by the Spirit that 'imprisonment' (lit. 'chains') and 'persecutions' awaited him (21.4, 10–11; 2 Corinthians 1.8; Philippians 1.17). More important than his life, however, was to 'finish' his 'course'. Athletic competition was a common metaphor for moral effort, and Paul is fond of using it to describe his apostolic toil (1 Corinthians 9.24; Galatians 2.2; Philippians 3.14; 2 Timothy 4.7). The 'ministry' (Gk, *diakonia*) Paul received was to proclaim the gospel about God's grace to everybody (Acts 9.15; Galatians 1.15), but in this context it might include delivering the collection for the Jerusalem believers (cf. 2 Corinthians 8.9; 9.13).

20.25. None of you . . . will ever see my face again: A formal announcement of departure was a staple element of a 'farewell discourse' (2 Timothy 4.6; 2 Peter 1.13; Luke 22.15–16). This is no more than Paul's human expectation; some of them did probably see him again (2 Timothy 4.20).

20.26–27. I am not responsible for the blood of any of you: For the expression see the note on 18.5. This recalls the watchman of Ezekiel 33.1–6. Paul declared his innocence because he had not hesitated to proclaim 'the whole purpose of God' (v. 27). In verse 21 this will of God is summed up in terms of repentance and faith.

20.28. Keep watch over yourselves and over all the flock: Jesus himself often uttered such a warning to look to oneself (Luke 12.1; 17.3; 20.46; 21.34). See also Acts 20.30. Leaders cannot expect people to be faithful without themselves being faithful. The 'flock' is a familiar biblical metaphor for God's people (Psalm 78.52, 70; Micah 5.4; Isaiah 40.11, etc.). So the elders are called 'shepherds'. This is the only time Luke uses the word 'overseer' (Gk, *episkopos*; Philippians 1.1; 1 Timothy 3.1; Titus 1.7), a title practically synonymous with 'elder' (*presbyteros*). In 1 Peter 2.25 both titles are applied to Jesus: 'the shepherd and guardian (overseer) of your soul'.

In the OT the idea of purchasing or acquiring is related to the theme of election (Isaiah 43.21). The phrase 'by His [God's] own blood' (NKJV) is surprising. But it can also be translated 'by the blood of his own', i.e. 'by the blood of his own Son' (NRSV; cf. Romans 8.32).

20.29. After I have gone, savage wolves will come in among you: Here the idea of going clearly means death, not Paul leaving the Ephesians. A farewell discourse often contained a prediction of future trouble after the death of the hero (2 Timothy 3.1–5; 4.3–4; 2 Peter 2.1–3). The warning continues the pastoral metaphor and it also reflects the warning of Jesus himself: 'like sheep among wolves' (Luke 10.3; 12.32; cf. John 21.15–17; 1 Peter 5.2). The warning was about hard-line Jewish Christian missionaries who were forcing the Gentiles to take up 'works of the law' such as circumcision and the Jewish calendar (2 Corinthians 11.4; Galatians 1.6–9; 6.12–13; Philippians 3.2–11).

20.30. Some even from your own group will come distorting the truth in order to entice the disciples to follow them: This is the danger from within the church (cf. 1 John 2.19). The desire of false teachers would be making the believers follow themselves rather than the Lord (Galatians 5.7). Paul's two Letters sent to Timothy in Ephesus show that his warning here was not an idle one (1 Timothy 1.6–7, 9–20; 4.1–3; 2 Timothy 1.15; 2.17–18; 3.1–9; cf. Revelation 2.1–7).

20.32. I commend you to God and to the message of his grace: That is, 'his word about his saving grace'. This word is able to bring believers to maturity ('building up'; Ephesians 4.12), until they attain to the promised inheritance, i.e. their final salvation (1.14, 18; 5.5). The leaders are no less subject to the authority of God's word than their flock.

20.33–34. I worked with my own hands to support myself: In Ephesus Paul had worked (probably with Priscilla and Aquila) to support himself and his companions. In Greek 'with my own hands' is emphatic; we can picture Paul holding up his hands before the elders. Thus Paul presented his own practice as an example of controlling greed for money.

20.35. It is more blessed to give than to receive: We do not find any such words in the Gospels but the Ephesians were familiar with the idea.

The Lord wants his followers to work hard for the benefit of others. The word 'must' implies divine necessity. Those words of Jesus which are not recorded in the Gospels but found in other early Christian writing, especially in other books of the NT, are called *'agrapha (logia)'*, a Greek expression meaning 'unwritten (sayings)' (1 Corinthians 9.14).

20.36–38. He knelt down with them all and prayed: The Jews usually stood to pray, so the kneeling posture indicates the solemnity of the occasion (cf. 1 Kings 8.54; Ezra 9.5). It was also a distinctively Christian way of praying (9.40; 21.5; Luke 22.41; Ephesians 3.14; Philippians 2.10). Since Luke portrays Paul's trip to Jerusalem in a way that recalls Jesus' trip there, the scene also reminds us of Jesus who 'knelt down and prayed' after his farewell discourse (Luke 22.41).

 ## Interpretation

Paul's journey to Macedonia and Greece

About this time Paul was having a hard time with the Corinthian church with regard to his apostolic authority. His own and Timothy's visit did not help to ease the tension, so he sent Titus with another letter (now lost). Unable to wait for his return, he went ahead to Troas hoping to meet him there. He was full of anxiety and physically ill, but he preached the gospel there and found that the Lord had opened 'a door' to him (2 Corinthians 2.12). But he could not put his heart into it. Failing to meet Titus at Troas, he decided to go to Macedonia himself (2 Corinthians 2.13). Paul met Titus in Macedonia who brought reassuring news to Paul's great relief and joy (2 Corinthians 7.6–7).

The Lord's day and the Lord's Supper

The Christians in Troas gathered together on the Lord's day to celebrate the Lord's Supper. This provided them with occasions for experiencing the presence of the risen Christ who had died for them and celebrating their God-given unity under the guidance of the Spirit. This formed the core of their Christian identity and the basis for their service both in the church and out in the world. The Church should surely be 'the salt of the earth' and 'the light of the world' but we first need to possess saltiness or brightness, i.e. our distinctive Christian identity, in order to be of any service to others. And we gain such identity from our act of gathering together and worshipping the same God in the name of one Jesus Christ. It would be foolish to expect a healthy and active church without making due effort to gather together and worship as one body of Christ (cf. Hebrews 10.25). To be sure, life together is never easy. Many Christians are frustrated by the problems within the Christian community. This leads some to say that the Church is unnecessary, or even harmful, to healthy Christian life. Yet giving up Christian *koinōnia* is giving up Christian life altogether, since God is accomplishing his work of redemption by bringing people together and making them learn how to live together peacefully in mutual love. Avoiding problems does not solve them. So, if the situation allows it, we have to make every effort to maintain proper Christian fellowship.

Paul as a model: Paul's farewell speech

Paul's farewell address to the Ephesian elders follows the typical pattern of the genre of farewell address:

1 he warns the elders about difficulties that lie ahead; and

2 he sets himself up as a model for the elders to imitate.

Paul very much stresses his own integrity and uprightness as a God-appointed minister. For Paul the gospel was not a matter of mere talk but of power (1 Corinthians 4.19–20). Thus, the work of proclaiming it involved not only words but also deeds (Romans 15.18), so that the Gentiles might hear him and imitate him. So he often told his Gentile converts to imitate him, just as he had become an imitator of Jesus (1 Corinthians 4.6, 16; 11.1; Galatians 4.12; Philippians 3.17), and commended them for doing so (1 Thessalonians 1.6). Christianity is not just an idea to accept but a 'way' of life to walk. Thus an indispensable part of becoming a good Christian leader is becoming a good Christian to set a good example for others to follow (1 Peter 5.3). The American mythologist Joseph Campbell once remarked that Christian ministers were at pains to explain the gospel with words when it is much more effective to let others see it. Or do we use so many words because we do not have much to display?

 STUDY SUGGESTIONS

Word study

1 What is the meaning of 'encouraging' in Paul?

   (a) 14.22; 16.40; (b) Romans 12.1; Ephesians 4.1.

Review of content

2 Why did Paul decide to go to Jerusalem by way of Macedonia?

3 When and for what purpose did the believers in Troas meet?

4 In his farewell speech to the Ephesians' elders, what did Paul say about his ministry and what warning did he give to the elders?

5 What word of Jesus did Paul quote which is not recorded in the Gospels?

Bible study

6 Read the following passages. What significance did 'breaking bread' have in the Early Church?

(a) Luke 22.19; 24.30, 35; (b) Acts 2.42, 46; 20.7.

7 Paul often puts himself forward as an example for the believers to imitate. What can we learn from Paul's example in the following passages?

(a) 1 Corinthians 4.6; 11.1; (b) 1 Thessalonians 1.6; Philippians 3.17.

Discussion and application

8 What do you think about Paul's bringing Eutychus back to life? Was it a miracle or can we explain it in different ways?

9 In his farewell speech Paul underscores his integrity as a pastor. Why do you think it is important?

Theological essay 4

Leadership in the Early Church and today

VÍCTOR HERNÁNDEZ-RAMÍREZ

The book of the Acts of the Apostles is also known as the 'Acts of the Holy Spirit' because it highlights the action of the Holy Spirit in pushing the Christian mission beyond all boundaries. It shows us especially the action of the Spirit upon the Church's leaders, on the testimony that presents the good news. That action often breaks cultural patterns, overcomes religious prejudices or resolves ethnic conflicts. It is the Spirit who pushes beyond these situations and moves the mission forward.

We shall now look at how the Holy Spirit can guide us in choosing leaders, in conflict management, in service to the weak, in integrating the personal with community and, finally, in adopting the pastoral approach that is required of Christian leaders.

Acts 1.15–16 Election of leaders

Churches, or communities of faith, often have an established system for the election of their leaders. Except at the very beginning of a religious movement, it is usual for a church to have defined rules and customs for choosing its leaders.

It is helpful to set out a way of choosing leaders, since it is important to define the means of access to power within an organization. Having recognized the usefulness of a system, however, we often find that the choice of leaders becomes a bureaucratic process that can pervert the purpose of leaders or create a minority class, an elite, with privileged access to power.

Against this phenomenon of the institutionalization of leadership – that is, rigidity and privileges in access to and use of power – we may set the teaching of the book of Acts, testimony to another way of electing leaders.

The story of the election of Matthias has a surprising element, because it starts with the 'anti-testimony' of Judas Iscariot. It takes an experience of failure and disappointment to show the need to elect a new apostle. It is striking that it is Peter who speaks, since Peter was also a traitor, someone who denied knowing Jesus in the darkest hour. The text describes the election of the twelfth apostle and Peter sets the criteria: it must be a man (Gk, *aner*) and must be someone who was with Jesus from his baptism with John until the day of his Ascension. Some people are critical of Peter's procedure, since it is apparently not guided by the Holy Spirit; instead the primacy of the apostolic group is imposed.

In any case, what the text allows us to learn about the election of leaders is the primacy of following Jesus. The following of Jesus is focused in the historical life of Jesus – his actions and teachings – and is the foundation of the apostolic witness. No one can be a leader through personal success or good intentions, but only through loyalty in following the resurrected Lord.

Acts 6.1–6 Service to the weak and the service of the word

It is commonly said that leadership is related to service. It is understood that the purpose of those who govern is to serve others. Modern societies – Western societies – have a common commitment to democracy, which insists that leaders must be elected by their citizens to serve the people.

However, it is also common for political leaders only to develop an interest in people during – or in relation to – a political campaign. It is said, with irony, that real democracy has a very short duration: the period of voting. After election day comes an exercise of power where leaders are directed by other interests and the common good is often overlooked.

In the exercise of political leadership it is very common to prioritize economic interests. For example, rulers swiftly offer aid to banks or financial institutions in an economic crisis at the expense of social assistance for the unemployed, or for health or education.

Jesus mentions kings who rule tyrannically yet claim the title of benefactors (Luke 22.25), and teaches the disciples that they should not be like that. Rather Jesus teaches that among the disciples the boss should be like a slave, someone who serves others. This criterion of service is essential to recognize among the skills of Christian leadership. But it must be service not limited to discourse, but demonstrated in action. When service is the purpose of leadership, this prevents power-seeking and reaching for the top position.

In the narrative of Acts 6, we find an important lesson about the connection between service and leadership. The election of deacons (slaves or servants) takes place as a result of conflict, a situation of controversy: the 'Greeks' are complaining about the 'Jews' because the Greek widows are not receiving the help they need. It seems that, as the church has grown, discrimination against a group or sector of society has developed. Some scholars hypothesize that there were two groups in Jerusalem, Jewish Christian 'Greeks' who were Greek-speaking and had a more critical attitude toward the Temple (as exemplified in the case of Stephen, the first martyr) and Jewish Christians, 'Jews' with a less critical approach to temple worship and represented by 'the Twelve'.

Thus the text tells us of a tense situation, which could be managed by dominant leaders in top-down style but yet is not so. The leaders – Peter and the rest of the Twelve – invite the entire community to participate and propose to elect seven people 'full of the Holy Spirit and wisdom'. The men elected are all from the Greek community party (Jewish Christians who are Greek), as is shown by their Greek names. We note that this is not a 'new ecclesiastical office', but a dynamic response to a real situation, which shows the implementation of the criterion of service set by Jesus (Matthew 20.20–28; Mark 10.35–45; Luke 22.24–27). This criterion of service, very important in the life and teaching of Jesus, was also common in Greek popular philosophy. For example, the truth of the teaching of Philo of Alexandria, a Jewish philosopher, was verified by his example of service.

A problem arises when the purpose of service becomes perverted in the exercise of leadership. This perversion is seen in contemporary societies – as democratically elected leaders tend to follow interests that are not for the common good. The writer Jose Saramago has said that we should have democratic elections to appoint or remove members of boards of multinational corporations and large financial institutions, because these people make decisions that affect the entire planet. As he thus suggests, the problem of democracy is that elections don't affect the real power in the world (economic power). Church institutions copy the practice of their contexts, so we should watch carefully what Christian leaders do. The lesson is that church leadership should work for the people's benefit and not for other interests (as the culture of capitalism indicates).

Indigenous communities in south-eastern Mexico – the Zapatista movement – say that leaders chosen by the people must exercise leadership in the following way: leaders must 'lead by obeying'. And they say that there are leaders who 'command commanding' and neither obey the will of the people they represent, nor seek the common good. In such cases – say the Zapatistas – the leaders must be removed and replaced by others with a different heart, a heart that has the humility and strength to serve, to 'lead (order) by obeying'. I think that the Indians of south-eastern Mexico have suitably updated the teaching of Jesus: anyone who wants to be above others must be their servant.

But how do we ensure that leadership, whatever the method of choice or the system of organization, is directed towards the principle of 'serving others'? Again we must remember the importance that Acts gives to the Holy Spirit's guidance. The apostles respond to a need among a neglected part of the community and the main leaders propose electing native leaders, who are 'full of the Spirit and of wisdom'. We will see that these deacons were leaders who knew the Scriptures and could discuss them with the priests (like Stephen), or could explain and share the gospel with foreigners or Gentiles (like Philip who speaks with the Ethiopian eunuch).

That 'fullness of the Spirit' refers to a quality that can be understood as a radical attitude of service. But service in two specific ways: service to the word, because the lives of the deacons are devoted to teaching the word of God and, at the same time, service to others, because they serve the tables 'caring for widows'. This form of service practised by the new leaders has a novelty: an openness to other people who are not of their circle. So, they are the first to cross ethnic boundaries and spread the gospel beyond the Jewish circle to the Samaritans and the Gentiles.

The filling of the Spirit, therefore, is expressed in actions of service to others, where the word of God is always present. The presence of the Spirit is the force that breaks the barriers of culture or race. Thus begins a programme which will accomplish the mission laid down by the risen Lord, to be witnesses from Jerusalem to the ends of the earth.

Acts 13.1–4 The mission as community and personal commitment

Dreams offer us a glimpse beyond the horizon; they show us a new horizon, that exists only as a possibility. In dreams we look at what does not yet exist, but has begun to take shape. And as the dream takes shape it forms something original, like a hidden seed that has begun to germinate.

There are dreams that are forgotten and there are dreams that arise and are shared, that make a group of people start to dream together. Those dreams become a project, a mission project. The mission of the church of Antioch in Syria to other lands was a dream of the entire community. It was a dream that came from the touch of the Holy Spirit and was under his direction. The text teaches us to recognize the specific situation that made this dream possible.

The situation of this community is very interesting, because it is the first church in the narrative of Acts to include both Jews and non-Jews. It is the first experience of the close mixing of people. People can recognize each other in the passage of days and weeks, as they live together closely, sharing meals and celebrations. It is in sharing living and time that they overcome their previous prejudices. This experience often involves difficulties, misunderstandings and – sometimes – conflict. But it is an experience that enriches us and teaches us to recognize the power of faith in common, precisely because we thereby recognize and respect the differences of others.

In this community of Antioch there were leaders who taught the word within this new experience of multiculturalism. Inside this dynamic experience of learning in multiculturalism emerged a dream mission: to go beyond the borders of the Middle East, beyond Syria to the northern cities of Asia Minor, closer to the centre of the Roman Empire. The text speaks of moments of prayer and fasting. Times of worship show us that an experience of multicultural Christian community can be possible only within a living spirituality, inside a life of communion with God.

Those elected to go beyond the borders are two of its best teachers: Barnabas and Saul. There are other teachers and prophets (the text portrays a diversity of origin and ethnicity among them), but the Holy Spirit draws these two. And the community is not selfish or closed to the project and so is willing to send two of its best men. It responds in obedience, in an atmosphere of prayer and fasting.

What we may realize immediately is that the Gentile mission is not a personal project of Paul's, but a community project of the whole church of Antioch. The text tells us that the Holy Spirit communicates with everyone, with the entire community, saying: 'Set apart for me Barnabas and Saul for the work to which I called them.' It is possible to talk of a dream or project of the entire community and say, therefore, that the economic and spiritual support for the missionary journeys of Paul came from the whole of the Antioch church.

This shows how intertwined were the dimensions of community and individual commitment: everybody was included, both the members and leaders. It was a synergy of personal dreams and the coordination of support from the entire community. Not only can we think about the material support and ongoing community prayers for Paul and Barnabas, but we can also think of the letters they exchanged, in the narrative of events, achievements and difficulties, as they preached the good news in the lands they visited.

The previous experiences of Paul and Barnabas as teachers at Antioch, a multicultural community, were important. They learned a lot from that 'experiment' of co-existence, conflict management and growth in a community where Jews and Gentiles learned to share everything.

Acts 20.17–36 Christian leadership always entails a pastoral attitude

There are different visions of leadership. It is a task that involves coordinating the talents and gifts of others. Leaders are models for following Jesus, teachers who convey practical wisdom based on the Bible, and inspirers of dreams about love for the kingdom of God.

But whatever vision of leadership we have for leaders in the Church (and I think the above are views that include features required for Christian leadership), the most important aspect is a 'pastoral spirit'.

Leadership is the exercise of power. It implies a certain influence over others, which requires great responsibility in its exercise. This responsibility is expressed as care for the growth of others and the community in general. The power of leadership, understood as helping to guide, teach, model to, share with and listen to members of a community, must be exercised with pastoral care.

And the pastoral approach is characterized by the attitude of service. Paul reminds the elders of Ephesus, in the farewell that takes place at Miletus, of their duty of service, which is the pastoral approach (Acts 20.28). Before the leaders of Ephesus, Paul appeals to the memory of his dedication to others and to the tears he shed during his teaching and accompaniment of others. He mentions the humility which he showed to others even though he was their teacher and pastor. He also stresses that he has preached 'anything that would be helpful to them', showing the attitude of service necessary for a preacher. The most important trait of leadership, the criterion that defines it, is the pastoral attitude of service. It is seen most clearly in the example of Jesus, who became a servant of others and taught us how to exercise leadership.

One of the most beautiful images of Jesus is as the shepherd, who gives his life for his sheep (John 10). It is an image that expresses criticism of religious leaders who have no interest in the welfare of people (for example, in John 9, where the priests are more concerned about the sabbath law, and forget the blind man who was healed by Jesus). Jesus was someone who put people above the traditions or rules of any institution, and that attitude brought upon him the hostility of the powerful. But that pastoral concern is the attitude of service that Jesus expects of every leader.

In conclusion, leaders are to take on pastoral care for others, being attentive to the growth of each individual and the whole community. This attitude of pastoral care derives not from any personal quality or power that enables the person to take on a leading role, but from the fact that the Lord has given his life for all. It is the love of Jesus Christ that motivates the pastoral devotion of the Christian leader.

Acts 21.1–36

Paul's arrival and arrest

 Summary

Paul arrives at Jerusalem and is welcomed by the leaders of the Jerusalem Church. A misunderstanding leads to his arrest.

 Notes

21.1–3. When we . . . set sail, we came by a straight course to Cos . . . we sailed to Syria and landed at Tyre: The journey was along the southwest coast of Asia Minor and then south-east to the Phoenician Tyre, an important centre of trade and industry. It will be helpful to follow the route on Map 3 (p. 190).

21.4. Through the Spirit they told Paul not to go on to Jerusalem: While waiting for the ship to unload the cargo (cf. v. 5: 'when our days there were ended'), the missionaries paid a visit to the disciples there. For the presence of believers in Tyre, see 11.19 and Luke 6.17. Paul himself had met them before (Acts 11.30; 12.25; 15.3).

The disciples probably misinterpreted the message of the Spirit, since Paul's decision to go to Jerusalem had also been made through the Spirit (19.21). Now the Spirit's city-by-city warning begins to be realized (20.23).

21.5–6. There we knelt down on the beach and prayed: See the note on 20.36.

21.7–9. We went into the house of Philip the evangelist, one of the seven: It is not clear whether they took another ship to Caesarea (RSV) or travelled there by road (NIV). The Greek can mean both, though the latter is more likely. Both Ptolemais (ancient Accho) and Caesarea were major ports along the eastern coast of the Mediterranean. Paul had probably visited the disciples in these cities (Ptolemais, 11.30; 12.25; 15.3 and Caesarea, 9.30; 18.22). Of course, Caesarea was the place of Cornelius's conversion (10.1, 24; 11.11). Here Philip, 'one of the seven', appears again after the conversion of the Ethiopian eunuch (6.3; 8.26–40). Luke calls

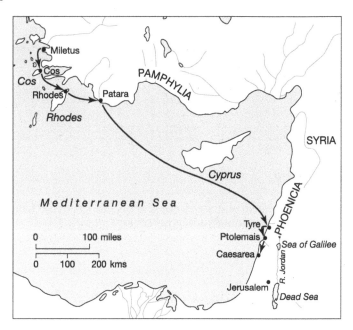

Map 3 Acts 21.1–3
Source: Tom Wright, *The New Testament for Everyone* (SPCK, 2011), p. 313.

him 'evangelist' (cf. Ephesians 4.11; 2 Timothy 4.5). Luke also mentions four unmarried prophetess-daughters of Philip but they do not play any role in the story.

21.10–14. I am ready not only to be bound, but even to die in Jerusalem for the name of the Lord Jesus: Agabus appears for the second time (11.28), now to predict Paul's destiny in Jerusalem. His symbolic action recalls those of OT prophets (1 Kings 11.29–39; Isaiah 20.2; Jeremiah 13.1–11; Ezekiel 4.1–8). The 'handing over to the Gentiles' echoes the prediction of Jesus about his own suffering (Luke 9.44; 18.32; 24.7) and about the destiny of Peter (John 21.18). We will see the fulfilment of this prophecy in Acts 21.33. So 'in every city' the Holy Spirit kept warning Paul of his impending affliction (20.23).

Once again, the believers misinterpreted the prophetic message and tried to dissuade Paul from continuing his journey to Jerusalem but failed. 'Breaking my heart' probably means 'weakening my resolution' (see the Jerusalem Bible); so Paul unambiguously declares his resolution once again: 'I, on my part, am ready' (the Greek is emphatic). The willingness to suffer 'for the name of the Lord Jesus' proves that Paul was a faithful disciple of Jesus (9.16; also 5.41; Luke 6.22; 21.12, 17). Paul's resolution also echoes the affirmation of the Jerusalem leaders (Acts 15.26). In a way, the emotional engagement between Paul and the rest recalls the struggle between Jesus and Satan in the form of Peter (Mark 8.32–38). In the end the believers gave up and left the matter with God. The phrase 'the Lord's will be done' is missing in Luke's version of the Lord's Prayer (Luke 11.2; cf. 22.42; Matthew 6.10).

21.15-16. After these days, we got ready and started to go up to Jerusalem: So the company finally arrived at Jerusalem. Mnason, Paul's host in Jerusalem, was a Cypriot Jew and 'an early disciple'. It is possible that he was one of those 'men from Cyprus and from Cyrene' who had preached the gospel to the Gentiles (11.20). As is seen clearly in the travel narrative, hospitality was an important part of the early Christian mission (9.43; 10.6; 16.15, 40; 21.4, 8; Luke 9.3–5; 10.4–12).

21.17. When we arrived at Jerusalem, the brothers welcomed us warmly: Luke keeps underscoring that Paul was not rejected by the Jerusalem church (cf. Romans 15.31).

21.18-20a. Paul went with us to visit James; and all the elders were present: Clearly, this was a more formal meeting. Paul's 'report' of 'the things God had done among the Gentiles' echoes an earlier report at the Jerusalem Council (15.12). It was not about what Paul himself had done but what God had done through him (14.27; 15.4; also 2.47; 8.26, 29; 10.1—11.8; Romans 15.18-19; Galatians 2.7-8). His point was well taken, so the leaders praised God for that.

21.20b-21. They have been told about you that you teach all the Jews living among the Gentiles to forsake Moses: Paul was warmly welcomed by the leaders but the overall atmosphere of the Jewish Christians was not so favourable to him, since they continued to be loyal to the Jewish way of life. The existence of many thousands of believers in Jerusalem recalls the episodes of mass conversion in the early days of the Church (2.41; 4.4; 6.7). Being 'zealous for the law' involved both zeal for observance of the Torah and hostility toward any perceived threat to it (22.3; 1 Maccabees 2.27; 2 Maccabees 4.2; Romans 10.2; Galatians 1.14).

The charge was apostasy (Gk, *apostasia*) from Moses, i.e. from the Torah. More concretely, Paul had been suspected of discouraging the Diaspora Jews from circumcising their children or from living according to the Jewish customs. It was clearly a false accusation, since he never gave such an instruction. Moreover, he himself had remained a good Jew: he had Timothy circumcised (Acts 16.3), had taken a Nazirite vow (18.18) and had observed the feasts (20.5, 7). His laxity toward the law only concerned the Gentiles. To be sure, Paul himself did not insist on behaving like a Jew and could mix with the Gentiles quite freely. Perhaps such flexibility could easily be misunderstood as promoting apostasy from the Torah.

21.22-26. Thus all will know that there is nothing in what they have been told about you, but that you yourself observe and guard the law:

Paul's presence in Jerusalem did not make things easy for the leaders of the Jerusalem church. The only solution was to demonstrate publicly how faithful a Jew Paul was. James advised Paul to show it by joining the Nazirite purification rites with four other men and paying the expense of shaving their heads. Paul had no qualms about acquiescing to James's suggestion for the benefit of the Church. See 1 Corinthians 9.19–23 for the self-effacing principle of Paul's conduct. So Paul did as advised, apparently, according to the prescribed regulations (cf. Numbers 6.1–21, especially v. 9).

The reminder of the apostolic decree by James is a bit odd (Acts 21.25; 15.23–29), since Paul himself delivered it to the Gentile churches (15.12, 22–26; 16.4). James probably mentioned it to bring out the possibility that Jewish Christians might have become impure by associating with Gentile believers.

21.27–30. The Jews from Asia, who had seen him in the temple, stirred up the whole crowd: Ironically, the measure to mollify the Jewish Christian suspicion sowed the seed for Paul's arrest. The Jewish crowd at the pilgrimage periods was quite volatile, especially when it came to such sensitive issues as the law and the Temple. It had already been illustrated by the stoning of Stephen by the angry crowd (7.57—8.1).

The accusation brought against Paul was twofold:

1 He was teaching against Judaism ('our people, our law, and this place'). So Luke links the incident with the widespread suspicion about Paul even among Christians.

2 But the immediate cause of the rage was not the Christians but 'some Jews from Asia' who misunderstood that Paul had profaned the Temple by bringing Gentiles into it.

The Gentiles were allowed up to the Court of the Gentiles but prohibited from going further into the temple precinct on the penalty of death. Paul was not with the Gentile Trophimus, but they assumed that Trophimus was in the Temple because they had earlier seen Paul with him in the city. The outraged Jews dragged him out of the inner courts (restricted to the Jews) to the Court of the Gentiles, perhaps to prevent any further pollution. The crowd began to beat him, with the intention of killing him there and then, as in the case of Stephen. This reminds us why Paul asked the Roman believers to pray for his deliverance from the unbelieving Jews in Jerusalem (Romans 15.31).

21.31–36. The tribune came, arrested him, and ordered him to be bound with two chains: The Roman army intervened swiftly, since such a dangerous situation could easily turn into a riot. (The report that the whole of Jerusalem was in an uproar seems a bit exaggerated.) The temple precinct was connected to the Fortress Antonia ('barracks') by two flights of steps (see Map 4, on p. 193). The tribune (lit. 'leader of a thousand') was the head of a 'cohort'. His name was Claudius Lysias (23.2). He thought Paul to be a criminal of some sort, so had him arrested and bound with chains. This fulfils the prophecy of Agabus (21.11; cf. 12.6). The tribune

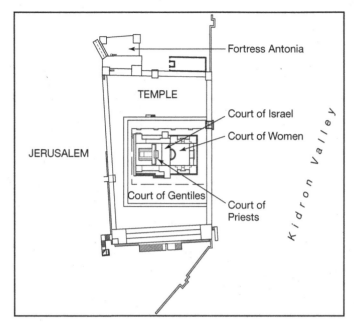

Map 4 Fortress Antonia and the temple precinct
Source: Adapted from Tom Wright, *The New Testament for Everyone* (SPCK, 2011), p. 253.

tried to find out the cause of the uproar, but it is unclear whom the tribune actually questioned, Paul or the crowd. In any case, the commotion made the investigation impossible and so he had Paul taken into the barracks. The shouting of the crowd echoes the cry which the crowd had shouted against Jesus (Luke 23.18; John 19.15; cf. Acts 22.22).

21.37–40. I am a Jew, from Tarsus in Cilicia, a citizen of an important city; I beg you, let me speak to the people: Paul's surprising knowledge of Greek prompted the tribune to consider the possibility that Paul might be a Jewish revolutionary from Egypt. (The tribune's remark in v. 38 is a positive conjecture, not a negative question.) This person had gathered thirty thousand men to the Mount of Olives to make an attack on Jerusalem. The procurator Felix had crushed them, but the Egyptian had fled, and now the tribune suspected this Paul might be the same man. Paul's self-identification was twofold:

1   he was a Jew, i.e. not a person who might defile the Temple;

2   he was a citizen of Tarsus, i.e. not an Egyptian revolutionary.

Paul then received the tribune's permission and spoke to the Jews in 'the Hebrew language', namely, in Aramaic (see notes on 6.1). A fluent Aramaic speech by a person suspected to have defiled the Temple attracted the immediate attention of the Jewish crowd, since not many Diaspora Jews were able to speak Aramaic. (Remember the Greek-speaking Jews, namely, the Hellenists, within the Church in Acts 6.)

 ## Interpretation

Paul's journey toward Jerusalem, like that of Jesus in the Gospel of Luke, was overshadowed by a growing sense of imminent suffering in Jerusalem. The Spirit kept warning Paul of the impending persecution, and Paul approached Jerusalem with a full awareness of it (20.23–24; 21.4, 11–14). Paul did what he could to avoid unnecessary trouble within the church, but he was arrested and beaten by the angry crowd in the temple precinct, before he was subsequently handed over to the 'Gentile' Romans. He had the Spirit-given conviction that he would be able to see Rome after his visit to Jerusalem (19.21), but he had no idea how it would materialize. From then on Paul would spend two years in Jerusalem and Caesarea as a prisoner. In the following stories, he would have to defend himself before the Jewish authorities, the Roman governors and King Herod, before his appeal to Caesar and subsequent travel to Rome.

Paul's journey to Jerusalem and subsequently to Rome takes up a quarter of the whole book of Acts. This makes us wonder why Luke devotes so much space to it. Luke does not give us any reasons, but we may venture a guess. First, we have already noted the fact that he describes Paul's journey to Jerusalem as a kind of parallel to that of Jesus: Paul was a faithful follower of Jesus who did not hesitate to sacrifice even his life to carry out God's will. Second, Paul stayed in Jerusalem and Caesarea as a prisoner defending his own innocence before both the Jewish and the Roman authorities. Luke repeatedly underscores that Paul was a Jew loyal to the faith of his ancestors on the one hand, and that he was an innocent citizen of the Roman Empire deserving neither death nor imprisonment on the other.

Christians in disagreement

In Acts 21 we observe two interesting cases of disagreement between Paul and other believers. Paul was determined to go on to Jerusalem, while other believers tried to dissuade him from doing so. Both believed that they were acting according to the guidance of the Spirit, but their actual courses of action were polar opposites. Many of us are quite familiar with situations like this: confessing the same faith but drawing different practical implications out of it. We all read the same Scripture but different groups of Christians have different stances on many important issues, both theologically and practically. For example, many Christian leaders in Korea say that Christians should lend unreserved support to the president who is a Christian elder. But others are very critical of him, saying that many of his policies run counter to Christian values.

God gives us revelations either in Scripture or through other means. Very often, however, we have to interpret them in order to find out what concrete course of action we are to take, like Peter in Caesarea or Paul in Troas. So the believers in Tyre and Caesarea mistook the prophetic prediction of persecution for a prohibition, while Paul took it to be a preparatory warning to make him ready to face what lay ahead. In the end the believers gave in, saying 'God's will be done'. In this way they recognized the possibility that they might be wrong and God's will in fact might lie somewhere else than in Paul's personal safety. This makes us cautious, since our interpretation of God's will is often influenced by our own desires or fears (Romans 8.26). It teaches us the importance of humility and sober acknowledgement of our weakness in finding out what God's will is in our lives. Such humility will often save us from unnecessary conflicts that hinder Christian fellowship. We also note the importance of open communication among Christians for finding out God's will for us all.

Faithful yet flexible

The apostles and elders in Jerusalem had their own problems to solve in their relationship with the non-believing Jews around them. Paul fully understood the situation, and so unreservedly followed the advice of James to perform a purification rite publicly in order to avoid unnecessary conflict with the more conservative Jewish Christians. Paul did so, not because it was mandatory but because he wanted to maintain the peace of the church in Jerusalem. He was a man of principle, but he was also ready to compromise, as long as it did not damage the truth of the gospel (1 Corinthians 9.19–23). What we need, therefore, is the ability to discern what is essential from what is not: are we trying to maintain our own position or are we trying to promote the truth of the gospel itself?

 STUDY SUGGESTIONS

Review of content

1 Why does Luke devote so much space to Paul's travels to Jerusalem and to Rome?

2 In what cities did the believers try to keep Paul from going to Jerusalem?

3 What was Paul's answer to the Spirit-prompted dissuasion of the believers?

4 What did James suggest to Paul to clear up the suspicion of the Jewish Christians?

5 Why did Paul agree to the suggestion of James?

6 Who were the men who initially stirred up the crowd in the Temple?

7 What two facts about himself did Paul reveal to the tribune?

Bible study

8 Read the following passages and see how the OT prophets used symbolic actions to proclaim their messages.

(a) 1 Kings 11.29–31; (b) Isaiah 20.2–5; (c) Jeremiah 13.1–9; (d) Ezekiel 4.1–3.

9 Read Romans 2.1–19. Is it true to say that Paul taught the Jews against the law (Torah)?

Discussion and application

10 Even sincere believers often face mutual disagreement among themselves. Can you think of any examples? What do you think is the best way of resolving the tension?

11 What do you think of Paul's decision to acquiesce to the suggestion of James? Is Paul's 'compromise' justifiable?

Acts 22.1–29

Paul defends himself before the crowd

 Summary

Paul shows himself to be a loyal Jew by recounting his earlier passion for the law and his conversion–calling. He reveals his Roman citizenship to the tribune.

 Notes

22.1–2. When they heard him addressing them in Hebrew, they became even more quiet: Paul's use of the Jewish language and Jewish style of address ('brothers and fathers') further underscores his solidarity with the Jews. Here the 'Hebrew' actually means Aramaic, the everyday language of the Palestine Jews of the day. For Gamaliel see the note on 5.34.

22.3–5. I am a Jew . . . being zealous for God, just as all of you are today: Paul's account of his past life in Judaism parallels his own words in his Letters (Galatians 1.13–17; Philippians 3.4–11; 1 Timothy 1.12–16). Here he makes two main points. First, he was 'born' in Tarsus but 'brought up' in Jerusalem and 'trained' (Gk, *paideuō*) under Gamaliel (see Acts 5.34; Luke uses the same verbs for Moses in 7.20–22). Second, he had been so zealous to God as to persecute the Church (Galatians 1.14; cf. Romans 10.2). For his persecution see the notes on Acts 9.1–2 (22.20; 26.10). Here Paul appeals to the common memory of the Jewish leaders: 'as the high priest and the whole council . . . can testify'.

22.6–11. About noon a great light from heaven suddenly shone about me: Paul recounts his conversion in his own words (9.3–9). Verse 9 ('saw the light'; 'did not hear the voice') seems to conflict with 9.7 where Paul's companions did hear the voice but did not see anything, but NIV is probably right in taking it in the sense of understanding rather than sensory perception itself (cf. John 12.29). Paul's question, 'What am I to do, Lord?' in v. 10 is an addition to the earlier version. Jesus' response (v. 10) is much expanded in 26.16. 'The glory (so the Greek; NRSV: "brightness") of the light' echoes Paul's own words in 2 Corinthians 4.6: 'God . . . has shone in our hearts to give the light of the knowledge of the glory of God in the face of Jesus Christ.'

22.12–16. The God of our ancestors has chosen you . . . you will be his witness to all the world: These verses recount Paul's commissioning through Ananias. Paul naturally did not refer to the vision of Ananias and his subsequent struggle (9.10–16). Instead, Paul accentuated that his conversion–calling had been mediated by such 'a devout observer of the law and highly respected by all the Jews living there'. Paul did not mention his being also a Christian (cf. 9.10). Here God is referred to as 'the God of our ancestors'. Paul also did not use the word 'Gentile' at this point but said instead the more general 'all men' in stating his own mission (cf. 9.15), probably to avoid premature provocation of his audience. Paul was to be 'a witness to all the world of what he had seen and heard': he had now seen the risen Christ and heard his voice. So having seen the risen Jesus was an essential qualification of a witness, since witness is about the resurrection of Jesus more than anything else (1.21–22; 1 Corinthians 9.1; Galatians 1.15–16). For the designation of Jesus as 'the Righteous', see Luke 23.47 (NRSV margin); Acts 3.14; 7.52.

22.17–21. Go, for I will send you far away to the Gentiles: Paul's praying in the Jerusalem Temple was not mentioned earlier but is included here, no doubt, to underscore his loyalty as a Jew. Would any Jew who had prayed in the Temple dare to defile it? (cf. Isaiah 6.1–10). Paul also did not say anything about the Jewish plot against him either in Damascus or in Jerusalem (Acts 9.23–25, 29–30). Instead he recounted his escape from Jerusalem and going to the Gentiles as part of God's plan. As for Paul himself, he would have stayed in Jerusalem; if the Jews would listen to anyone, it would be to someone like him: a zealous persecutor of the Way now turned into its witness (vv. 19–20). But the Lord had a different plan for him: he had called Paul to send him 'far away to the Gentiles' (v. 21). So his being the apostle for the Gentiles was in obedience to 'the God of our ancestors'.

That Paul was an apostle specifically for the Gentiles is reflected in many places in his Letters (e.g. Romans 11.13; Galatians 1.16). Here Stephen is called 'martyr'. In this context it should be understood as 'witness' but it would soon gain the meaning 'martyr' as we use it in English.

In Acts 9.17–18 Ananias's mediation of the Spirit was followed by Paul's baptism, but here Paul only mentioned his baptism for the forgiveness of sin without saying anything about the Holy Spirit. We should remember that Luke does not have any intention of systematizing the conversion process.

22.22–23. They shouted, 'Away with such a fellow from the earth!': Apparently, the mention of Gentiles in v. 21 triggered the outburst (21.36). The suspicion was that Paul was extending salvation to the Gentiles without requiring them to take up 'the yoke of the law' and the angry crowd would not allow this. They now demanded that Paul be killed. Shouting, throwing off their cloaks and flinging dust into the air all express their rage (2 Samuel 16.13; Job 2.12; Revelation 18.19; cf. Acts 7.58; 22.20). This recalls the murderous cries of the Jerusalem crowd against Jesus (John 18.40; 19.6, 12, 15).

22.24–29. This man is a Roman citizen: The commander could not understand Paul's speech given in Aramaic. The outrage of the crowd probably confirmed his initial conviction that Paul must have committed some serious crime. So he thought that the only way to find out the truth was to interrogate him under torture. In Greek it is unclear whether the 'thongs' were for binding (so NRSV) or for scourging. If the latter (Lat. *flagellum*), it could prove fatal. For Paul's experience of beating see 2 Corinthians 11.24–25. Such a treatment was forbidden for a Roman citizen, and this time Paul did not miss the chance to assert his citizenship (cf. Acts 16.37).

Under Claudius, Roman citizenship was widely purchased, and the acquirer usually took the name of the emperor. The commander's name, Claudius Lysias, also points in that direction. The commander's comment about the purchase of his citizenship (v. 28) implies sarcasm about Paul debasing such a privilege. The fearful reaction of the commander recalls the reaction of the Philippian authorities (16.38).

 Interpretation

This speech is the first of Paul's 'defence' (Gk, *apologia*) of his loyalty as a Jew (Acts 24.10–21; 26.2–23). It repeats the pattern discernible in earlier stories of trial: the Jews accuse Paul but the Roman authorities declare his innocence (18.12–17, in Corinth; 19.23–41, in Ephesus). The defence speech was a well-established rhetorical genre of the day (25.16; 1 Corinthians 9.3; 2 Corinthians 7.11; Philippians 1.7, 16; 2 Timothy 4.16; 1 Peter 3.15).

Paul and the Jewish tradition

In a real sense, Jerusalem was the centre of Christian life for the Early Church. Throughout Acts and especially in the extensive stories of Paul's confrontation with the Jewish leaders in Jerusalem (Acts 21—26), Luke keeps underscoring the importance of Jerusalem and Jewish tradition for Christians. Paul's radical move was certainly different from that of his Jewish contemporaries, and that led them to misunderstand him as a religious renegade who was teaching against the law and against the Temple. Luke is confident in affirming that that is simply not true. Paul's activity did move beyond the traditional boundary, but that was precisely because he was faithful to the hope of Israel. Ironically, Paul's enthusiasm for the

Gentile mission was the very outcome of his loyalty to the promise of God for his own people Israel (Romans 9—11). He went back to the root of Israel's faith, i.e. to the faith of his ancestors such as Abraham and David, to find out that God's promise included the Gentiles from the first.

Luke makes it clear that the Church cannot exist without Israel. Without Jerusalem, there could have been neither Antioch nor Rome. It does not mean that traditions should be respected simply because they are traditions. The Jews were in error in many respects, and the Christians were courageous enough to point it out, as did the prophets of old and Jesus in the Gospels. Paul did the same in his own way (Romans 2). But they all did so in the creative and responsible spirit of ascertaining the true meaning of the tradition in their lives, not for the sake of criticism itself. It is true that such a message offended the selfish pride of some (or many) Jewish traditionalists of the day, but no one can say that Christianity has abandoned the tradition to create a new religion out of the blue.

Paul as a Roman citizen

In Jerusalem Paul escaped scourging by claiming his right as a Roman citizen. Some think that his attitude was different from that of Jesus, who never escaped suffering by asserting his rights. Did he then ignore Jesus' teaching that we should turn the other cheek also, if anyone strikes us on the right cheek? But we should remember that this word of Jesus speaks of willing acceptance of unjust treatment when it cannot be avoided. Jesus did not forbid us from escaping meaningless and avoidable sufferings. If possible, Jesus himself avoided unnecessary confrontation with his opponents. Peter hid himself from the Jewish authorities and the Hellenist Christians fled Jerusalem to save themselves from persecution. And they acted wisely. Paul believed that his mission was not to face a heroic death in Jerusalem but to go to Rome and witness there. So he used his God-given privilege for the service of that mission. In Philippi he calmly suffered flogging instead of utilizing his right. But later on he revealed his citizenship before his release, clearly to save believers there from unnecessary hassles or persecutions. Later he would use his right once more to appeal to Caesar, when it was clear that he could not expect a fair trial among the Jews and appealing to Caesar was the surest way of going to Rome. Yes, Paul did use his right as a Roman citizen, but he always did so in the service of the gospel, not for the sake of his own personal benefit. Whatever gifts he had, he used them not to please himself but to build up the Church.

? STUDY SUGGESTIONS

Word study

1   To whom does the 'brothers' refer in both Acts 22.1 and 22.5?

Review of content

2   What is the major burden of Paul's self-defence here?

3   What two points did Paul make in his account of his past life in Judaism?

4   What are the differences between 22.9 and 9.7?

5   Why did the crowd demand that Paul be killed?

6   Why was the commander afraid when he learned about Paul's Roman citizenship?

7   In what sense was Paul's enthusiasm for the Gentiles the expression of his loyalty to the Jewish tradition?

Bible study

8   Read 22.21 and Galatians 1.16. Also read Acts 13.45–47, 18.6 and 28.24–28. How are the Jewish rejection of the gospel and Paul's mission to the Gentiles related to each other?

Discussion and application

9   Christian witness should be based on God's revelation in Scripture. But it is also an act of testifying to what the witnesses themselves have seen and heard (22.14–15; 4.20). Which of these two dimensions (the Scriptural revelation and experience) is more prominent in your church?

10   How can we explain the 'discrepancies' between the different accounts of Paul's conversion? Does that affect the reliability of Luke as a historian? Why, do you think, did Luke leave those differences instead of tidying them up?

Acts 22.30—23.35

Paul before the Sanhedrin and the plot to kill him

 Summary

Paul defends himself before the Sanhedrin. He is then taken to the governor Felix in Caesarea.

 Notes

22.30. He brought Paul down and had him stand before them: Since Paul's case clearly involved Jewish religious matters, the commander brought in the Sanhedrin to find out exactly (cf. 21.34) what Paul was 'accused' of (cf. 24.2, 8, 13, 19; 25.11, 16; 28.19). In the Gospel of Luke the Sanhedrin (Gk, *synedrion*) assembled once for the trial of Jesus (22.66), and his disciples followed suit: the Jerusalem apostles (Acts 4.15; 5.21), Stephen (6.12, 15), and now Paul himself, just as Jesus had foretold (Luke 21.13).

23.1. Up to this day I have lived my life with a clear conscience before God: This is in fact the point Paul tried to make in his previous speech (22.2–21; cf. 26.19). Here 'to live' (Gk, *politeuomai*) literally means 'to be a citizen' or 'to live as a citizen' and thus more generally, 'to conduct one's life' (Philippians 3.20).

23.2–5. Are you sitting there to judge me according to the law, and yet in violation of the law you order me to be struck? This high priest Ananias (AD 47–59) was actively pro-Roman; he was later killed by the radical Jewish revolutionaries (called *sicarii* after the type of dagger (*sicarius*) which they carried) at the outset of the Jewish war in AD 66. Paul's reflexive reaction is an allusion to Deuteronomy 28.22, and the reference to 'whitewashed wall' echoes Ezekiel 13.10 (cf. Matthew 23.27). The task of the high priest was to find out whether Paul had violated the law or not, but he himself was breaking the law by treating Paul as a criminal even before having heard the witnesses. Paul's confession of ignorance in v. 5 is puzzling; some take it to be a prophetic critique of the high priest's hypocrisy. In any case, Paul's subsequent quotation of Exodus 22.28 demonstrates his faithfulness to the Scripture.

23.6. I am on trial concerning the hope of the resurrection of the dead: Here Paul explicitly identified himself as a Pharisee (26.5; Philippians 3.5). Invoking the resurrection of the dead functioned in two ways. On the surface, it was a rhetorical ploy to extricate himself by creating a division among the assembly. On the other hand, it also stated a central teaching of the Church: the resurrection of Jesus marks the realization of the hope of Israel. Rhetorically useful or not, Paul did not fail to testify to the resurrection of Jesus, just as he did before Agrippa (26.5).

23.7-10. The Sadducees say that there is no resurrection: The Sadducees only accepted the Torah, the first five books (Pentateuch) of the Scriptures to be the Scripture and they did not believe such ideas as resurrection, angel or spirit because they could not find them there. They thought such ideas had been imported from Zoroastrianism, ridiculing the Pharisees as 'Persianizers' (4.2). Not surprisingly, the assembly was divided (Gk, *eschisthe*) into two at Paul's self-identification as a resurrection-believing Pharisee, with the result that some Pharisaic teachers of the law 'argued vigorously' (NRSV: 'contended') in defence of Paul: 'We find nothing wrong with this man' (cf. 23.29; 25.18; 26.31). Resurrection was the central tenet of the Christian message, and it was only natural that the Sadducees, who did not believe it, stood out as the chief persecutor of the apostles (4.1-4).

But as in the case of Gamaliel (5.33-40), even the Pharisaic openness to resurrection and spiritual experiences was far from enough; even they would not accept the real point that Paul tried to make: the resurrection of Jesus from the dead. The second half of v. 9 (the remark about the angel) may reflect a distorted perception of Paul's encounter with the risen Jesus on the Damascus road. After all, the Sanhedrin was not much different from the excited mob at the courtyard (22.23). Once again, the commander had to rescue Paul from their hands.

23.11. So you must bear witness also in Rome: Throughout his career, visions played an important role in Paul's ministry (9.4; 16.9; 18.9-10; 22.17; 27.23-24). The vision gave Paul encouragement and the assurance that God's sovereign will was at work behind his turbulent life: 'You must (Gk, *dei*) bear witness also in Rome'.

23.12-15. The Jews joined in a conspiracy and bound themselves by an oath neither to eat nor drink until they had killed Paul: The fact of the conspiracy is mentioned no less than three times in the narrative (vv. 12, 14, 21). The identity of these 40 people is not clear: a Pharisaic fraternity (*haburah*) or a band of *sicarii* employed by the high priest? The plan was to have Paul appear before the Sanhedrin again under the pretext of a closer examination and kill him as he was brought out of the barracks. There was little chance of success and high risk but they were so desperate.

23.16–22. But do not be persuaded by them, for more than forty of their men are lying in ambush for him: The episode is very dramatic and easy to follow. The appearance of Paul's 'sister's son' is tantalizing, but we hear no more about Paul's family relations, either here or otherwise. We are also curious how Paul's nephew got wind of the plot and how he obtained access to the barracks. Since Paul was an unconvicted Roman citizen, he seems to have been allowed to receive visitors (cf. 24.23; 28.17, 30; 2 Timothy 1.16–17; Philippians 2.25). In v. 18 Paul was called 'prisoner' for the first time, but it was the centurion that carried out Paul's order! (v.17). The commander apparently took the matter seriously, and made up his mind at once about what to do next.

23.23–35. Get ready to leave by nine o'clock tonight for Caesarea with two hundred soldiers, seventy horsemen and two hundred spearmen: The size of the troop seems too large for just a single prisoner, but it only shows how seriously the commander took the matter, especially in light of the increasing fanaticism of the Jewish nationalists of the day. The word translated 'spearmen' (Gk, *dexiolaboi*, 'holding in the right hand') is otherwise unattested and its meaning is unclear. It may refer to 'light-armed troops' of some kind.

The commander, identified as Claudius Lysias, sent a letter to the governor Felix. On the whole his letter outlined the circumstances fairly accurately. But in v. 27 he skilfully passes over his attempt to flog Paul before the discovery of his being a Roman citizen and moves quickly to the inquiry by the Sanhedrin. His statement of Paul's innocence remains the typical Roman attitude in Acts: 'he . . . was charged with nothing deserving death or imprisonment' (v. 29; 18.15; 26.31). The immediate point was that the charge of Paul's defiling the Temple proved groundless after all.

Antipatris was built by Herod the Great in honour of his father, Antipater. It was about 37 miles from Jerusalem. At Antipatris the infantry returned to Jerusalem and left the cavalry to accompany Paul; Paul apparently no longer needed such a heavy escort. It was about 25 miles from Antipatris to Caesarea.

The governor asked about Paul's origin to ascertain legal jurisdiction of the case (cf. Luke 23.6–7). The reason is not clear, but he decided to take up the case even after he had learned that Paul was originally from the province of Cilicia. Paul was detained in the palace built by Herod the Great, which now served as the governor's headquarters (Lat., *praetorium*; Gk, *praetōrion*; cf. Mark 15.16; John 18.28; Philippians 1.13). This was the beginning of Paul's two-year imprisonment in Caesarea.

 Interpretation

This is Paul's second self-defence before the Jews. Now it was given more formally before the Sanhedrin, not before the angry crowd. Paul's defence focused on the hope of resurrection, and that split the whole council into two with the result that the hearing was cut short in confusion. The following episode of the Jewish plot against Paul and his subsequent transfer to Caesarea emphasizes the Jewish antipathy and the Roman (Gentile) goodwill toward Christianity, which is a theme typical of Luke.

God visits Paul

At the end of Paul's defence before the Sanhedrin, God visited Paul to encourage him (23.11). Of course, this is not the only time for him to have such an experience. In fact, Luke makes it clear that God visited Paul to encourage him and make him strong: in Troas (16.9), in Corinth (18.9–10), to send him out of Jerusalem to protect him (22.17), to send him to Rome (23.11), and to give him assurance of deliverance from shipwreck (27.22). Especially when Paul was in serious trouble or in deep despair God appeared to him and gave him assurance of protection. Yet God's promise was not that he would keep Paul out of trouble but that he would keep him safely in hardship, so that he might fulfil his mission as the apostle to the Gentiles. God did not spare him from life-threatening dangers (21.31, 36; 23.12–15). And Paul himself fully knew that 'it is through many persecutions that we must enter the kingdom of God' (14.22).

Divine providence in everyday life

There is nothing 'miraculous' in the story of Paul's rescue from the plot of the Jews against him. His nephew got wind of it, and told Paul. Paul in turn informed the Roman commander about it and the commander did whatever he could to save Paul from the attempt by the Jews to assassinate him. God surely delivered him from the Jews but he did so through the natural course of everyday life. Sometimes he does use 'extraordinary' things to carry out his purpose (16.25–40), but many a time he does his work in 'ordinary' ways through human beings.

Even today we hear numerous reports of extraordinary things that God is doing throughout the world. Of course, we can thank God for such remarkable works, but that should not blind us from perceiving the hand of God working silently but diligently through those people who faithfully fulfil their duty in their own everyday lives. Jesus warns us that performing miracles is not the sure guarantee that we are doing God's will (Matthew 7.21–23). The bottom line for us is 'God's will be done', whether miraculous or not.

 STUDY SUGGESTIONS

Word study

1 What is the meaning of the metaphor 'whitewashed wall' (Ezekiel 13.10; Matthew 23.27)?

Review of content

2 Why was Paul so angry with the high priest?

3 Why did Paul's remark about resurrection cause a split among the council members?

4 How did the Lord encourage Paul in the night vision?

5 Who informed the commander about the Jewish plot against Paul?

6 What was the view of the commander about Paul's case?

Bible study

7 Read **(a)** 23.3 and **(b)** Matthew 23 and Romans 2. What is the major point of criticism in these passages?

8 Read Acts 23.12–15; 22.22–23 and John 16.2. What can we learn from these passages about the zeal of the Jews for God and the law?

Discussion and application

9 Was Paul right to be angry with the high priest? Is anger always wrong or is there such a thing as 'righteous anger'?

10 Paul's mention of resurrection was intentional. What do you think of Paul's 'tactic'?

Acts 24.1–27

Paul before Felix

 Summary

Paul is accused by Tertullus, representing the Jewish leaders, before Felix and defends the continuity of the Christian belief with the Jewish faith.

 Notes

24.1–9. A pestilent fellow, an agitator among all the Jews throughout the world, and a ringleader of the sect of the Nazarenes. He even tried to profane the temple, and so we seized him: The high priest and the elders went to Caesarea and had Tertullus the lawyer indict Paul before the governor. The accusation consists of three parts. The first part is a *captatio benevolentiae*, a rhetorical device to win the favour of the judge by saying good things about him (vv. 2–4; cf. 24.10; 26.2–3). But his words of thanks for 'peace' and 'reform' amounted to outright flattery, since in reality Felix was not thanked but hated by the Jews for his cruel treatment of them. He brought a kind of 'peace', but only through ruthless suppression of the people.

The indictment was twofold:

1 As a troublemaker belonging to the Nazarene sect (Gk, *hairesis*). The word could be used either neutrally (party) or negatively (sect, faction) as here. But it had not gained the modern meaning of 'heresy' by this time; Paul had been stirring up riots and thus was politically dangerous. Being a messianic revolutionary was a serious charge to make before the Roman governor. As usual in Luke–Acts (Luke 23.2–5; Acts 16.20; 17.6; 19.40), Tertullus was playing upon the Roman governor's fear of rebellion. Verse 5 is the only place in the New Testament where the Christians are referred to as the 'Nazarenes'.

2 Paul tried to desecrate the temple (21.29). Tertullus turned the picture upside down: the mob violence of the Jews became a legal and orderly act of official arrest, while the commander Lycias was the one

who violently interrupted the process, according to the Western text tradition (verses 6b and 7. See the NRSV marginal note).

24.10–13. Neither can they prove to you the charge that they now bring against me: Paul also paid his respects to the governor but his word of good will was much more moderate (v. 10). Paul denied the charge of treason. His point is that he simply did not have time to stir up riots since he had arrived at Jerusalem only recently. And he did not come to Jerusalem as a troublemaker but as a worshipper; he never caused trouble anywhere in Jerusalem. See 21.17–30.

24.14–16. But this I admit to you, that according to the Way, which they call a sect, I worship the God of our ancestors, believing everything laid down according to the law or written in the prophets: Paul's response to the charge of his being 'a ringleader of the sect of the Nazarenes' is more nuanced. He admitted (lit., 'this I do confess') that he was following 'the Way', which the Jews called a 'sect'. But he denied that the Way was a deviation from the faith of the fathers. First, Paul was worshipping the same God of the fathers. Second, he believed in the Scriptures, since the Way was proclaiming Christ as the fulfilment of God's promises written in the Scriptures. Third, he continued to hold the same hope of the Jews about the resurrection of both the righteous and the wicked (Daniel 12.2; John 5.28–29; Revelation 20.12–13). This hope also involved belief in the judgement of God, and that was why he was making every effort to keep his conscience clear before God and people (23.1). It is not clear, however, if the Pharisees held to the general resurrection of both the righteous and the wicked.

24.17–21. They found me in the temple, completing the rite of purification, without any crowd or disturbance. But there were some Jews from Asia: Paul's aim here was to discredit the Sanhedrin as witnesses: he was in Jerusalem to bring alms and offerings to his nation and, therefore, he was ceremonially clean. He was not involved in any disturbances either. The commotion was actually instigated by some 'Jews from Asia' (21.27). So those eyewitnesses should have been here to testify, if they wanted to accuse him of desecrating the Temple. To be sure, he later stood before the Sanhedrin, but they could not find any wrongdoing in Paul; it was only that a dispute broke out when Paul announced his belief in the resurrection of the dead (23.6). Thus, those present here in the court were in no position to testify against Paul, either about his stirring up the crowd or desecrating the Temple. The only thing that could be ascertained was Paul's belief in resurrection.

24.22–27. At the same time he hoped that money would be given him by Paul, and for that reason he used to send for him very often and converse with him: Felix found himself in a dilemma. He was acquainted with 'the Way' well enough to know that Paul had not done anything wrong, but he had other motivations too. He was expecting a bribe from Paul on the one hand (v. 26) and he also wanted to please the Jews (v. 27).

Lysias was probably only a pretext for adjourning the case, since he never came to Caesarea.

Paul was kept in prison, now with 'free custody'. Drusilla was a daughter of Herod Agrippa I. She had formerly been married to Azizus, king of Emesa, but was enticed by Felix. Her brother Herod Agrippa II and her sister Bernice appear later in the story (25.13, 23; 26.30).

Felix often talked to Paul (v. 26), and once with his Jewish wife, Drusilla. Paul's subject was 'faith in Christ Jesus'. More specifically, Paul preached on 'justice, self-control, and the coming judgement'. The infamous cruelty of Felix showed his lack of righteousness; the unlawful marriage of the two evidenced their lack of self-control. And Paul made it clear that they would have to face God's stern judgement. No wonder Felix became afraid and cut the conversation short. Some interpreters explain the three subjects of Paul's sermon as corresponding to the three stages of salvation: righteousness (already given by faith), self-control (present life of obedience), and the judgement to come.

Taking bribes was against the Roman law, but local governors seldom kept it. For various reasons he must have considered Paul to be a man of means. So he kept Paul in prison for two years, exceeding the maximum legal period of confinement. His leaving Paul in prison seems to have been a failed effort to appease the Jews. According to the Jewish historian Josephus, he was summoned back to Rome because of his violent suppression of the clash between the Jews and the Greeks.

 Interpretation

This chapter reports Paul's third self-defence, once again before a Jewish authority but now in the Roman court, not in the Jerusalem Sanhedrin. The beginning scene is typical: the Jews made every effort to make Paul as politically dangerous as possible before the Roman governor, while Paul simply pointed out that such accusations did not make sense under the circumstances.

Paul's positive confession makes it clear that he too served the same 'God of our ancestors' and believed the same Scriptures (the law and the prophets) but in a different way, namely, 'according to the Way, which they call a sect'. Paul did not specify this crucial difference at this point, since his purpose here was to show the continuity of Christian faith with Jewish belief. The Christians served God as the one who raised Jesus of Nazareth from the dead and they believed the Scriptures basically as the witness to the Messiah who was none other than Jesus. They maintained the same hope of the resurrection of the dead, but here Paul carefully refrained from relating it to the resurrection of Jesus as he did in 1 Corinthians 15.

Once again, Paul summed up the Jewish (and the Christian) faith in terms of the hope of resurrection, a theme which receives special treatment throughout Acts. This hope is closely related to the belief that God will judge every person according to their deeds (17.30–31). It was an integral part of faith both in Judaism and in Christianity (Psalm 62.12; Jeremiah 32.19; Romans 2.6; 1 Peter 1.17) and provided a strong stimulus for maintaining proper conduct here in this life, as Paul shows in v. 16.

Felix adjourned the court without just cause. In the event Paul had to be in custody for nearly two years. Luke also tells us that he expected money from Paul and tried to please the Jews at the same time. This shows the sheer unreliability of the Roman authority. Luke presents the Roman officials in a much better light than the Jewish leaders but it does not mean that they deserved unreserved trust. Now we know why Paul needed special encouragement from the Lord (Acts 23.11). Also noteworthy in this chapter is Paul's courage in confronting the governor with the message of justice, self-control and the future judgement. Paul's testimony must have been taken quite personally, as Felix's fear indicates.

 ## STUDY SUGGESTIONS

Word study

1   Read the following passages where the word 'agitation' is used. What is the nature of the Jewish accusation of Paul?

   (a) Luke 23.19, 25; Acts 19.40; **(b)** Acts 15.2; 23.7, 10.

Review of content

2   What are the two major charges brought against Paul by Tertullus?

3   What are the three points Paul raised to prove his loyalty to the Jewish tradition?

4   What was Paul's aim in recounting the circumstances of his arrest in the Temple?

5   What was the nature of Felix's dilemma?

6   What did Paul preach to Felix about?

Bible study

7   Paul says that he came to Jerusalem 'to bring to my nation alms and offerings' (Acts 24.17). Read Paul's own words in 1 Corinthians 16.1–4 and Romans 15.25–27 about the collection. Why was it so important for Paul?

8   Read Matthew 16.27; Romans 2.6–11; 1 Peter 1.17. How can you reconcile the teachings of God's judgement according to deeds with God's unconditional grace?

Discussion and application

9 Proclaiming the gospel often involves the demand of repentance. Paul did not shun such responsibility even before those in power. Can you think of situations in which you are tempted to blunt the sharp edges of the gospel to avoid uncomfortable confrontation with others?

10 Paul had to remain in prison for two years due to the opportunistic attitude of Felix. How are Christians to react when we are put in a helpless situation by the fault of someone else?

Acts 25.1–27

Paul before Festus and Agrippa

 Summary

Standing before Festus, Paul finally appeals to the emperor. And he defends himself once again before King Agrippa.

 Notes

25.1–5. Let those of you who have the authority come down with me, and if there is anything wrong about the man, let them accuse him: Festus was the governor of Judea from AD 60 to 62. The new governor paid a courtesy visit to Jerusalem, the centre of Jewish life. This prompts another plot to kill Paul. Unlike the earlier plot (23.12–35), now the chief priests and the leaders were the initiators of the plot. After two years of Paul's imprisonment, emotions against him were running even higher. But here Festus was fair enough not to allow such an abnormal procedure, although he later changed his attitude a bit in favour of the Jews (cf. 25.9).

25.6–7. The Jews . . . surrounded him, bringing many serious charges against him, which they could not prove: With the Jews surrounding Paul, the arrangement must be threatening to him. The charges were many and serious, as had always been so (21.28; 24.5–6), but the undeniable fact remained: they had no proof for their accusation.

25.8. I have in no way committed an offence against the law of the Jews, or against the temple, or against the emperor: Paul's position was firm (22.1–21; 23.1, 6; 24.10–21); his conscience was as clear as ever (23.1; 24.16). He was innocent of any religious or political crime. The specific mention of the emperor prepares the way for Paul's final appeal to him.

25.10–12. 'I appeal to the emperor' . . . 'You have appealed to the emperor; to the emperor you will go': Giving way to his desire to please the Jews, Festus suggested a retrial in Jerusalem, but Paul knew all too well that no fair trial would be possible by the murder-breathing Jews. He had also sensed the changed attitude of the governor and knew that Festus' judgement would be seriously affected by his desire to appease the Jews (24.27). Paul now had no other choice but one: the only hope of getting a fair trial was to exercise his right as a Roman citizen, so he appealed to the emperor. Not that he wanted to save his life; he just wanted to get a fair trial. After consultation, the request was granted. Interestingly, the name 'Caesar' is mentioned eight times in this chapter in three forms: *Kaisar*, *Sebastos* (Lat., *Augustus*, vv. 21, 25) and *ho Kyrios* ('the Lord', v. 26). This Caesar was none other than the infamous Nero, but he had not yet shown any sign of cruelty.

25.13–22. Agrippa said to Festus, 'I would like to hear the man myself.' 'Tomorrow', he said, 'you will hear him': Agrippa was Herod Agrippa II, the son of Agrippa I (12.1), the grandson of Herod the Great and the brother of Drusilla (24.24). He was in an incestuous relationship with his sister Bernice. This overtly pro-Roman family paid a state visit to the new Roman governor.

It is not clear why Festus introduced Paul's case to Agrippa. Was he trying to extricate himself by handing the matter over to Agrippa or was he simply presenting the case as a kind of amusement? In any case, Festus summarized the events recorded in 24.27—25.12 for Agrippa. First, he refused the request of the Jews to have Paul tried in Jerusalem (vv. 15–16). Second, the charges brought against Paul only concerned the Jewish religion and the question about 'a certain Jesus, who had died, but whom Paul asserted to be alive' (vv. 17–19). Third, for lack of knowledge about the Jewish religion he asked Paul if he would be tried in Jerusalem, but Paul instead appealed to be protected (from the Jews) in order to await the emperor's decision, and he granted the request (vv. 20–21). But his remarks that the Jews asked for a sentence (25.2–3, 15) and that he acknowledged the rightness of Paul's defence (25.18–19) were not true. He also omitted his politically motivated proposal that Paul be tried in Jerusalem (25.9, 20).

25.23–27. Therefore I have brought him before all of you, and especially before you, King Agrippa, so that, after we have examined him, I may have something to write: Now the chained Paul stood before Agrippa and Bernice who were present with great pomp (Gk, *phantasia*), and Festus once again summarized the case for the audience. He rightly mentioned the repeated requests by the Jews that Paul be killed and his failure to find any crime deserving death (23.29; 25.18; 26.31; cf. Luke 23.15, 22).

Now the governor mentioned the lack of 'something to write' to Agrippa, since it was 'unreasonable to send a prisoner without indicting the charges against him' (v. 27). His statement was not quite true, since the Jewish leaders had made very specific accusations against Paul. What he lacked was tangible evidence for such charges. Part of his dilemma was that the charges brought by the Jews were of a political nature, while the real point of dispute was an intra-Jewish, religious one.

Interpretation

This chapter reports Paul's hearing before another governor, Festus (vv.1–12), the meeting of Festus and King Agrippa and Bernice (vv. 13–22) and the beginning of the hearing (vv. 23–27). Paul's speech itself is recorded in Acts 26.

With the change of governor, the Jews made another plot to kill Paul and asked Festus to bring him back to Jerusalem to be tried again by the Jewish authorities. Festus initially saw no reason for such an anomalous procedure, so he refused their request. Luke does not say much about the hearing before Festus, since it was basically the repetition of the earlier one conducted by Felix. The only thing it confirmed was that the Jews were unable to present any substantial evidence for the charges brought against Paul.

It was during this hearing that Paul finally appealed to Caesar, which marked one of the most crucial moments in the long career of Paul. Paul already had the conviction that he would bear witness to the gospel in Rome as he had done in Jerusalem (23.11), but now it became clear that he would go to Rome as a prisoner to stand in the emperor's court.

It is somewhat unusual that Luke describes in detail the conversation between Festus and Agrippa and the introductory speech of Festus at the hearing. The primary purpose of such an extended report seems to be to underscore the innocence of Paul in the face of the Jewish accusation against him. Festus's words sum up the matter very clearly: 'King Agrippa and all here present with us, you see this man about whom the whole Jewish community petitioned me, both in Jerusalem and here, shouting that he ought not to live any longer. But I found that he had done nothing deserving death' (vv. 24–25; cf. vv. 18–19).

STUDY SUGGESTIONS

Review of content

1 What was Festus' answer to the request of the Jews that Paul be transferred to Jerusalem?

2 How did the attitude of Festus change by the time of this trial?

3 What was Paul's response to the Jewish accusation and the suggestion of Festus?

4 What was Festus' pretext for having Paul tried again before Agrippa?

5 What is Luke's purpose in reporting the conversation between Festus and Agrippa in detail?

Bible study

6   Many a time Paul had to stand before the tribunal. Read the following passages. What sort of tribunals appear in the New Testament?

   (a) Acts 18.12; 25.6, 10; **(b)** Romans 14.10; 2 Corinthians 5.10.

7   We have many members of the Herod family in Acts, including two women. Who are they? And what is their relationship with one another (Acts 4.27; 12; 25—26)?

Discussion and application

8   In later chapters of Acts the Jewish people play the role of Paul's chief opponents. It must have been very hard to have to endure the accusation of his own people, while Paul himself wanted to remain a faithful Jew. As a modern Christian, can you think of any such situations around you?

9   It must have been frustrating for Paul to observe the changed attitude of the initially fair Festus. Can you think of any similar situations around you?

Acts 26.1–32

Paul's defence before Agrippa

 Summary

Paul declares his Jewish loyalty by recounting his past as a Pharisee, his conversion and his proclamation of the Way afterwards. Paul boldly proclaims Jesus as the fulfilment of the promises before the governor and the king.

 Notes

26.1–3. I consider myself fortunate that it is before you, King Agrippa, I am to make my defence today against all the accusations of the Jews: Agrippa, the guest of honour, gave Paul permission to speak and Paul began his defence with the customary motion of an orator (12.17; 13.16; 21.40) and a typical *captatio benevolentiae* (24.2–4). Strictly speaking, the Herods were Edomites, but practically they were considered Jews. Paul referred to Agrippa's familiarity with the Jewish customs as an advantage for his case.

26.4–5. They have known for a long time . . . that I have belonged to the strictest sect of our religion and lived as a Pharisee: Paul appealed to the knowledge of his Jewish accusers about his past as a zealous Pharisee (22.3; 23.6).

26.6–7. And now I stand here on trial on account of my hope in the promise made by God to our ancestors: Paul was on trial because of his hope of resurrection, but it was the hope 'in what God had promised our fathers', and the Israelites were now awaiting the fulfilment of the promise. His point is: 'I am now on trial precisely because I remain loyal to the faith of our fathers.' The repeated use of 'our' underscores his solidarity with his fellow Jews.

26.8. Why is it thought incredible by any of you that God raises the dead?: The question is an aside. Paul probably meant the general idea of resurrection but it could not be separated from the specific belief that God raised Jesus from the dead. It was through the resurrection of Jesus that

God revealed himself as the one who 'raises the dead' (26.23; Galatians 1.1; Romans 4.17; 8.11).

26.9–11. Indeed, I myself was convinced that I ought to do many things against the name of Jesus of Nazareth: Compared to 22.4–5, Paul's words in these verses are much harsher (8.1, 3; 9.1–2). Ironically, what his accusers were doing to Paul now was what he himself had been doing to the followers of Jesus before his conversion. 'I myself was convinced' reflects regret about his blindness.

26.12–15. I saw a light from heaven, brighter than the sun, shining around me and my companions: This is the third account of Paul's Damascus experience. This account clarifies that the light enveloped all the travellers (cf. 9.7; 22.9) and that all fell to the ground (cf. 9.4; 22.7). However, nothing is said about Paul's blindness and what happened afterwards. 'It hurts you to kick against the goads' was a proverb expressing the foolhardiness of opposing God-ordained destiny. Paul also clarified for his Greek audience that the risen Jesus spoke in the Hebrew (i.e. Aramaic) language.

26.16–18. I have appeared to you . . . to appoint you to serve and testify to the things in which you have seen me and to those in which I will appear to you: These verses combine earlier accounts and describe Paul's commission as given directly from Jesus on the spot (cf. 9.6, 15–16; 22.14–16, 17–21). The command to stand up and the promise of rescue echo prophetic commissions (Ezekiel 1.28—2.7; 1 Chronicles 16.35; Jeremiah 1.8, 19). Paul would bear witness not only 'to the things in which you have seen me' but also 'to those in which I will appear to you'.

Paul's mission covered both Jews and Gentiles. His message was about:

1 turning from darkness to light or from Satan to God, which is a familiar metaphor for conversion (9.35; 11.21; 13.47; 14.15; 15.19; Luke 1.79; 2.32; Ephesians 5.8; Colossians 1.12–14; 1 Thessalonians 5.5);

2 (present) forgiveness of sins;

3 (future) inheritance (NRSV: 'a place') among the saints; and

4 faith in the risen Jesus Christ as the means to attaining such blessings.

26.19–22a. I was not disobedient to the heavenly vision: The renewed address, 'After that, King Agrippa', signals the real point of Paul's defence. Verses 19–22a sketch Paul's career since his conversion: in Damascus (9.20–25) and in Jerusalem (9.26–30). We hear nothing in Acts about his mission 'in all Judea'. 'Not disobedient' means 'enthusiastically obedient'.

Paul's message was doubly offensive to the Jews. First, he preached repentance and salvation not only to the Jews but to the Gentiles also. Second, he demanded that their repentance be proved by their deeds, just as John the Baptist had called for 'fruits worthy of repentance' (Luke 3.8; Romans 2). This was the same as saying that the external badges of Jewish identity such as circumcision, Jewish calendar and table manners were meaningless unless they were accompanied by an appropriate life of obedience (Romans 2.25).

In a nutshell, the real reason for antipathy against Paul was his Gentile mission. For Paul it was God's will revealed to him through the heavenly revelation, but the Jews considered it as a threat to their faith at its core. Inevitably, the Jews kept attempting to kill him but without success so far, since God had been protecting him. So he could continue his testimony to both Jews and Gentiles. 'To small and great' probably refers to the various ranks of his audience.

26.22b–23. I stand here . . . saying nothing but what the prophets and Moses said would take place: Here we have a nice summary of the early Christian *kerygma* (proclamation): the death and resurrection of Jesus Christ as the fulfilment of God's promise in the Scripture (cf. 1 Corinthians 15.3–4). Paul's point is that there was nothing anti-Jewish in his proclamation, since his message concerned the fulfilment of what the prophets and Moses had promised: the suffering and resurrection of Christ/Messiah (2.25–36; 3.18, 21–25; 4.11; 8.32–35; 13.33–37; Luke 24.26; cf. Psalms 2, 16, 118) as well as his proclaiming light both 'to his own people and to the Gentiles' (Acts 2.32; Isaiah 49.6; cf. Acts 13.47). For the idea that Christ is the 'first fruit' (NRSV: 'the first') of resurrection, see 1 Corinthians 15.20–21.

26.24–25. I am speaking the sober truth: Festus considered Jesus as plainly dead (25.19), and for him Paul's talk of the resurrection of Jesus was simply too much. For an obtuse Gentile such as Festus Paul's message of the cross and resurrection was nothing but sheer madness (cf. 17.32; 2 Corinthians 5.11, 13; cf. 1 Corinthians 1.18, 24). Paul spoke as a learned man, but the Roman governor could not understand him. Here Luke's description of Paul reminds us of an ideal philosopher of the day who spoke what was true and reasonable with boldness.

26.26–29. King Agrippa, do you believe the prophets? I know that you believe: Paul could not get through to the Roman governor, so he now turned to King Agrippa. Here Paul appealed to the common knowledge about Jesus, since the Jesus event did not happen 'in a corner' (cf. 12.18–19). So he could speak 'with boldness' (NRSV: 'freely'; see 4.13). Paul was almost confronting Agrippa, touching on the latter's belief in the Scripture. He might have nominal faith in the Scripture, but that was far from being enough to enable him to see its fulfilment in the death and resurrection of Jesus of Nazareth.

For Agrippa, the conversation had become too personal, so he backed away. But Paul went on with his bold challenge not only to him but to 'all who are listening to me today' that they become Christians like Paul himself.

26.30–32. This man is doing nothing to deserve death or imprisonment: Paul's last defence before Agrippa led to the final conclusion that he had done nothing deserving imprisonment or death, thereby confirming the earlier verdicts by the commander (23.29) and the governor Festus (25.25). It is interesting to note that the movement here resembles the trial of Jesus: Jesus too was declared innocent three times by Pontius Pilate (Luke 23.4, 14, 22) with the agreement of Herod the Tetrarch (23.6–12).

 ## Interpretation

The whole of Acts 26 is Paul's defence speech delivered before Festus and King Agrippa, the last apart from the one before the Jewish leaders in Rome. This speech mostly repeats the points made in his earlier speeches (22.1–21), but in more detail:

1 respectful introduction (vv. 2–3);

2 his zeal as a Jew (vv. 4–8);

3 persecution of the Way (vv. 9–11);

4 conversion and calling (vv. 12–18);

5 subsequent commitment to the calling (vv. 19–20);

6 recent state of affairs (vv. 22–23).

What is noteworthy in this chapter is the unusually personal tone of Paul's speech specifically addressed first to Festus and then to King Agrippa. So in this last defence readers get the impression that Paul did not so much defend himself as proclaim the gospel to those in the court.

Paul's mission and message

In this apology Paul made it clear that his mission covered both Jews and Gentiles. His message for the Gentiles was also described in more traditional terms: repentance and turning to God and deeds consistent with repentance (v. 20). Though Luke does not tell us anything about his activities in Judea, such a description fits well with the picture of Paul's mission drawn in Acts which typically started with the Jews in the synagogues before turning to the Gentiles. It is true that Paul had a specific mission as the apostle to the Gentiles, but it need not mean that he should not preach the gospel to the Jews. His goal was to proclaim the word to as many people as possible, and that explains why he 'became as a Jew' to the Jews, 'in order to win the Jews' (1 Corinthians 9.20).

Resurrection as the stumbling block of faith

Paul's boldness had much to do with his conviction that the Christian message deals with objective truth, and so it is 'true and reasonable'. However, it is also true that Christians proclaim many things that go beyond human reason. Resurrection is one such claim. People think that resurrection from the dead runs counter to human, scientific reason and thus cannot be true. But Christians do believe that God raised Jesus from the dead, so consider it as 'sober truth'. For this reason the gospel can only be apprehended by faith, faith in the God who gives life to the dead (Romans 4.17). Paul declares that the cross of Christ is a folly to those who are perishing but the power and wisdom of God to those who are being saved (1 Corinthians 1.18, 24). It is important that we should communicate the gospel in a way that is intelligible to our audience, but our eagerness to communicate should not lead us to remove the 'stumbling block' of the gospel itself and turn it into something that can be apprehended by human reason alone, i.e. without faith.

Unlike earlier apologies, Paul's speech here contains very personal exchanges, first between Paul and Festus and then between Paul and Agrippa. Paul's talk of resurrection prompted Festus to interrupt Paul's speech to Agrippa and cry out to him, 'You are crazy!' Paul confidently denied the charge, affirming that he was telling 'sober truth'. Then he addressed King Agrippa more personally, demanding 'Do you believe the prophets, King Agrippa?' Understandably, Agrippa was upset, but Paul did not balk but concluded his speech with a bold challenge: 'Whether quickly or not, I pray to God that not only you but also all who are listening to me today might become such as I am – except for these chains' (v. 29).

 ## STUDY SUGGESTIONS

Review of content

1 According to Paul himself, why was he standing on trial before Agrippa?

2 What are the major differences between Paul's account of his conversion in this chapter and the earlier stories in Acts 9 and 22?

3 What are the four elements of the message Paul was called to preach?

4 What was the real reason for the antipathy of the Jews toward Paul?

5 What did Festus say at Paul's mention of resurrection?

6 What was the verdict of Agrippa?

Bible study

7 Read Acts 26.23 and 1 Corinthians 15, especially vv. 20–21. What does it mean that Christ is the 'first fruit' of resurrection?

Discussion and application

8 What do you think about the statement that resurrection presents one of the greatest stumbling blocks of Christian faith?

9 We noted above Paul's courage in maintaining such a personal and even confrontational tone toward Festus and Agrippa. What do you think is the ultimate ground of such courage (cf. Romans 1.16–17; Luke 1.4)?

Acts 27.1—28.16

Paul sails for Rome

 Summary

Paul sails for Rome. He has to undergo fierce storms and a shipwreck, before he finds himself in the capital of the empire.

 Notes

27.1–8. Embarking on a ship of Adramyttium that was about to set sail to the ports along the coast of Asia, we put to sea: Luke devotes a large space to the report of Paul's voyage and shipwreck on his way to Rome (27.1—28.15). Here the 'we' passages resume (cf. 21.18; 28.16; see notes on 16.10) and, not surprisingly, the eyewitness character of the narrative is frequently noted. The centurion in charge of the prisoners was Julius. He belonged to the Augustan Cohort, and was depicted as being very kind to Paul throughout the voyage (27.3, 43). The company went on board a ship from Adramyttium (a city of Mysia) on its return journey. 'Aristarchus, a Macedonian from Thessalonica', who had accompanied Paul on his way to Jerusalem (20.4; cf. 19.29), was also on board. He probably accompanied Paul all the way to Rome (Colossians 4.10; Philemon 24).

The ship kept to the east and to the north of Cyprus, and then along the coast of Asia Minor to reach Myra in Lycia (see Map 5 on p. 223). There they transferred to an Alexandrian ship sailing for Italy. Sailing from Egypt to Italy carrying wheat, it was probably a grain ship (27.38), since Rome was dependent on Egypt for her grain supply. They sailed from Myra up to a point off Cnidus, beyond which they would be out in the open sea without protection of land. Facing the north-westerly wind, the ship had to turn south and sail under the lee of Crete (v. 7), until they arrived 'with difficulty' at 'a place called Fair Havens' (v. 8).

27.9–12. Sirs, I can see that the voyage will be with danger and much heavy loss: The 'Fast' refers to the Day of Atonement which fell on the tenth day of Tishri (September/October). The Mediterranean was dangerous for sailing and thus practically closed during the winter months. So Paul offered a piece of common-sense advice as a seasoned sea traveller, but it was ignored by the majority. Those in charge of the ship wanted to winter

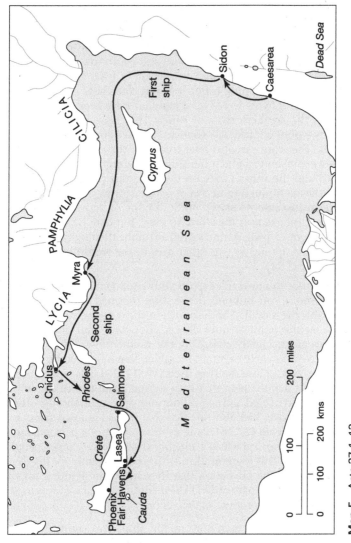

Map 5 Acts 27.1–12
Source: Tom Wright, *The New Testament for Everyone* (SPCK, 2011), p. 331.

in Phoenix, since Fair Havens was inconvenient for spending the winter due to its easterly and north-easterly winds.

27.13–20. When neither sun nor stars appeared for many days, and no small tempest raged, all hope of our being saved was at last abandoned: The initial fair weather was deceptive, and they were soon caught up with 'a violent wind' (Gk, *typhonikos*, from which the word 'typhoon' came). The name 'northeaster' translates *eurakylōn*, a combination of the Greek *euros* ('south-east wind') and the Latin *aquilo* ('north wind'). Instead of reaching Phoenix as planned, the ship lost control and began to drift helplessly.

The crew undergirded the ship to prevent it from breaking up (the operation is called 'frapping'), but it is not clear how exactly they did it. The sandbars of Syrtis were two dangerous bays between Cyrene and Carthage on the northern coast of Africa. They were still a fair way off but the crew would not take any chances. The 'sea anchor' literally means 'vessels', but the word can also refer to one of the sails. Then successive measures were taken to lighten the ship: abandoning the cargo the next day (v. 18) and the ship's tackle on the third day (v. 19). But all to no avail, and they continued to be swept by the storms without any means of navigation (no sun, no stars), until all hope of deliverance was gone (v. 20). In v. 20 Luke uses the word 'to save', but here it simply refers to deliverance from shipwreck, not 'salvation' in the theological sense of the word. The same applies to two other uses of the word in the following narrative (vv. 31, 34).

27.21–26. I urge you now to keep up your courage, for there will be no loss of life among you, but only of the ship: They had not eaten for a long time; probably the food had been spoiled by the water or they were unable to cook it. At the point of utter despair, however, Paul offered a word of encouragement. Lightly chastising the foolhardiness of the majority (27.10), he tried to cheer them up by saying that all would be delivered, although they would lose the ship itself (vv. 22, 25). His confidence was based on God's definite plan that Paul should stand before the emperor (23.11). This plan of God had been confirmed once again through a timely vision, in which God had also revealed that he had granted safety to all those sailing with Paul (27.24). Paul, expressing a strong personal faith in God ('an angel of the God whose I am and whom I serve'), urged people to trust him (27.25). This identification with God was partly for his Gentile fellow passengers. The prediction that they must run aground on some island may have been part of God's revelation or Paul's common-sense deduction from God's promise of deliverance.

27.27–32. Unless these men stay in the ship, you cannot be saved: Sensing that the ship was finally approaching land, the sailors attempted to escape using the lifeboats but the attempt was thwarted by Paul; he clearly saw that their expertise was indispensable for the survival of the passengers. In Paul's day, 'the Adriatic Sea' referred to much broader areas of the Mediterranean. The modern 'Adriatic Sea' was called 'Gulf of Adria' then. Here and in the next episode, Paul's confident leadership stands out quite clearly.

27.33–38. Therefore I urge you to take some food, for it will help you survive; for none of you will lose a hair from your heads: The passengers had been in despair and gone without food for a long time. Now Paul assured them of their survival once again, this time encouraging them to take food (27.22–26). For the expression 'not losing a hair from one's head' see 1 Samuel 14.45; 2 Samuel 14.11; 1 Kings 1.52; Matthew 10.30; Luke 21.18.

Paul's motion (taking the bread, giving thanks to God and breaking it) reflects the usual Jewish (and Christian) practice of saying grace at table but, interestingly, it also reminds us of Jesus at the Last Supper and other similar occasions in the Gospels (Luke 9.16; 22.19; 24.30). So 'all of them were encouraged and took food for themselves'. Naming the number of the passengers recalls the feeding miracles of the Gospels (Mark 6.44; Luke 9.14). Throwing the wheat into the sea was yet another measure to lessen the danger of shipwreck by making the ship ride higher.

27.39–44. And so it was that all were brought safely to land: This section describes the attempt to ground the ship on the shore, the inescapable shipwreck and the eventual deliverance of all the passengers. Loosening the steering-oars seems to mean loosening them from the securing ropes in order to use them. But approaching the shore, the bow of the ship got stuck fast into the muddy bottom of the sea and the stern (the rear part of the ship) broke up under the impact of the pounding waves. Since they were not far from the shore, the soldiers tried to kill the prisoners for fear of their escape (cf. 12.19; 16.27), but their plan was stopped by the centurion who wanted to save Paul's life. So by swimming or on planks or on pieces of the broken ship, everyone reached land in safety, thus bringing the long and adventurous voyage to a close.

28.1. The island was called Malta: The Phoenician name 'Malta' (Gk, *melitē*) means 'refuge'. What an interesting coincidence!

28.2–6. They changed their minds and began to say that he was a god: The 'natives' translates *barbaroi*, which the Greeks used to denote those who did not speak their language (cf. Romans 1.14). The weather was terrible, but the islanders were very kind to the company. Paul tried to make himself useful by helping to tend the fire, but a viper from the brushwood fastened itself on to his hand. 'Justice' refers to the Greek goddess Dike; the natives thought that she was taking vengeance on Paul for his wrongdoing: 'Though he has escaped from the sea, Dike has not allowed him to live.' But the viper did not harm Paul at all, so the natives changed their minds and hailed him as a god. This incident recalls what happened to Paul and Barnabas in Lycaonia (Acts 14.6). God was protecting Paul, so he could stand before the emperor.

28.7–10. Paul visited him and cured him by praying and putting his hands on him: The 'leading man of the island', named Publius, showed extreme hospitality to the company, though it is not clear whether the 'us' refers to all the passengers or only to the Christians around Paul. It is also unclear whether this 'leading man' was a Roman magistrate or just a local patron. In Acts we often see Paul associating with the leading persons of a place (13.7; 16.22; 17.19; 18.12; 19.31). The 'fever and dysentery' probably refers to the so-called 'Malta Fever', which usually lasted for many months. Paul's healing the father of Publius led to an unexpected healing ministry for the sick of the island. This recalls Jesus' healing of the mother-in-law of Peter which had also attracted the crowd for healing (Luke 4.38–44). The islanders once again returned this favour by providing for the need of the travellers, though it is not clear exactly what 'many honours' mean.

28.11–15. The believers from there, when they heard of us, came as far as the Forum of Appius and Three Taverns to meet us: These verses describe the last stage of Paul's journey to Rome. They spent the three months of the winter season (from mid-November to mid-February) on the island and boarded another Alexandrian grain ship which was bound for Rome (it had also spent the winter on the island). The figure head of the 'twin brothers' (Gk, *dioskouroi*) refers to the twin sons of Zeus, Castor and Pollux, the gods of sea voyages and the patrons of seamen.

The ship stopped at Syracuse, the capital of Sicily, and then at the port of Rhegium at the toe of the Italian peninsula. Then the ship sailed 320 miles to the north to arrive at Puteoli in the Bay of Naples, probably due to the centurion's official business. As in Sidon, Paul was once again allowed to greet fellow Christians there (27.3).

Somehow Christians in Rome had learned of Paul's arrival and came down along the Appian Way to meet him. Some walked 32 miles from Rome as far as the 'Three Taverns', a halting place on the Appian Way; others walked 10 miles further to 'Forum Appius' ('the market-place of Appius'). It was three years since Paul had sent a letter to the believers in Rome (Romans 1.9–13; 15.22–32). So Luke makes it clear that Paul was not the first person to bring the gospel to Rome.

28.16. When we came into Rome, Paul was allowed to live by himself, with the soldier who was guarding him: At this point the 'we' passages come to an end, though it seems that Luke stayed on in Rome for some time (Philemon 24; Colossians 4.14). In Rome Paul was given what was called *custodia militaria*, similar to the modern 'house arrest': he lived in his own private house and was free to receive guests, though he was chained to a soldier all the time (Acts 28.20).

 ## Interpretation

People have always been fascinated by stories of sea voyages the adventures of Odysseus in Greek literature, the story of Jonah in the Old Testament, and the frequent storms of the Sea of Galilee in the New. We are also familiar with many such stories in modern times such as *Robinson Crusoe* by Daniel Defoe and *Gulliver's Travels* by Jonathan Swift, as well as the heart-breaking stories of the sinking of the *Titanic*. The last phase of Luke's history is occupied by one such story: Paul's turbulent sea voyage to the capital of the empire.

We do not know for sure why Luke devotes so much space to Paul's journey to Rome, but throughout the narrative we cannot miss Paul's calm confidence in God's protection and his leadership, which shines out at times of crisis. In a way, Luke's portrayal of Paul resembles Jesus who, without losing composure, commands the storms to be stilled and thereby saves his disciples.

Literary conventions and historical truth

A comparison of this narrative with other Greco-Roman travel stories shows ample use of classical motifs typically associated with sea voyage, storm and shipwreck. These were regular elements of the popular romances of the Hellenistic period. From this sober observation, some scholars jump to the conclusion that the story of Paul's sea voyage is thus unhistorical. But reading Luke's narrative we feel that there is nothing in the story that is inherently improbable; on the contrary, the popularity of the literary convention indicates the frequency of such experiences. We can believe that Luke recounts the story as it really happened, but we can also acknowledge his use of literary conventions and techniques of the day in telling his story.

Faith that works

Throughout the narrative Luke depicts Paul as a sort of prophetic figure. He received God's prophecies and saw them fulfilled (27.10, 21, 24–25, 34, 44). God appeared to him to give him assurance (27.23–25), and he in turn gave advice (27.10, 33) and assurances to others (27.22, 36). There were many life-threatening dangers, but God's will triumphed, the will that Paul must stand before the emperor to witness (27.24). Paul did not exercise supernatural power to control the storms as Jesus had done in the Gospels, but his calm and confident demeanour evokes the image of Jesus in the Galilean boats (Luke 8.22–25). Here we see what faith in God can do in difficult situations. In Paul's case, it proved more effective by being combined with his ample experience. Paul steered through the dire situation by putting his experience to wise use while firmly believing in God's assurance. Sure, God often performs miracles to save those who believe, but that is not the only way for our faith to work: it can show its power all the more strikingly as we are going through the tempests of life in confident endurance. He believed in God, and did whatever he could to overcome the hurdles and carry out God's will for him.

STUDY SUGGESTIONS

Word study

1 What does the 'Fast' mean in Acts 27.9?

2 What does 'to save' mean in this particular context (27.20, 31, 34, 43)?

Review of content

3 What pieces of advice did Paul give to others during the voyage?

4 What measures did the crew take to save the ship?

5 How did Paul know that all of the passengers would survive the shipwreck?

6 Why did the centurion order the soldiers not to kill the prisoners?

7 How did the native people of Malta change their opinion about Paul?

8 How far did the Roman Christians travel to meet Paul?

Bible study

9 Read Mark 4.35–41; Matthew 8.23–27; Luke 8.22–25. What similarities can you find between Jesus and Paul?

Discussion and application

10 The natives of the island were unusually kind toward the company of people with Paul (28.2). Some Christians unwisely tend to belittle the goodness shown to them by non-Christians. What do you think is the right attitude toward the 'good' non-Christians around you?

11 God surely does deliver his people from all sorts of dangers, but not always. Peter was delivered from prison by God's angel, but James died without any such intervention. What are your thoughts on this?

Paul in Rome

 Summary

Paul unsuccessfully preaches the gospel to the Jews in Rome and announces the sending of salvation to the Gentiles. For two years Paul proclaims the gospel boldly without hindrance.

 Notes

28.17–20. I have asked to see you and speak with you, since it is for the sake of the hope of Israel that I am bound with this chain: Once again Luke depicts Paul as defending himself and proclaiming the gospel of Christ before the Jewish leaders in Rome. So in Rome too Paul followed his usual pattern of beginning his mission with the Jews. His defence recapitulates his earlier defences in Jerusalem and Caesarea. First, he had been loyal to the Jewish people and custom (22.3–21; 24.11–13). So Paul underscored his solidarity with the Jews ('our people' and 'our ancestors' in v. 17 and 'my nation' in v. 19). Second, he had been declared innocent by the Romans (25.8, 11). Third, he had to appeal to the emperor due to the objection of the Jews (25.10–12). Fourth, he was on trial for the sake of the hope of Israel (23.6; 24.14–15, 21; 26.6–8, 23). Here we first learn that the Romans had actually wanted to release him (28.18; cf. 26.32).

28.21–22. But we would like to hear from you what you think, for with regard to this sect we know that everywhere it is spoken against: The Jewish leaders in Rome had not heard any news about Paul's case from Jerusalem, but they had some unfavourable hearsay information about 'this sect' (Gk, *hairesis*), and that explains their interest in hearing Paul's views. We get the impression that there had not been much contact between the Jews and Christians of Rome.

28.23. Testifying to the kingdom of God and trying to convince them about Jesus both from the law of Moses and from the prophets: Setting a date gives the meeting between Paul and the Jewish leaders an official tone. Proclaiming the kingdom of God and proclaiming Jesus was one and the same (28.31). What Paul did was to prove the messiahship of Jesus from the Scriptures, as he had been doing with the Jews (cf. 17.2–3; 18.5).

28.24–28. Let it be known to you then that this salvation of God has been sent to the Gentiles; they will listen: The response to Paul's message was a mixed one, but what does Luke mean that 'some were convinced'? Did they become Christians? Or does he simply mean that they were willing to give Paul's point a try? Paul's message created disagreement (Gk, *asymphonoi*) among the Jews, but for Paul the situation must have been quite a disappointing one, so he denounced them by quoting the Scripture.

The citation was from Isaiah 6.9–10 (LXX), and Paul attributes it to the Holy Spirit. This passage was widely used by the New Testament writers to allude to the Jewish rejection of the gospel (Mark 4.12; Matthew 13.13; Luke 8.13; John 12.39–40).

As before in Pisidian Antioch (13.46), Corinth (18.6) and Ephesus (19.8–10), now for the last time here in Rome Paul announced that the gospel of salvation would go to the Gentiles and they, unlike the Jews, would listen to it. Placed at the end of the narrative, this announcement seems to carry a solemn note of finality, anticipating the ultimate separation of Christianity and Judaism.

28.30–31. He lived there two whole years at his own expense and welcomed all who came to him, proclaiming the kingdom of God and teaching about the Lord Jesus Christ with all boldness and without hindrance: The 'two whole years' seems to refer to the period of waiting before Paul eventually stood before Caesar. 'At his own expense' can also be rendered 'at his rented house' (NIV). So Paul lived in his own rented place, and was free to welcome guests.

Luke's narrative ends with two triumphant notes: 'with all boldness' and 'without hindrance'. Boldness was the hallmark of the Spirit-filled witnesses (4.13, 29, 31; 9.27; 13.46; 14.3; 18.26, etc.), and the fact that Paul testified to the word without hindrance reminds us of the efficacy of God's will which could not be thwarted by any human means, as Paul himself once remarked: 'Remember Jesus Christ, raised from the dead, a descendant of David – that is my gospel, for which I suffer hardship, even to the point of being chained like a criminal. But the word of God is not chained' (2 Timothy 2.8–9).

 Interpretation

God's Messiah rejected by God's people

The conclusion of Acts strikes a sad note, as it touches on the problem which troubled the earliest (Jewish) Christians so much: the rejection of the gospel by the Jews and its subsequent move into the Gentile territory. On the one hand, there was no denying that the majority of God's people rejected Jesus of Nazareth as their Messiah, and that provided an ironic opportunity for the Gentiles to enter the undeserved feast of salvation. Paul's mission among the Gentiles illustrates this quite clearly. Now Rome, not Jerusalem, was becoming the centre of the Christian movement. On the other hand, this should not be taken to mean that Christianity was a mere 'sect' deviating from the orthodox Judaism. As Paul's apologies underscored repeatedly, the Christian gospel was about the very hope of Israel, especially the hope of resurrection. What the Christians claimed was that this very hope was now being fulfilled through the death and resurrection of Jesus. So it all turned around Jesus: to accept Jesus of Nazareth as God-appointed Messiah or not, that was the question. Under the circumstances, it is not surprising at all that the first thing Paul did in Rome was to invite the Jewish leaders and clear up some misunderstandings about his attitude toward the traditional faith of the Jews. We can imagine that an extended version of Paul's conversation with the Jewish leaders in Rome would not be much different from what he says in Romans 9—11, the Letter he sent to the Christians in Rome three years before his final arrival there.

But the final note of Acts is not a sad one. Luke concludes his book with Paul in Rome, doing his best as a witness of Jesus and thereby fulfilling for his own time the programme set by the risen Jesus: 'But you will receive power when the Holy Spirit has come upon you; and you will be my witnesses in Jerusalem, in all Judea and Samaria, and to the ends of the earth' (Acts 1.8). Many feel that Luke cuts short his story rather prematurely, but we can also say that enough has been said to accomplish the purpose Luke had set at the beginning of his project, namely, to show the 'truth' of the gospel (Luke 1.4). For Luke 'the things about Jesus' are not true simply because it is historically or philosophically so; the truth of the gospel means, more than anything else, power, i.e. the power of God's Holy Spirit. This power, first shown through the ministry of Jesus of Nazareth, especially his death and resurrection, now expresses itself through those who faithfully follow God's will in the name of this Jesus who is now the Messiah of Israel, the Lord of all, and the pioneer of life and salvation for all those who obey him. It is God's will that this gospel should spread towards the end of the earth, so throughout the book Luke has been at pains to show the unhindered progress of this gospel through the bold testimonies of the Spirit-filled witnesses, even in the face of life-threatening challenges. Luke's last words of his book admirably sum up what he has been trying to say all along about the nature of the gospel and its witnesses: 'with all boldness and without hindrance'.

STUDY SUGGESTIONS

Review of content

1 What was the first thing Paul did in Rome?

2 What are the main points of Paul's apology before the Jewish leaders?

3 Why were the Jewish leaders interested in listening to Paul?

4 What are the other places in the NT where the same Isaiah passage is quoted?

5 How does Luke summarize Paul's message preached in Rome?

Bible study

6 Read **(a)** 21.28; 23.29 and **(b)** Romans 3.1–8. Theologically speaking, what sort of misunderstanding was current about Paul and his gospel?

7 Read Isaiah 6.9–10. Are there any differences between the passage and the words quoted by Paul in Acts 28.26–27? What do you think is the major point Paul tries to make by quoting this passage?

Discussion and application

8 Christianity is not a deviation from the hope of Israel. How does this apply to us modern, non-Jewish Christians?

9 Luke ends his story with the triumphant note of 'with all boldness and without hindrance'. Can you say that this is still true today? What are the things that weaken our confidence in the gospel? What do you think are the major hurdles in spreading the gospel today?

Key to study suggestions

1.1–11

1 p. 10, Interpretation, 'Witnesses need power'.
2 p. 7, note on 1.3b.
3 p. 6, note on 1.1a.
4 p. 7, note on 1.4c; p. 8, notes on 1.8.
5 p. 8, note on 1.8a.
6 p. 8, note on 1.11a.
7 p. 7, note on 1.5b.
8 p. 7, note on 1.6.
10 p. 8, note on 1.9b.

1.12–26

1 p. 13, note on 1.14a.
2 p. 13, note on 1.16a.
3 p. 12, note on 1.13b.
4 p. 14, notes on 1.16.
5 p. 17, Interpretation, 'The restoration of the twelve'.
6 p. 16, Interpretation.
7 pp. 17–18, Interpretation, 'The Scripture has to be fulfilled'.

2.1–13

1 p. 20, note on 2.1a.
2 p. 22, note on 2.10.
3 p. 20, note on 2.2b.
4 p. 23, Interpretation, 'The coming of the Holy Spirit'.
5 p. 22, notes on 2.7a; 2.13.
6 p. 24, lines 3 to 7.
7 pp. 23–4, Interpretation.

2.14–41

1 p. 27, note on 2.21.
2 p. 26, note on 2.16; p. 29, Interpretation.
3 p. 30, from line 4.
4 p. 28, note on 2.33.
5 p. 28, note on 2.36.
6 p. 29, note on 2.38.

2.42–47

1 p. 32, notes on 2.42; p. 33, notes on 2.46.
2 As above.

3 p. 33, note on 2.44–45; Interpretation, the third paragraph.
4 p. 33, note on 2.46.
5 p. 33, Interpretation, the second paragraph.

3.1–26

1 p. 36, note on 3.11.
2 p. 36, note on 3.15a; p. 38, Interpretation, 'The apostles display the power of the living Jesus'.
3 p. 37, Interpretation, 'Healing of a lame man'.
4 p. 35, note on 3.6; p. 36, note on 3.16a.
5 p. 37, notes on 3.17–18.
6 (d) p. 35, note on 3.6; (e) p. 123, note on 14.9.
7 p. 37, note on 3.22–23.

4.1–31

1 p. 48, note on 4.12.
2 p. 48, note on 4.13.
3 p. 47, note on 4.1; p. 50, Interpretation.
4 p. 48, note on 4.10.
5 p. 49, note on 4.22.
6 p. 48, note on 4.10.

4.32—5.16

1 p. 54, note on 4.36–37.
2 p. 53, note on 4.32; p. 55, Interpretation.
3 p. 54, note on 5.2.
4 p. 54, note on 5.13–14.
5 p. 54, note on 5.5; p. 55, Interpretation.
6 p. 55, Interpretation, 'Peter's shadow'.

5.17–42

1 p. 64, note on 5.17.
2 p. 65, note on 5.31.
3 p. 66, Interpretation, 'The threat continues'.
4 p. 66, line 1; pp. 66–7, Interpretation, 'Gamaliel'.
5 p. 64, note on 5.19.
6 pp. 66–7, Interpretation, 'Gamaliel'.

6.1–15

1 p. 68, note on 6.1a.
2 p. 69, note on 6.4.
3 p. 68, note on 6.1b.
4 p. 69, note on 6.6.
5 p. 70, notes on 6.11 and 6.13–14.
6 p. 70, note on 6.12.

7.1—8.1a

1 pp. 73–4, notes on 7.2–16.
2 p. 74, note on 7.35.
3 p. 75, note on 7.47–48.
4 p. 75, note on 7.53b; p. 77, Interpretation, 'The law-breaking Israel'.
5 p. 74, note on 7.22.
6 p. 75, note on 7.42.
7 p. 75, note on 7.51.
8 p. 75, note on 7.53b.

8.1b–40

1 p. 85, Interpretation, 'Magic'.
2 p. 82, note on 8.27.
3 p. 80, note on 8.1b.
4 p. 80, note on 8.4.
5 p. 84, Interpretation, 'Philip evangelizes Samaria'.
6 As above.
7 p. 80, note on 8.5.
8 p. 83, note on 8.39 (Matthew 5.10–12).

9.1–30

1 p. 88, note on 9.13–14.
2 p. 87, note on 9.2b.
3 p. 87, note on 9.4; p. 91, Interpretation, 'Saul meets the risen Jesus'.
4 p. 88, note on 9.15.
5 p. 89, note on 9.28.
6 p. 90, notes on 9.35; 9.42; p. 92, Interpretation, 'Peter in Judea'.
7 pp. 90–1, Interpretation, 'Saul meets the risen Jesus'.
8 pp. 91–2, Interpretation, 'Grace in power'.

10.1—11.18

1 p. 94, note on 10.3.
2 p. 97, note on 10.36a.
3 p. 94, note on 10.2; p. 100, Interpretation, 'Good works and God's grace'.
4 p. 95, note on 10.15.
5 p. 97, note on 10.44.
6 p. 98, note on 11.18.
7 p. 100, Interpretation, 'Jews and Gentiles in the New Testament'.
9 p. 96, notes on 10.34–35.

11.19–30

1 p. 103, note on 11.30.
2 p. 104, Interpretation.
3 p. 102, note on 11.20.
4 p. 104, Interpretation.

5   p. 102, note on 11.22.
6   p. 103, note on 11.27.

12.1–25

1   p. 106, note on 12.1.
2   p. 107, note on 12.7.
3   p. 108, Interpretation.
4   p. 107, note on 12.17a.
5   p. 108, note on 12.21–23.

13.1–12

1   p. 111, note on 13.1.
2   p. 112, note on 13.8.
3   p. 111, note on 13.2b.
4   p. 112, note on 13.5b.
5   p. 113, Interpretation, 'The confrontation'.

13.13–52

1   p. 115, note on 13.15.
2   p. 116, note on 13.17.
3   p. 115, note on 13.15.
4   p. 115, note on 13.16.
5   p. 119, Interpretation, 'Paul's first sermon'.
6   p. 116, note on 13.27–29.
7   p. 118, note on 13.50.
8   (a) God's unconditional gift; (b) separation from the power of sin; (c) justification does not depend on external, ethnic identity but on faith in Jesus Christ.

14.1–28

1   p. 123, note on 14.13–14.
2   p. 124, note on 14.21.
3   p. 122, note on 14.1.
4   p. 123, note on 14.11–12.
5   p. 124, notes on 14.16–17.
6   p. 124, note on 14.19.
7   p. 124, note on 14.22.
8   p. 126, Interpretation, 'Entering God's kingdom through suffering'.
9   p. 125, note on 14.23.
10 p. 126, Interpretation, 'The Gentile idolatry and Paul's Jewish exhortation'.

15.1–35

1   p. 130, note on 15.7–11.
2   p. 129, note on 15.1–2.
3   p. 129, note on 15.3–4.

4   p. 130, note on 7–11.
5   p. 131, note on 15.19.
6   p. 131, note on 15.20.
7   p. 130, note on 15.14.
8   p. 129, note on 15.1–2.

15.36—16.10

1   p. 137, note on 16.6–8.
2   p. 136, note on 15.36.
3   p. 136, note on 15.37–38.
4   p. 138, Interpretation, 'Evangelism and pastoral care'.
5   p. 138, line 1.
6   p. 137, note on 16.1–2.
7   p. 137, note on 15.41.

16.11—17.15

1   p. 142, note on 16.16–18.
2   p. 141, note on 16.14.
3   p. 142, note on 16.19.
4   p. 142, note on 16.20–21.
5   p. 143, note on 17.2–3.
6   p. 144, note on 17.6–7.
7   p. 144, note on 17.6–7.

17.16–34

1   p. 150, note on 17.22.
2   'Areopagus' means the 'Rock of Ares'. According to Greek myth, Ares, the god of war, was tried on the rocky hill for murder.
3   p. 149, note on 17.17.
4   p. 150, note on 17.22.
5   p. 150, note on 17.24–25.
6   p. 151, note on 17.31.
7   p. 151, note on 17.32–34.
8   p. 151, note on 17.30.

18.1–28

1   p. 154, note on 18.2
2   p. 155, note on 18.9–11.
3   p. 155, note on 18.12–17.
4   p. 154, note on 18.3; p. 158, Interpretation, 'Paul as a tentmaker'.
5   p. 156, note on 18.25–26.
6   p. 157, note on 18.27–28.
7   p. 154, note on 18.2.

19.1–44

1   p. 170, note on 19.11–12.
2   p. 169, note on 19.2–3.

3 p. 170, note on 19.9–10.
4 p. 171, notes on 19.18, 19–20.
5 p. 172, note on 19.25–27.
6 p. 173, note on 19.37–39.
7 p. 169, note on 19.4

20.1–38

1 p. 177, note on 20.1–3a. (a) consolation, comfort; (b) exhortation, admonition.
2 p. 177, note on 20.3b–4.
3 p. 178, note on 20.7.
4 p. 182, Interpretation, 'Paul as a model: Paul's farewell speech'.
5 p. 180, note on 20.35.
6 p. 178, note on 20.7; p. 181, Interpretation, 'The Lord's day and the Lord's Supper'.
7 p. 182, Interpretation, 'Paul as a model: Paul's farewell speech'.

21.1–36

1 p. 194, Interpretation.
2 p. 189, note on 21.4 (Tyre); pp. 189–90, notes on 21.7–9 and 21.10–14 (Caesarea).
3 As above.
4 p. 191, note on 21.22–26.
5 p. 192, lines 5–6.
6 p. 192, note on 21.27–30.
7 p. 193, note on 21.37–40.
8 p. 190, note on 21.10–14.
9 p. 191, note on 21.20b–21.

22.1–29

1 p. 197, note on 22.1–2.
2 p. 197, 'Summary'.
3 p. 197, note on 22.3–5.
4 p. 197, note on 22.6–11.
5 p. 198, note on 22.22–23.
6 p. 199, note on 22.24–30.
7 p. 199, Interpretation, 'Paul and the Jewish tradition'.
8 p. 198, note on 22.12–16.

22.30—23.35

1 p. 202, note on 23.2–5.
2 p. 202, note on 23.2–5.
3 p. 203, note on 23.7–10.
4 p. 203, note on 23.11.
6 p. 204, note on 23.16–22.
7 p. 202, note on 23.2–5.
8 p. 203, note on 23.12–15.

24.1–27

1 (a) p. 173, note on 19.40; p. 207, note on 24.1–9; (b) p. 129, note on 15.1–2; p. 203, note on 23.7–10.
2 p. 207, note on 24.1–9.
3 p. 208, note on 24.14–16.
4 p. 208, note on 24.17–21.
5 p. 208, note on 24.22–27.
6 p. 209, line 7.
8 p. 209, Interpretation.

25.1–27

1 p. 212, note on 25.1–5.
2 p. 212, note on 25.10–12.
3 p. 212, notes on 25.8, 10–12.
4 p. 213, note on 25.23–27.
5 p. 214, Interpretation.
7 p. 106, note on 12.1; p. 213, note on 25.13–22.

26.1–32

1 p. 216, note on 26.6–7.
2 p. 217, note on 26.12–15.
3 p. 217, note on 26.16–18.
4 p. 218, lines 6–7.
5 p. 218, note on 26.24–25.
6 p. 219, note on 26.30–32.
7 p. 219, Interpretation, 'Resurrection as the stumbling block of faith'.

27.1—28.16

1 p. 222, note on 27.9–12.
2 p. 224, note on 27.13–20; p. 225, notes on 27.33–44.
3 pp. 222–5, notes on 27.9–12, 21–26, 27–32, 33–38.
4 p. 224, note on 27.13–20.
5 p. 224, note on 27.21–26.
6 p. 225, note on 27.39–44.
7 p. 225, note on 28.2–6.
8 p. 226, note on 28.11–15.
9 p. 227, Interpretation, 'Faith that works'.

28.17–31

1 p. 229, note on 28.17–20.
2 p. 229, note on 28.17–20.
3 p. 229, note on 28.21–22.
4 p. 230, note on 28.24–28.
5 p. 230, note on 28.30–31.
6 p. 192, note on 21.27–30; p. 204, note on 23.23–35.

Index

This index contains only the more important names of people and places and the main subjects which occur in Acts or which are discussed in this Guide. As the names of God and Jesus appear on almost every page, only a few, major subheadings are listed against them for convenience. **Bold print** indicates those pages or sections where a subject is discussed in detail.